George Sanders and Josh Packard

THE AIR WE BREATHE

sociology of religion

Kendall Hunt
publishing company

BRIEF CONTENTS

	About this Book	ix
	About the Authors	xi
CHAPTER 1	Religious Universes and Spiritual Lives	1
CHAPTER 2	Becoming Religious: Navigating Beliefs, Negotiating Expressions	31
CHAPTER 3	Religion and Economics and the Worlds between Them	67
CHAPTER 4	Religion and Equality for All: African American Activism	95
CHAPTER 5	The Religious Right	119
CHAPTER 6	Sexed and Sexual Souls	141
CHAPTER 7	The End of Religion As We Know It, or Just a New Beginning?	169
CHAPTER 8	From Chapels to Arenas	191
CHAPTER 9	Past Religion but Post-Secular	215
CHAPTER 10	Trends in Religious Affiliation	241
	Glossary	255
	Bibliography	259
	Index	265

TABLE OF CONTENTS

About this Book   ix

About the Authors   xi

CHAPTER 1   Religious Universes and Spiritual Lives   1

    Key Terms   1
    Objectives   1
    What is Sociology?   1
    Types of Sociological Analysis   4
    Levels of Analysis   7
    What does Religion Do?   11
    Abrahamic Religions   16
    Islam   18
    Buddhism and Hinduism   21
    Denominations   24
    Religious "Nones"   25
    Discussion Questions   29

CHAPTER 2   Becoming Religious: Navigating Beliefs, Negotiating Expressions   31

    Key Terms   31
    Objectives   31
    Religiosity   32
    Social Construction   37
    Is Religion in Decline?   41
    Religious Socialization   47
    The Religious Economy   57
    Church and Sects   63
    Discussion Questions   65

CHAPTER 3   Religion and Economics and the Worlds between Them   67

    Key Terms   67
    Objectives   67
    Social Stratification   67
    Rationalization   75
    Weber's Thesis   80

Consumerism and "Liquid Religion"   88
Liquid Religion and Commitment   91
Discussion Questions   93

CHAPTER 4 Religion and Equality for All: African American Activism   95

Key Terms   95
Objectives   95
Introduction   95
Agency and Structure   97
Racial Equality   101
After Slavery   103
Institutionalized Racism   107
The 1950s and Beyond   111
Black Power   113
The Social Gospel   115
Discussion Questions   118

CHAPTER 5 The Religious Right   119

Key Terms   119
Objectives   119
Introduction   119
Christian Evangelicalism and Christian Fundamentalism: Some Basics 121
Historical Background on Fundamentalism   123
Millenarianism   125
Fundamentalism in the 20th Century   127
Fundamentalism as it is Lived Today   130
The Rise of Televangelism   133
TV Becomes Political   134
Neoliberalism   138
Discussion Questions   140

CHAPTER 6 Sexed and Sexual Souls   141

Key terms   141
Objectives   141
Women in the World   141
Religion and Women   143
Gender and Sex   144
Religion and Gender   148
Separate Spheres   152
Women at the Forefront   155
Masculinity   158
Sexual Expression   159
What Is Normal?   161
LGBTQ   164

Complexity 167
Discussion Questions 168

CHAPTER 7   The End of Religion As We Know It, or Just a New Beginning?   169

Key Terms 169
Objectives 169
Introduction 169
Society Divinized 174
Civil Religion 179
Privatization of Religion 183
Therapeutic Religions 185
What Are We Celebrating Now? 190
Discussion Questions 190

CHAPTER 8   From Chapels to Arenas   191

Key Terms 191
Objectives 191
Introduction 191
The Theory of McDonaldization 192
Megachurches 200
Seekers 204
The "Business" of the Megachurch 207
Another Perspective 209
The Key Difference 212
Discussion Questions 213

CHAPTER 9   Past Religion but Post-Secular   215

Key Terms 215
Objectives 215
The Radical Lack 215
Postmodern Religion 217
Postmodernity 222
Heaven's Gate 227
Edge Religions 230
Conclusion 238
Discussion Questions 239

CHAPTER 10 Trends in Religious Affiliation   241

Key Terms 241
Objectives 241
Introduction 241
Where Are We Now? 243
How Did We Get Here? 247

So, Where Are We Going?   249
Stepping Boldly Into the Future   251
Discussion Questions   253

Glossary   **255**

Bibliography   **259**

Index   **265**

ABOUT THIS BOOK

At the beginning of every semester that we teach Sociology of Religion, we ask our students one simple question, "Of all of the electives available to you, why did you sign up for this class?" While we get a few students responding with banal answers relating to the time the class is offered or that a friend was already in the course, the majority of my answers indicate a sincere desire to learn more about a subject they know to be important yet have very little training in understanding. As one of our students put it, "Religion is a part of our culture and influences nearly everything to some extent, but I don't really know how it works or ever really even think about it much. It's like the air we breathe. It's always around, interacting with everything, but I don't really ever think about it much, and when I do, I find that I don't really know much." It is this impulse to unpack, decode and explain "the air we breathe" that drives us to teach Sociology of Religion.

The book you are holding in your hands is the result of a long-running conversation between its authors. We have each taught the sociology of religion for a number of years and have always found ourselves wanting a textbook that more closely mirrored the approach we took in the classroom. When we teach about religion, we teach it from an explicitly sociological perspective. That is, we are trying to figure out how religion fits into the other major social institutions, or how it is socially constructed or how the intersectionality of gender, race and class affect belief and participation or any other of a number of topics that fill our classes.

These conversations ultimately became the foundation for the organization of this textbook. In fact, we even work-shopped the various chapter ideas with our classes to see which topics resonated most with them and which questions they felt were the most useful in helping them to understand the sociological side of religion.

The result is that you'll find chapters organized around topics that are relevant and the sociological knowledge and theories that you need to know in order to understand those topics is woven throughout. This is the opposite approach of many textbooks that organize chapters around theories and leave the application up to you.

We want you to be able to offer something new to the ongoing discourse in our society about the role of religion. Whether the conversation is about the how religion influences politics, what role religion plays in international terrorism, how gender roles are developed and challenged or any number of other relevant conversations that are going on in our society about religion, we want you to be able to offer a unique, sociological perspective about this vital social institution.

Our approach is reflected in the main title of this book, *The Air We Breathe*. Religion is not a discrete institution that is separated from all of the other social institutions that make up our society. It is not as though we can treat religion as a sort of thing or object to be scrutinized and evaluated. While we are scientists in every sense of the word, it is not possible to excise religion from society, situate it in a laboratory, and then slice it up and expose its inner "truth." In our society, religion is far too embedded in all of our social institutions: the family, government, education, and many others. It is a part of all of us, even those of us who do not profess to be religious. Religion pervades our culture – it is part of the air we breathe.

ABOUT THE AUTHORS

Josh Packard, Ph.D.
Vanderbilt University, 2008

When I was an undergraduate, I had the opportunity to visit a synagogue, a church and a mosque in the same semester for one of my courses. I remember being struck by their remarkable similarity. I found myself coming back, time and again, to the ways that people managed to organize their religious expressions in remarkably consistent ways even if those expressions were directed at unique expressions of God. This, to me, suggested something about the universality of religion. I did not know it at the time, but I was taking my first steps toward a sociological understanding of religion.

I remember, distinctly, my early conversations with friends, parents and pastors about the connections I saw between the role of ritual, the construction of belief and the common distinctions that religious systems made between the sacred and the everyday. I struggled to explain what I was thinking and they, as often as not, struggled to understand. Indeed, it is difficult to explain the sociological perspective of religion to others. It is, perhaps, too intimate for most religious people to be able to think abstractly about and too unfamiliar for the non-religious to fully grasp.

When George and I sat down to think about how we could remedy this gap for our own students, we hit on the idea of a textbook that would deal with real questions and issues in the study of religion. For me, this textbook is a natural fit with the kind of research and scholarship I already do. I began my formal research into religion with my dissertation, which was later turned into a book, *The Emerging Church: Religion at the Margins*. More recently, I wrote, with a student of mine, *Church Refugees: Sociologists Reveal Why People are DONE with Church but not their Faith*. Both of these books, and the articles and presentations that make up the rest of my research take a pragmatic approach. I had a question that I wanted to answer.

It helps that I work at The University of Northern Colorado where the sociology department has an explicitly applied focus. We take the approach that a sociological understanding of the world helps our students to do their jobs better and create a more critical, well-informed citizenry. I believe those values represented in my own scholarship and department are present in this textbook as well. As I wrote, outlined chapters and tracked down references, I often found myself returning to those early conversations I had as an undergraduate. I wanted this textbook to be a helpful way to frame conversations about religion from a sociological perspective.

With all of that in mind, I hope you find this book to be, above all else, *useful*. I know that writing it has been immensely valuable for me and the conversations I continue to have with my students, colleagues, friends and family.

George Sanders, Ph.D.
Vanderbilt University, 2008

Like many undergraduate students, I did not enter college with a clear goal. So I found myself exploring many different classes across the university curriculum. The problem wasn't that I was dissatisfied with a particular topic, discipline, or major. It was the opposite. Just about everything I studied held some attraction or fascination for me. The more I ventured across different academic terrains, the more I became curious about what else there was to know. The first couple of years I probably declared a new major every single semester.

College, in some ways, is a real-life adventure. There we can take responsible risks and allow ourselves to be challenged, setting aside what we think we know and what we take for granted as being "real" or "true."

This is what I like most about the sociology and specifically the sociology of religion. For those whose religion occupies a central place in their lives - who are guided by their religious principles and practices - their truth is incontrovertible and their reality is well structured. And yet we recognize that in an increasingly diverse society, people's truths and realities vary significantly. To me the sociology of religion makes space for that fact. Sociology provides the empirics, the tools, and the scientific *bona fides* for making sense out of multiple realities and multiple truths. In doing so, sociology delicately balances the relative with the absolute.

These presuppositions guide all of my research, which to this point has examined the role of the sacred in a consumer-driven, postmodern context. For me personally, the highlight of my scholarly explorations has been the manner in which we as a society have proven quite capable of realizing transcendence and a sense of enchantment in spite of an environment saturated by rationalizing mechanisms.

Oakland University has been a welcome and welcoming setting for my work. Situated outside the city of Detroit, the region is, in spite of reasonable expectations, undergoing a kind of miraculous resurrection. It is nothing short of inspiring, something keenly reflected in my students; they are committed to realizing transformation and they refuse to abandon their wide-eyed wonder. Indeed, I'd have to say that those students are pretty darn awesome.

CHAPTER I

RELIGIOUS UNIVERSES AND SPIRITUAL LIVES

Why do people have religion in the first place and what does sociology have to do with it?

KEY TERMS

- Cultural-ethnic Jew
- Islamophobia
- Polity
- Religious "nones"
- Sacred canopy
- Solipsism

OBJECTIVES:

- Understand what sociology is.
- Grasp the importance of multiple perspectives existing simultaneously.
- Understand what religion is, and how/why this relates to and can be studied as a social institution.

WHAT IS SOCIOLOGY?

Let me begin by telling you a true story . . . As an undergraduate, I majored in philosophy, and after graduation, I took some time off to work before deciding to go back to school. Then I enrolled in a graduate program in psychology and began serving as the research assistant for one of my psychology professors on one of her projects. I was always curious about why the professor approached her study the way she did and probably asked way too many questions until one day she said to me, "George, I've enjoyed having you on my research team and you have been an asset, but you know what? You're really not a psychologist. I think at heart you are a sociologist."
My response?

It was, "What is a sociologist?" I had never taken a sociology class, and, to be perfectly honest, I do not think I had ever even uttered the words "sociology," "sociological," or "sociologist" in my entire life.

My psychology professor was kind enough to put me in touch with a colleague of hers in the sociology department. He very graciously and generously agreed to sit down with me the following week. The first question

I asked him was, "What is sociology and what does a sociologist do?" His reply was this: "Sociology is the scientific study of social groups." Then he paused and thought about what he wanted to say next. "A sociologist is *someone who is in awe of the ways people transform their individual existence into something wondrous and meaningful with the help of others around them.*"

©vichie81/Shutterstock.com

It wasn't a technical definition, but it was a pretty good one nonetheless. In fact, that answer resonated deeply with me, and to this day, it has shaped the way I think about what sociology is and what it does. Sociology is a science, to be sure. Thus, we use systematic, empirical methods to make sense of collectivities, organizations, communities, and institutions. Sociology is interested in how groups come into existence, develop some stability, and change over time. Sociology is also interested in how groups shape us as individuals and influence our actions and our thoughts. It is also about the way individuals work within groups and help to create groups and change groups. Last but certainly not least, sociology examines how we as human beings come together to create systems of meaning and how this leads people to create lives that are fulfilling and purposeful.

©View Apart/Shutterstock.com

I am fairly positive that you have heard the phrase "try walking in someone else's shoes." My parents used that phrase a lot, especially when I would get too judgmental about other people or feel that my way of thinking was the best way of thinking. They would say, "Well, George, don't judge someone else before you've walked a mile in their shoes." The value they were trying to instill in me was that it is important to not get too caught up in our own thoughts and our own values. We should always strive to understand what it is like for other people, particularly people who are different from us, to get along in life.

Well, in order to properly conduct sociology, we have to walk in other people's shoes. We must try hard to recognize that our version of events and our experience of reality is rather limited and narrow. There is a multitude of different perspectives in our world, and it is imperative to do our best to understand those perspectives. After all, we understand our own views on life. We've got those down pat. The challenge is to make sense of the way others see things.

©hikrcn/Shutterstock.com

So, in a sense, sociology is a unique science: it is a *moral* science. It is moral because we are obligated to set aside our own biases and our own values in order to really comprehend the ways other people feel about life. It is moral because when we begin to do that, it affects how we ourselves feel, think, and act. When we understand the challenges and opportunities that people around us face, we naturally begin to empathize with them. We begin to recognize that underlying all of the wonderful differences others have, there is a common desire to create a life that is meaningful and happy. It is hard, in such circumstances, not to develop a sense of compassion for people who face difficulties and struggles, and it is equally difficult not to experience joy when others experience positive things in life.

In sociology, we have many different ways of talking about just how complicated life really is . . . intersectionality, dedifferentiation, mutual constitution, multivariate correlation, polyvocality, just to highlight a few "ten-dollar" words that all point to the same thing: life is complicated. Reality is complicated, and even truth can be fuzzy. In today's world, sociologists tend to agree with this profoundly simply truth. That can make understanding the way society works, a daunting challenge. It would be naïve and simplistic to think otherwise.

One of the core concepts in sociology comes from C. Wright Mills: the sociological imagination. This refers to the ability to think about society as though you were completely unfamiliar with it. In doing this, we should aim to defamiliarize or make strange all of the things we take to be routine, normal, and ordinary. We should try and always question what we take for granted as common sense. The sociological imagination also implies that we need to see how individual stories are tied to the bigger events and forces in our world. We ought to be able to see how our own individual autobiography is a product of the social environment.

So, sociology, in my view, is a moral science. However, it is nonetheless a science. This means that as sociologists, we employ reliable, empirically credible, and scholarly rigorous approaches when we are conducting our research. In order to accurately and realistically understand individuals, communities, and institutions, we draw on methods that will lead us to valid findings. If I conduct an experiment with an organization, for instance, someone else should be able to come along and replicate my study. Thus, the methods a sociologist uses in a study ought to be transparent to others in the field.

TYPES OF SOCIOLOGICAL ANALYSIS

As you might imagine, there are a wide variety of empirical methods that sociologists draw on when conducting research. There are two broad classifications of methods: quantitative and qualitative. Quantitative methods utilize data in order to conduct statistical analysis. For instance, a sociologist might collect information from people that can be quantified in numerical terms such as age or region of the country. People might be asked questions that exist on a scale, such as when we ask how religious someone is

©MSSA/Shutterstock.com

on a scale from 1 to 5. Alternatively, there are a number of surveys already in existence that contain information that can be calculated. The General Social Survey is administered to thousands of people every year and contains hundreds of variables that sociologists can then use to conduct statistical analyses. The General Social Survey and the U.S. Census are both examples of datasets that sociologists use to conduct quantitative research.

Qualitative research relies on information that is more difficult to quantify. There are a wide variety of approaches qualitative researchers use in their work. A sociologist might observe people in a group and describe their interactions. A more in-depth strategy is called "participant-observation," in which a sociologist actually takes part in a group and combines her or his own observations with some knowledge of what it was like to actually take part in the group. For example, Josh and I have each conducted participant-observation research by attending various worship services at churches around the country. The key to good participant-observation research is making sure you have a good grounding in the sociological imagination and even some theories that give you some initial indication of where to look for interesting and important interactions.

©Andreser/Shutterstock.com

Additionally, a qualitative researcher will often include interviews with people. More often than not, interviews in qualitative research ask people to answer open-ended questions (or questions that cannot be answered with a simple one word or "yes" or "no" reply). Open-ended questions begin with phrases such as "Tell me about . . ." or "What is it like . . ." so that interviewees can provide some depth to their answers.

These two forms of qualitative research are very common in sociological research on religion and focus on how people make decisions or why they do the things they do. In short, it is a way of investigating the process of meaning-making with regard to religion.

For example, Josh recently completed a large-scale interview project to understand how people come to see themselves as still aligned with a Christian identity but refuse to attend an institutional church. This complex process is simply not something that could be captured in a survey.

Another approach a qualitative researcher might take is with "content analysis." With this approach, a researcher is usually examining some document or text in order to look for patterns that show up. One might, for instance, examine church bulletins to see what kinds of information different churches include.

Quantitative research, on the other hand, typically relies on closed-ended answers so that the responses can easily be classified or categorized and transformed into numerical data. The most common quantitative method is the survey. Surveys are perhaps the most popular form of data collection but present severe limitations when trying to understand something as inherently personal as religious affiliation.

©thodonal88/Shutterstock.com

Of course, one can combine strategies and methods in order to better understand what is taking place sociologically. In my own Sociology of Religion class, I require students to attend multiple faith communities and do a little bit of participant-observation, interviewing, and content analysis. As we prepare to go out into the field, I ask students to come up with a list of questions they might ask people for interview purposes such as "How long have you been attending this church/temple/synagogue?" or "What kinds of rituals do you participate in when you are at your church/temple/synagogue?" These questions allow students to get a good overview of how the faith community is organized and how involved people tend to be.

But students also develop observational questions that they can note down rather than actually ask someone about. These are things such as: What is the proportion of women and men in the congregation? Are most people young or old? Even observing how people dress when they attend or how physically involved they get (do they kneel a lot, bow, clap, dance?) can be very informative when talking about religious groups.

These methods are not the only ones sociologists use to acquire and interpret information needed to conduct proper research. They represent just a handful of popular strategies. The goal of any research strategy though is to develop an ethical and scientifically valid means for accurately representing a particular social phenomenon, situation, or process. Ultimately, as a sociologist, it is important to recognize that different kinds of research provide different kinds of information. Throughout this book, we have relied on sociologists who have conducted both quantitative and qualitative research since both forms can contribute to a broader understanding of the sociology of religion.

©supergenijalac/Shutterstock.com

Sociology is a uniquely wide-ranging discipline. More specifically, the sociology of religion shares some overlapping features and characteristics with many other disciplines including: psychology, economics, political science, communications, philosophy, and, of course, religious studies. Thus, if you are someone who is not a sociology major or you are someone who appreciates interdisciplinary types of work, the sociology of religion is a valuable entry point into sociology more broadly. Most sociologists of religion are attuned to the contributions a variety of academic fields can make in understanding the importance, value, and significance religion has to society at large.

LEVELS OF ANALYSIS

Some sociologists like to make a distinction between micro-levels of analysis (the communications and behaviors that take place on an interpersonal level) and macro-level sociology (the large-scale social structures and forces that take place on national, global, institutional, governmental, or cultural levels). I personally tend to de-emphasize this distinction and see it as one that is arbitrary and less helpful.

For instance, I live in Detroit, Michigan. When the economy turned sour a little over a decade ago, many automobile and automobile parts companies closed down their factories or moved them to other countries where they could pay lower wages to their employees. When this took place, I knew a number of students had parents who were laid off. The effects were so widespread that unemployment in this region soared. For quite some time, there were far more job applicants than there were available jobs. As you might imagine, my students were directly impacted since many relied on parents to help them pay for their college tuition. Now, all of a sudden, they had to seek employment that provided them with 20, 30, and even 40 or more hours of paid work a week so they could continue to afford to go to school. This impacted their sleep patterns, and many struggled to find time to complete their homework, write their papers, and prepare for their exams. More than a few of my students struggled and saw a decline in their grade performance. So, you can see how the macro-level changes in the economy impacted the micro-level behaviors of students. The macro and micro are both part of the same sets of flows and forces that are always moving, which shape how we think, act, and feel at any given moment.

It is important to always be able to try and connect the macro with the micro to best understand the institution of religion. In Josh's study about the "Nones" that I referenced earlier, for example, he explicitly situates the movement of people away from institutional religion as a part of a larger trend going on in our society. People are abandoning social institutions on a broad scale and finding new ways to organize their social lives. As he shows, religious institutions are not immune to these larger social forces.

©Who is Danny/Shutterstock.com

Sociology provides us with a kind of metaphorical lens through which to view religion. In order to fully comprehend religion from a sociological perspective, one must appreciate the ways in which we can alter the focus from the macro to the micro but always with the awareness that we are looking at essentially different areas of an expansive, ever-changing system.

On a macro level, we might train our lens on different religions such as Buddhism, Islam, or Judaism. We might examine regional differences and ask questions such as: Are there parts of the country that are more likely to have people who attend Christian houses of worship? Are people who identify as being of the Hindu faith more likely to live in cities or suburbs? Do people who attend Jewish synagogues get married at earlier ages than people who attend Muslim mosques? Do Christians have higher or lower levels of income and higher or lower levels of education than Buddhists? All of these are examples of sociological questions that attempt to understand religion at a macro level. We are examining large-scale trends that relate religion with another variable. This is one of the most common areas of sociological research: that is, looking at how religion either influences (an)other social variable(s) or how (an)other variable(s) affects religion. There are a wide variety of variables that we can look at: geography, income, education, gender, age, ethnicity, family structure, and many, many more.

Just to give you an idea of some of these patterns, let us identify a few at the outset. Chaves (2004) has pointed out that there are over 300,000 congregations in the United States alone, while most are small (they have less than 100 members). However, more people tend to belong to larger churches (averaging over 400 members). Chaves also notes that a little over half of the congregations identify as "conservative" in nature. These are macro-level descriptions of patterns in the United States.

©My Good Image/Shutterstock.com

Another macro-level finding reveals that participating in religion appears to be related to good psychological health. Ellison et al. (2001) found that the frequency of prayer, a belief in God and a belief in an afterlife, and regular participation and involvement in a faith community all point to increased mental health and an overall sense of positive well-being.

Generally speaking, the more conservative a religious group is, the more likely they are to believe in Heaven and Hell. Also, the more conservative a religious group is, the more likely its members are to be frequent churchgoers and committed members overall. Finally, in the same study, the more conservative a religious group is, the more likely they are to adhere to the traditional family structure, the more likely they are to get married and have children at an earlier age, and the more likely they are to remain married (Roof and McKinney, 1987).

Sometimes, macro-level data can appear to be contradictory. For instance, while there used to be a correlation between income and religious affiliation (specifically, the higher one's income, the more likely one was to be affiliated with a more liberal religious organization), that does not appear to hold any longer (Stark and Finke 1992). Yet, the Pew

Research Forum has examined income and religion and found that Jews and mainline Protestants tend to have higher incomes than more conservative Christian religions. The reason the studies seem to contradict one another is that the first study only looked at a few Christian organizations and the second took into account a wider variety of religions.

Or consider this: there is a general correlation between how involved one is with one's religion and where one's political attitudes lie. According to the sociologist of religion Mark Chaves: "Actively religious Americans are more politically and socially conservative than less religious Americans. Active churchgoers support more restrictions on legal abortion, endorse more traditional gender roles, and vote Republican more often than less religious people" (2011: 94). Furthermore, Chaves notes that the correlation between religious participation and conservatism has grown stronger over time. Chaves also notes a widening gap between the social and cultural attitudes of people who identify as more religious and the attitudes of those who are less religious and nonreligious.

The aforementioned are all examples of macro-level patterns that exist in the United States (and we discuss other patterns throughout this textbook). They describe general tendencies of large groups of people. What is important to remember is that these are *general tendencies*. There are always exceptions to the rule. So, for example, another macro-level pattern is the following:

Church attendance is positively correlated with age—that is, as people grow older, the more likely they are to go to church (Chaves, 2004).

Again, the fact that people are more likely to attend a church as they age is a general tendency. This means that if we were to randomly select a small group of people out of the American population, we would find that more often than not, older persons would be more likely to say that they went to church on a regular basis. Conversely, more often than not, younger people would say that they did not go to church on a regular basis. Does that mean that we would also find some young people who go to church regularly and some older people who do not go to church? Of course, we would. That is because we are only suggesting that the pattern predicting aging with higher rates of church participation is more likely to be the case.

©withGod/Shutterstock.com

Now, if we refocus our sociological lens to look at another level of religion, we might opt to scale down somewhat. Instead of looking at an entire religion, we might look at a specific group within a religion. A denomination refers to the subgroup within a religion. The core tenets of the religion are shared between denominations, but there are important self-identified distinctions between denominations. So, if we were to take the religion Christianity and divide it into denominations, we would come up with a list that would include, but not be limited to: Lutherans, Presbyterians, Roman Catholics, Baptists, Jehovah's Witnesses, Seventh Day Adventists, Episcopalians, and so on. Within each of these denominational orders, there are single units that are called congregations (in other words, individual churches or parishes). When we narrow our focus to examine behaviors within a specific congregation, we are then more likely to take a micro-level approach and examine individual behaviors.

This focus on broad trends at the micro or macro level is really at the heart of sociology. When Josh explains this concept to his class, he tells them that sociologists are like gamblers. Most of our lives we are inundated with a very psychological, individual-based explanation for the world around us, but sociologists are trained to look at trends, themes, and patterns. We make claims such as "American churches are very racially segregated." Of course, as his students often point out, they can actually name a racially diverse church they have attended or know about. But the presence of one racially diverse church does not negate the overall trend. He asks his students, if we picked one church, at random, from among all the churches in this country, who wants to bet that it would be racially diverse? In that moment, you can see what sociologists care about. They might lose a bet or two, but over time, they will come out ahead. As the great sociologist Howard Becker (1998) reminds us in his book *Tricks of the Trade*, all outcomes in the social world are possible, but not all outcomes are probable.

So, now that we have discussed some of the core things that sociologists do, let us turn to the case of religion . . .

WHAT DOES RELIGION DO?

Some might argue that it is not the purview of the sociology of religion to answer the question, "Why is there religion in the first place?" Instead, they might say that addressing that question should be left for the theologians, the philosophers, or perhaps even the psychologists. Sociologists think otherwise. Religion is, after all, a social enterprise and involves groups coming together. In fact, the Latin word from which we derive our own word "religion" is *religare*, which roughly translates to bind together. Religion is an institution that is inherently social. Thus, some sociologists attempt to address the functions of religion.

Peter Berger, one of the foremost sociologists of religion, says that religion serves as a **sacred canopy**. I have always liked that image. For me, it evokes a sense of comfort, like a warm blanket, but it is one that protects and reassures many of us. The sacred canopy is a metaphor for religion: it is an institution that functions to protect us from feeling like existence is meaningless and from what philosophers call solipsism. The word solipsism sounds complicated, but I think it will become clear in a discussion about one of my favorite French philosophers Rene Descartes.

Sacred canopy An institution that functions to protect us from feeling like existence is meaningless; a metaphor for religion.

©Eugene Sergeev/Shutterstock.com

During the 1600s, the period in which Descartes was writing, philosophers were very concerned with "deep" concepts such as knowledge and reality. They were interested in answering questions such as: How do we know what is really real? Is there any way we can have certainty about the world around us? Are there truths that apply to everyone, all of the time?

Descartes attempts to answer these questions in a very short book he called *The Meditations*. In it, he takes us, his readers, on a journey, to explore whether or not we can even be sure of our own existence—something we generally take for granted. The work is a kind of thought experiment in which he writes in the first person and suggests that we imagine ourselves right there with him along his journey.

©Everett-Art/Shutterstock.com

He begins with a description of his present . . . He is comfortably sitting alone one evening, warming himself by his fireplace. Painting a picture of what it must feel like to be cozy and content with nothing much to do other than turn one's thoughts to philosophical questions, he begins by pointing out something we all know but rarely think about: we take for granted that the "reality" we are in is, in fact, real. Yet, he asks, how can we know this for certain? Reality is, of course, filtered through our five senses: taste, touch, smell, sight, and sound. Those five senses are not perfect. We have all of us been fooled by our senses. Perhaps you have experienced the mild delight and surprise of optical illusions in which we think we see one thing until something else is revealed. Or, if you are like me, you feel the vibration of your cell phone in your pocket, indicating that you have received a text, only to pull it out to read your text and discover there is no message. Or, maybe you thought you heard your name in a crowded room or saw something from the corner of your eye when nothing turned out to be there.

So, our senses trick us all of the time, and since we access what we call "reality" through our senses, Descartes wonders, how can we really know if there is in fact a reality at all? Maybe, he argues, *everything* we *think* we see, hear, and touch is an illusion. Maybe there is some alien force that is intentionally tricking us into believing what we see, hear, and touch is real when in fact it is not. Or, maybe we are dreaming and everything is taking place in the imaginary spaces of our dreams.

Tap your fingers on your chair—how do you know that the feeling of your fingers against the solid object and the sounds emanating from your "tap" are really real? Is it possible that the "you" you think yourself to be, is something else altogether? Is it possible that you are right now dreaming and not really reading the words on this page? Is it possible that "you" are something that lives in a laboratory attached by various cables and cords to a computer that is merely programming you into thinking you see, hear, and feel your fingers tapping against your chair?

Philosophers came to call this the brain-in-a-vat dilemma—illustrated well in the movie *The Matrix*. In the movie, we follow the main characters moving about, speaking, and interacting with others in a fairly recognizable reality. Yet, we later learn that their reality is one that is merely a projection of a vast computer network. It is a virtual

> **Solipsism** The belief that we live in a completely isolated reality, in which we can never know for certain whether or not we or anything/anyone else around us is real.

reality, and the "real" reality is that bodies are lying in state, each in its own individual cell attached to a central hub via nodal connections.

Returning to Descartes' conundrum, **solipsism** refers to the belief that we live in a completely isolated reality in which we can never really know for certain whether or not we are real, the people around us are real, or whether anything around is real. For what it's worth, Descartes escapes his solipsism by asserting that because he is able to think these things, wonder about the nature of reality, and question whether he is really real, there must be one thing that is real—the person doing the thinking, wondering, and questioning. So, he concludes *cogito ergo sum* or "I think therefore I am."

©GaudiLab/Shutterstock.com

While Descartes is satisfied with his resolution, philosophers today continue to argue about the possibility of solipsism. In fact, some sociologists of religion do as well—including Peter Berger, the man who came up with religion as a "sacred canopy." For Berger, one of religion's primary functions is to protect us from solipsism so that we do not feel alone in the universe. Religion reminds us that there is an existence that transcends our own experience; that is, there is a reality that is greater than the very limited one we have access to through our senses.

The American philosopher Richard Rorty has this wonderful image that he uses to talk about the inherent social nature of humans that I'll paraphrase here: our lot in this existence is to cling together with one another against the dark. Or, in the words of Peter Berger, religion is what protects us from the "lurking irrealities" of meaninglessness and the ever-present possibility that we can die at any time. Religion, therefore, is a way for people to come together to help us make this life significant even in times when the banality of waking up, showering, going to work, coming home, fixing dinner, going to bed, and doing it all over again seems like all there is to our existence. As Berger writes: "Religion is the audacious attempt to conceive of the entire universe as being humanly significant" (Berger, 1967: 28).

Religion not only protects us from feeling alone in our own little realities, it situates us within broader system of meaning in which we connect with one another and with our divinity. Religion tells us that we are not only *not alone* but that we *matter*. When I use the word "matter," I mean that we matter to another. Others find us significant and worthwhile. If your religion involves God (since not all religions do), then religion says that you matter to your God. You live a life that is worth living. There is nothing more reassuring than that very premise.

Extending this a step further, there is nothing more reassuring to the foundations of living life together than knowing that we all, collectively, matter. The study of religion is at the heart of sociology. The founding of the discipline, in fact, is intimately intertwined with understanding why religion exists in every society. One of the key insights early sociologists, like Emile Durkheim and his teacher, Auguste Comte, had in this regard was that a shared sense of common belief is at the heart of creating a society. Thus, in the process of providing meaning for individuals, the meaningfulness of the group is created and re-created over and over again.

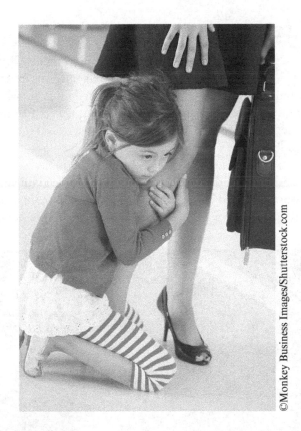

©Monkey Business Images/Shutterstock.com

Now that we have discussed some of the things that religion does by answering the question "What is the function of religion?" let us turn to answering a different question, one that is just as basic, but one that is equally complex: "What are some concrete examples of religions?"

Here, we will provide only a very cursory overview of some major religions. It would be impossible to address the depth and breadth of any one of these even in an entire volume of books. So, we just want to provide a comparative summary of just a few features. No religion is a monolith. In other words, every religion contains an enormous variety of different subgroups all with different rites and rituals, belief systems, priorities, values, and the like.

If you identify with a religious group, then you know how complex and layered and nuanced your own religion is. If you do belong to a religion, then you know that all of the years you spent taking part of that religion have culminated in an appreciation and understanding of your religion that outsiders can only begin to approximate.

Recognizing that we can never fully grasp the importance and value of religions other people have of religions that are not our own can cause us to react in one of two ways. We can easily become overwhelmed with frustration and throw our hands up in the air in resignation. Or, we can embrace our sociological imagination and befriend our curiosity. When we do this, we can better appreciate the wonder of a diverse religious landscape. Then we can delve into our own lifelong explorations of the different ways people cling together against the dark (to again borrow from Richard Rorty).

ABRAHAMIC RELIGIONS

In the United States, religious life is dominated by "the Big Three": Christianity, Islam, and Judaism. That is, when we look at the most popular religions in America, the vast majority of the population belongs to one those three. All three are what we refer to as the Abrahamic tradition. Abraham and his ancestral lineage are featured prominently within each of those three religions. According to Genesis, God ordered Abraham to sacrifice his son Isaac, but God intervened at the last minute and told Abraham that as a reward for his trust in God, he would be given a long lineage of descendants—namely the Jews. Then for some of the authors of the New Testament, Jesus' lineage is traced back to Abraham, and in the Islamic tradition, Abraham leads a long list of prophets culminating in the Prophet Muhammad, who is the founder of Islam.

©Elena Schweitzer/Shutterstock.com

Judaism is one of the world's oldest religions having been around for about 3,000 years. Like Islam and Christianity, it is a monotheistic religion (the belief in one God). Their worship services take place on Saturdays, which is considered the Sabbath (the Sabbath, or "Shabbat," begins at sunset on Friday). Seasonal rituals are a significant part of most Jews' lives and include Rosh Hashanah or the Jewish New Year, and Yom Kippur, which is the holiest day of the year. Yom Kippur includes a period of fasting and worship and is considered the day on which people atone for their sins. Other holidays include the eight days of Hanukkah, or the Festival of Lights, and Passover.

©CREATISTA/Shutterstock.com

Sacred texts for the Jews are the Torah (the first five books of the Bible) and the Talmud, which is a commentary on the Torah written over 2,000 years ago. The clerical leaders in synagogues are rabbis, and outside Orthodox Judaism, women in addition to men can be ordained as rabbis.

One of the most important rites of passage for young Jews is the Bar Mitzvah for boys (at 13 years of age) and the Bat Mitzvah for girls (who are 12). The celebration of these events signals the age at when an individual becomes solely responsible for her or his development as a member of the religion responsible for her or his growth in the religion (rather than the parents' responsibility).

Jews also try and keep kosher by consuming food that has been blessed by a rabbinical authority during the preparation or manufacture of that food.

It is also worthwhile to note that approximately half of American Jews are considered "**cultural-ethnic Jews**" (Johnstone, 2004). These individuals are Jewish by birth or marriage who identify as Jewish but do not belong formally to a synagogue. When we include this group, there are roughly 10 million Jews in the United States.

Christians are by far the largest segment of religious adherents in the United States. The Old and the New Testament make up the sacred text of the Bible. Christians generally hold worship services on Sunday and believe that Jesus was the son of God who was crucified to atone for their sins. The primary holidays for Christians celebrate the birth of Jesus on Christmas and his resurrection on Easter.

> **"cultural-ethnic Jews"** Someone who is Jewish by birth and/or marriage, identifies as Jewish, but does not belong to a synagogue.

Christians must be baptized in order to be ritually accepted into the religion. Most Christians believe in an afterlife, and most belief that Jesus will return to earth in his second coming.

In the United States, there are quite a number of subgroups in the Christian religion, something which we discuss throughout this book. Indeed, because Christians make up the bulk of our country's religious followers, we will spend little time at this point addressing the Christian religion. Much of the work in the following chapters will relate to Christianity primarily due to the religion's significant impact on our society and its infusion into American culture.

ISLAM

While there has been growing attention to Islam in the past decade, the proportion of Muslims in the country remains quite small. Muslims make up only about 1% of the American population. Worldwide though, Islam is the second largest religion (behind Christianity).

In the United States, only a minority of Muslims are of Arabic descent, which runs counter to many people's assumptions about Muslims. Even more Muslims' ethnicity is tied to the Indian subcontinent. Two, a significant portion of Muslims are African American (about 25%) (Smith, 2012). Furthermore, at least 10% of slaves brought from Africa were Muslims (Ibid.).

©Taraskin/Shutterstock.com

The two largest subgroups of the Islamic religion are the Shias and the Sunnis, and the two are divided primarily according to who they believe Muhammad chose as his successor.

In Islam, the Prophet Muhammad, who was born in Mecca and lived in the 6th and 7th centuries, is considered to be the last prophet God sent to earth in order to establish Islam. Muhammad followed the lineage of other divine prophets that include Adam, Abraham, and Jesus, among others. The Quran, which represents Muslims' sacred text, is believed to represent God's revelation to Muhammad.

Muslims worship in mosques, which are headed by Imams. While women in Islam do not lead worship services, they can and often do assume leadership roles within their faith communities.

Muslims are guided by what are known as the "Five Pillars" at the heart of Shari'a Law: one should acknowledge that there is no god but God; one should pray five times daily; one must participate in almsgiving; there is fasting from dawn until dusk during the month of Ramadan; and one must at some point make a holy pilgrimage (the Hajj) to Mecca in one's lifetime.

We will revisit the topic of The Nation of Islam in a later chapter, but it is useful to know a few things about it at the outset. It is an American denomination of Islam, and it began in the 1930s with Elijah Muhammad as its first prominent leader. In the early years of the Nation of Islam, African American followers believed they were the "Lost Tribe of Shabazz" and descendants from the Middle East. While some of Elijah Muhammad's teachings were considered controversial such as his assertion that White people are descendants of the devil, generally speaking, he advocated a message of self-pride and empowerment. Malcolm X converted to Islam while serving time in prison and was a member of the Nation of Islam until he broke from them following a pilgrimage to Mecca. (Malcolm X was assassinated in 1965.) Today, the Nation of Islam continues to work to empower African Americans through encouraging healthy lifestyles, economic empowerment, and dignified and honorable behavior. The current head of the Nation of Islam is Louis Farrakhan, and he helped organize the Million Man March in 1995 in Washington D.C. One of the primary goals of the event was to bring attention to economic inequality that continues to plague American communities, particularly in African American communities.

Like immigrants of European ancestry, Muslim immigration has taken place in waves, the first of which occurred in the late 1800s. The second wave took place during the 1930s, when the Ford Company was experiencing tremendous growth and was in need of labor. To this day, Dearborn, Michigan, where Ford is headquartered, maintains a sizable Muslim population within its demographic. There have been multiple waves of immigrants since then, and some contend that in the past couple of decades, we have witnessed a rise in immigration in part due to political tensions and social turmoil in the Middle East and Africa.

©txking/Shutterstock.com

After 9/11, many Americans conflated, or equated, Islam with terrorism. Thus, for those Americans, Muslims were treated as though they were all the same and a threat to the country's national security. This kind of overgeneralization is a problematic and troubling issue for a variety of reasons, not least of which is the way in which the actions of a minuscule portion of highly radicalized Muslims get projected onto millions of peaceful, well-intentioned individuals. Just think about how Christians might feel if non-Christians demonized Christians for the actions of people such as the KKK (who self-identify as Christians), or the dozens of Christians who have bombed abortion clinics or murdered doctors at abortion clinics, or Eric Rudolph, who set off bombs during the Atlanta Olympics that resulted in two deaths and over 100 serious injuries.

Generally speaking, America is much more religiously diverse nowadays and also more tolerant of religious diversity. However, it should be noted that survey data show that Christians are less tolerant of Islam on average than they are of other religions (Chaves, 2011). Today, many Muslims must endure religious prejudice and suspicion on the part of non-Muslim Americans and that is in combination with heightened governmental attention and even surveillance. Indeed, "Islamaphobia," or the irrational fear of Muslims, unfortunately continues to be a factor in the United States. In spite of the irrationality of villainizing Muslims and disparaging Islam, "Law enforcement agencies in the immediate aftermath of 9/11 kept thousands of Muslims under surveillance and closely monitored the actions of major Muslim organizations . . . Roughly 83,000 people from predominantly Muslim nations were forced to register with the government, and nearly 50,000 people of mainly Muslim backgrounds were deported" (Moosa, 2012: 563). Also, there were a number of communities around the country that fought the construction of new mosques, and when, in 2010, a mosque near Ground Zero in Lower Manhattan was proposed, a furor erupted.

Much Islamaphobia is a result of treating a very diverse and heterogeneous population of Muslims as essentially all the same and linking all Muslims to the actions of a very few extremist terrorists. One need to merely read the Quran to learn that Islam is a religion that is no different to the other major religions in the world: kindness, peace, love, and compassion are the central virtues of each of those religions. Islam is no different.

BUDDHISM AND HINDUISM

Hinduism is considered to be the oldest major religion in the world. It is unusual since there are no shared doctrinal principles, no common theology, and no set of shared rituals.

Many Hindu practitioners believe in multiple gods and goddesses while others are monotheistic. Different subgroups of Hinduism are typically distinguished based on their respective beliefs in a particular *primary* deity though, such as Shiva, Vishnu, or Krishna. Also, they can be differentiated according to their primary sacred text, whether it is the Vedas, the Bhagavad Gita, or the Upanishads. However, for the most part, the different orders within Hinduism all acknowledge the importance of a variety of deities, and they all tend to recognize the significance of multiple sacred texts.

©Dangdumrong/Shutterstock.com

Almost all Hindus advocate the ethical principle of nonviolence, and for many believers, this extends to all sentient beings. Thus, vegetarianism is common but not entirely universal among them.

The religion has its origins in India, and the majority of Hindus reside on the Indian subcontinent. However, Hindu practitioners can be found across the globe. In spite of that, less than 1% of Americans identify as Hindu.

About 2,500 years old, Buddhism is not quite as old as Hinduism, though both religions trace their origins to India. Also, like Hindu practitioners, Buddhists make up less than 1% of Americans. However, the interest in mindfulness meditation, which has its roots in Buddhism, is helping to spur greater interest in the religion (also, celebrities who have converted to Buddhism likely make the religion more palatable to Americans and may contribute to its growth).

Buddhism is generally a nontheistic religion. That is, the vast majority of Buddhist subgroups do not worship a divinity, and a belief in a god is not a requirement to being Buddhist. Also, many people incorrectly assume that Buddhists believe in reincarnation as it is generally understood, but that is not the case for most practitioners, particularly in American Buddhism.

The religion traces its roots to the story of a prince named Siddhartha Gautama (he was not called the Buddha, which translates to "Awakened Being," until later). Against his father's wishes, he ventured out into the world beyond the palace and discovered that part of what it means to be alive is to have to deal with old age, sickness, and death. This fact is the first of the Four Noble Truths: life inevitably includes suffering. We can try all we can to avoid this simple fact by denying it, by numbing ourselves with sex, food, alcohol, or drugs, or by just accepting it.

Buddhists believe that the root of emotional and spiritual suffering stems from our attachments. What we cling to is the desire to not have to go through suffering (the Second Noble Truth). When things are going well in our lives, we want it to stay that way, and when things are not going so well, we want things to be different.

©LeshaBu/Shutterstock.com

However, there is a path of freedom from suffering (this is the Third Noble Truth), and the way we attain freedom is through the Noble Eightfold Path (the Fourth Noble Truth). The Eightfold Path is a set of guidelines for practices such as meditation and ethical behavior.

There are a wide variety of subgroups within Buddhism. Most groups hold certain teachings of the Buddha to be sacred, such as the Dhammapada. In the United States, most Buddhists are part of either the Zen tradition or the Theravedin. You may be familiar with the Dalai Lama, who is part of the Theravada School of Buddhism. In both schools of Buddhism, followers aim to become enlightened like the Buddha. The Zen school is influenced by the teachings of Bodhidharma, who advocated that Buddhists ought to first allay the suffering of others before allowing themselves to be free of suffering. He felt that since all beings are interconnected, the suffering of even one being creates suffering for others.

Both schools emphasize the importance of meditation and believe that all people have a Buddha nature within them that can be realized through meditation and other practices. Worship styles vary greatly though generally services include a period of chanting, meditation, and a "dharma talk" (something akin to a Christian "sermon"). Important holidays include the Buddha's birthday as well as Bodhi Day (which celebrates the historical Buddha's awakening).

©Kitja Kitja/Shutterstock.com

So, now that we have looked briefly at some of the major religions in America and across the globe, let us discuss the ways sociologists make sense of religions as institutional structures.

DENOMINATIONS

In the sociology of religion, it is helpful to understand the ways in which different religions break down into other groups and subgroups. For instance, Christianity is a religion with different subgroups that include Catholics, Baptists, Methodists, etc. So, at the very top level of our organizational chart, we have religions, and in the United States, the largest three in order of the number of adherents are: Christianity, Judaism, and Islam.

Within each religion, there are multiple denominations. Because most Americans identify as Christians, generally when we talk about denominations, we are only referring to subgroups within the Christian religion. Over 70% of Americans identify with some form of Christian religion (and the rate would be much higher when taking into consideration the number of Americans who were raised Christians but no longer identify as such). Because of this, much of our discussion regarding the structures within religion pertains primarily to Christian religions. However, there are certainly subgroups of Judaism (Orthodox, Conservative, and Progressive primarily) as well as of Islam (primarily Sunni and Shiite).

Different denominations adhere to different forms of organization. The way a religious organization is structured and governed is called its **polity**. There are, generally speaking, three different forms of polity, and we can map out how the leadership of a given organization corresponds to the lay people (or nonclergy) in each. [Note: What might be a source of confusion is the fact that each of the three forms of polity is also name of a Christian denomination. Here, though, when we are discussing polity, we are not referring to the denominations. Each of the three forms of polity is a technical term referring only to the governance and structure.]

Polity The way in which religious organizations are structured.

©winui/Shutterstock.com

In the episcopal form of organizational structure, there is a clear top-down hierarchy that is fairly linear. Catholics, Anglicans, and Episcopalians all have an episcopal polity. These structures include leaders of a given parish, such as a priest. Then above the priest is a bishop, and the bishop oversees multiple priests. In the Roman Catholic Church, there are also archbishops who oversee multiple bishops. Cardinals are above them, and, of course, at the very top is the Pope.

The Presbyterian polity is also is a top down hierarchy; however, each level is represented by a group of people who represent another group below them. In this form of organization, each church elects a group of leaders called a session. Multiple sessions select who to represent them at the level of the presbytery, and at the highest level is the general assembly.

A congregational polity is one in which each congregation, parish, church, or group is separate and autonomous in their decision-making from other congregations, groups, etc. There are more than 300,000 individual congregations in the United States. (i.e., synagogues, mosques, temples, churches). Most congregations are tied to a national denomination, but an increasing number of Protestant congregations maintain no denominational ties (about one in five) (Chaves, 2011).

Before we conclude this chapter, we need to address an important group of people who make up a growing segment of the American population: religious "nones."

RELIGIOUS "NONES"

The United States is often assumed to be a "Christian nation," and a lot of people think that it goes back to our very founding. However, two prominent sociologists note that, in 1776, regular religious participation stood at only 17% (Finke and Starke, 1992). The same sociologists also noted that since that time, religious participation has steadily climbed. In fact, if we are judging by the percentage of people who are active in a religious community, the United States is among the most religious countries when compared to other Western, industrialized countries.

©CHOATphotographer/Shutterstock.com

But that is changing.

The sociologist of religion Mark Chaves has analyzed an enormous amount of data involving Americans and their religiosity (2011). Among his findings, he discovered that Americans still believe in heaven and hell and in God or a higher power at almost the same high levels they always have. But, fewer people believe in the Bible as being the inerrant word of God. Interestingly, Smith also found a correlation between levels of education and belief in biblical inerrancy (the higher the rates of education, the less likely people were to believe in it).

According to Chaves (2011), 40% of Americans say that they attend a religious service at least weekly, but that figure represents how frequently people self-report their attendance. More accurate figures, which tell us how frequently people actually attend on a weekly basis, are closer to 25%. The number of people who report that they never attend religious services has increased, and more and more children and teens report that parents have never taken them to a religious service.

In 2015, the Pew Research Center on Religion and Public Life released data from a comprehensive study that examined trends in Americans' religious lives over time. (retrieved from URL: http://www.pewforum.org/2015/05/12/americas-changing-religious-landscape). Some of their findings were quite surprising. Particularly interesting to sociologists of religion was the statistic related to what are often called religious "nones." Religious nones are people who do not identify with a religion. Religious nones include the growing number of people who identify as "spiritual but not religious." Those people make up only a small minority of Americans, but most of the "spiritual but not religious" people tend to be younger. According to Chaves (2011), about 18% of people between the ages of 18 and 39 identify as such.

The reason we refer to them as "nones" is because often when someone is filling out a form that asks them to report their religion, there is a list of religions with a checkbox next to each. The list might include Catholic, Jew, Muslim, and Protestant. At the bottom of the list, there is an option for "none," which allows the person completing the form to report that they are not religious or do not identify with any particular religion.

©CLS Digital Arts/Shutterstock.com

Thus, sociologists simply refer to "religious nones" as a shorthand way of talking about people who do not identify with a religion. Historically, in the United States, the number of religious nones has been very small—almost to the point that religious nones were considered outliers or marginal cases hardly worth talking about. In 1957, only 3% of Americans were **religious "nones"** (Chaves, 2011). However, in 1957, it was not as socially acceptable to identify as a "none." Also, many people equate identifying as religious aligns oneself with conservatives and evangelicals, which many people are not willing to do (Ibid.). Nevertheless, America has seen an unprecedented rise in the number of religious nones, and not only are there more religious nones than ever before, but also the speed at which the number of religious nones increased is nothing short of astounding.

A little more than one in five American adults are now considered religious nones. When we narrow it down to age group and just look at one generation, the millennials (people who were born between 1981 and 1996), the number of religious nones is a remarkable one in three.

One in four religious nones identified as either atheist (believes there is no divinity) or agnostic (unsure of whether or not there is a divinity). Thus, one of the likely conclusions is that most of the religious nones are spiritual but not religious. That is, they may believe in God or have been raised in a particular religion but presently do not belong to a faith community.

The Pew data also revealed something else that was unprecedented in American history. The percentage of people who identify with a religion other than the one in which they were raised is higher than it has ever been: 42%.

From these data, we might make a couple of generalizations. First, while the United States has long been one of the most religious countries in the industrialized Western world, it is increasingly becoming less so. European countries have long had lower levels of religious participation than we have had here in North America, but that appears to be changing rapidly. Second, these changes are largely fueled by young adults, which means that these patterns are likely to grow even stronger as they pass

> **Religious "nones"** A growing group of people who identify as spiritual but not religious.

©Rawpixel.com

on their values to their children in the future. We discuss some of the reasons for this unprecedented growth in religious nones in a later chapter.

As we set out through the rest of this book and your class, it is important to keep the aforementioned discussions in mind. Rather than a set of terms, ideas, and concepts to be memorized, it is crucial to understand the sociological perspective. It is important to become conversant with the ways that sociologists think about religion, belief, and religious systems. Will it be helpful to understand something about the world's most popular religions discussed earlier? Of course. But only insofar as it helps us to understand the applications of the theories and examples we use later.

If sociologists are doing their jobs well, they are uncovering patterns, dynamics, and social forces in one time and place that apply to others with a similar context. This is as true for sociologists who study religion as it is for sociologists who study

©TungCheung/Shutterstock.com

stratification or family or gender or anything else. Our purpose in the following chapters is not to negate anyone's personal understanding and experience with religion but rather to enhance that understanding by exploring the social forces that help to structure our personal beliefs and choices.

DISCUSSION QUESTIONS

1. What is Sociology? Give an example of something a person who identifies as a sociologist might say (draw on concepts discussed in this chapter).
2. What are the types of sociological research? Compare and contrast the two, and give an example of a topic that would be well suited for each.
3. What are the sociological levels of analysis? Give two examples of people/places/things that fit into each category. Additionally, give an example of how one level can directly affect another level (think of the example of George's students from the chapter).
4. What has Chaves noted as the correlation between religion and conservative politics? Use proper terminology.
5. According to Berger, how does religion protect us from solipsism?
6. What are "The Big Three" religions in the United States? Name two things they all have in common. Which one is the largest (having the most members)?
7. What is **Islamophobia**, how did it come about, and why is it problematic?
8. Compare and contrast Hinduism and Buddhism.
9. Explain the three forms of polity.
10. Who are religious "nones," and what is their significance to the more recent social research of religion in the United States? Why do we use the term "none?"

Islamophobia The irrational fear of Muslims.

CHAPTER 2

BECOMING RELIGIOUS: NAVIGATING BELIEFS, NEGOTIATING EXPRESSIONS

Are religious people crazy?

KEY TERMS

- Achieved
- Ascribed
- Economist perspective
- Functional differentiation
- Institutions
- Liminal period
- Plausibility structure
- Proselytizing
- Privatized
- Reaffirmation
- Reify
- Relativistic
- Religiosity
- Religious pluralism
- Rite of passage
- Roles
- Secularization
- Social Construction
- Social drift theory
- Socialization
- Symbol

OBJECTIVES:

- Understand what it means to be religious in today's American culture, as well as what it means to be secular. Know why people adhere, or not, to a particular religion.

- Grasp the reasons why some people stay with their ascribed religious beliefs, and why others choose to convert to another religion, or a lack thereof one. Also, understand the processes involved in these phenomena.
- Understand why religion as a social institution is important, ultimately because generations and generations of people have deemed it so.

RELIGIOSITY

What does it mean when someone asks you whether or not you are "religious?" Does it mean you maintain a formal membership with a particular faith community? Does it have to do with whether or not you believe in God? Do you think the person asking you is trying to find out whether or not you pray or go to mosque or a church? Clearly, there are a lot of ways to interpret the word "religious." So, the question is: how do we as sociologists widen our attention from just the individual in order to find out how "religious" Americans are? Has that level of religiousness changed over time?

©Kjetil Kolbjornsrud/Shutterstock.com

There are multiple approaches we can take. For instance, we might ask: Has the percentage of Americans who profess a belief in God changed over time? This question attempts to address the issue of religion as a belief. Or, we might ask a question that attempts to understand people's actions with a question such as: Has the percentage of Americans who attend a church, temple, or synagogue on a weekly basis changed over time? Both of these questions address two different ways we can talk about religiousness (though we will use the term "religiosity").

If someone has ever asked you whether or not you are **religious**," then you know that the question is problematic because it is so vague. What one person calls "religious" may not seem all that religious to someone else, and vice versa. We could, for instance, be talking about beliefs, or we could be talking about behaviors, and depending on which one is at stake, we could get completely different answers.

In fact, the issue is even more complicated.

The sociologist Charles Glock (1965) actually developed five different dimensions for thinking about how "religious" one is or is not (i.e., levels of religiosity). That is, one might reasonably measure how religious someone is in five different ways. We will discuss each of the five briefly.

"Religious,"
Socially constructed idea to describe the level at which someone is or is not religious; measures vary.

The first dimension of religiosity is ritual. This dimension of religiosity pertains to the actual behaviors one participates in or performs that are related directly to one's religion. If your religion requires that two times a year you should fast (refrain from eating) from sunup to sundown, do you actually do it? What about prayer? If your religion has a place for prayer in daily life, do you pray? If so, how often do you pray? Do you regularly study the Bible or the Torah or the Quran? Do you regularly attend worship services that are relevant to your faith?

The second dimension of religiosity Glock identifies is intellectual. Here, Glock wants us to recognize that one's knowledge of religion is an important component to being a religious individual. How much do you know about the history of your religion? Do you know about all of the various stories and people who are portrayed in the Bible, Torah, or Quran? Do you know how your religious denomination developed over time and how it is organized on a national or even international level? Knowledge too is an important feature of religiosity.

©Saida Shigapova/Shutterstock.com

Belief is the third dimension of religiosity. How strongly do you identify with the central tenets of your religion? Do you believe pretty much everything you are supposed to believe? Are there some things your faith community professes as important beliefs or values that do not align with your own beliefs? Even within certain beliefs, there may be some latitude for believing something more strongly or less strongly. You may believe, for instance, with great certainty that there is a divinity, but when it comes to your belief in an afterlife, you may feel a little less sure. So, when we measure levels of belief, we must first have a reference point. Since by definition, Christians believe Jesus was the Messiah, we might ask Christians to what extent they felt that belief was true. Or, we might ask them to tell us how important that belief is when compared to other core Christian beliefs.

The reference point will, of course, change depending on one's religion. Thus, if someone is a Buddhist, it would not make sense to ask them whether or not they believe Jesus was the son of God. Similarly, it would not make sense to ask Christians to tell us about their beliefs in the Four Noble Truths (a central tenet in Buddhism).

The fourth dimension of religiosity is consequential. This dimension relates to how much your religion affects you in everyday life. Do you find yourself acting in certain ways or saying certain things that you may not have were it not for your religion? Does your religion impact the way you feel about people in general? If, for example,

©Cylonphoto/Shutterstock.com

you came across someone who was asking for money, would you respond in a certain way because of your religion? In short, the consequential dimension of religiosity attempts to get at how much of a factor your religion has on influencing how you think and act as you go about your day-to-day business.

The final dimension is experiential. What kinds of physical, emotional, or spiritual experiences do you have? Are they mystical? Do they make you feel like you are on an emotional high? Do you have what some people might refer to as religious experiences? This dimension is increasingly a focus for individuals in today's society, so we will devote a little more time to it than the others.

The emphasis on experientialism in today's religious culture can be attributed to the privatization of religion. That is, a consequence of religion becoming something increasingly intimate and internal and less of a topic for public or social conversation is that we become more reliant upon our own experiences and insights for a sense of right and wrong (and other religious values). Some sociologists argue that, as a result, we increasingly rely on how things, encounters, events, and so on make us *feel*. Thus, we are increasingly reliant on our bodies and how things make us feel inside our bodies. We can even come to have a kind of *embodied knowledge* in which we trust what we sometimes have referred to as our instincts, emotions, intuitions, or gut feelings. So, the tendency people have is to notice more and more contexts that make us feel comfortable and secure and avoid environments and situations that make us feel uneasy or anxious. The body, in other words, has become a prominent tool that helps us interpret the world as well as navigate the social environment.

©Poprotskiy Alexey/Shutterstock.com

You may consider the ways in which when people go shopping or to a restaurant they often expect more than merely obtaining a product or some nutritional sustenance. Rather, people want to feel as though they also got an experience from going out. Sociologists talk about this with the concept of experiential consumption. Experiential consumption is the idea that when people purchase something, they are also expecting that they will feel something emotionally or bodily. Take, for example, the ways that some stores that sell outdoor recreational goods include a rock-climbing wall on which customers can practice. Or, it can be something as simple as going into a store that sells lotions or other bath products and being surrounded by soothing scents that can lead customers to feel tranquil and relaxed.

©Peter Bernik/Shutterstock.com

The rise in experiential consumption in restaurants and stores can also be seen in the religious sphere as well. Many churches, for instance, highlight their abilities to stage what can feel like a theatrical production. Rather than sitting in hard-wooden pews, churchgoers are comfortably ensconced in movie-theater-style, cushioned chairs. Rather than relying on a small choir and a piano or organ to provide the worship music, some churches utilize something that might resemble a rock band with guitarists, a set of vocalists, bass player, and drummer to fill out the musical ensemble. Instead of having someone speak at a podium and read the announcements, some places put together a short film to do the job. All of these things contribute to making religion an experience that absorbs people and allows them to feel as though they are in touch with the sacred on an emotional and physical level.

©Syda Productions/Shutterstock.com

The importance of these embodied rituals and experiences can be perhaps most profoundly identified when people lose their faith or change religious traditions. Lynn Davidman (2014) investigated how the lives of ex-Hasidic Jews changed after they left their faith. She showed how the rituals and practices that once connected people to each other became a significant source of disconnection between people who lost their faith and their previous communities. In this juxtaposition, we can see clearly just how important these shared rituals are in creating and sustaining faith on a daily basis.

In sum, when we ask about how religious someone is or is not, that is, their level of religiosity, we must be careful about what specifically we mean. Being religious for one person may be quite different for another. Additionally, different religions emphasize different dimensions of religiosity. It is, therefore, important to qualify how we define religiosity as sociologists do, and it is equally important to be sensitive that others may have different requirements, expectations, or values that reflect their own religious traditions. This is because religiosity is something that is socially constructed: an idea we will turn to now.

SOCIAL CONSTRUCTION

We will frequently use the phrases "**socially constructed**" and "social construction" throughout this text. While it may seem apparent what the concept refers to, it is helpful to elaborate a bit on what we mean when we use those terms.

In 1966, Berger and Luckmann, two of the most important sociologists of religion, published their book *The Social Construction of Reality*. Now, to be clear, they were not suggesting that the concrete world that you can go out and touch and see is nothing more than an illusion fabricated by society. Instead, they want us to recognize that the ways we *think about* reality are socially constructed.

> **"Socially constructed"** Something that does not exist except in the fact that collective "we" think it does.

Take a fairly straightforward example of people's taste in music. I might play you a song that I really, really like, and you, after listening to it, might really, really dislike it. We both heard the same song. So, why do we have different preferences in music? I grew up listening to one style of music, and you grew up listening to a completely different style of music. We were both exposed through our parents and our friends to different kinds of music, and that exposure helped to influence our tastes. Therefore, we can say that musical preference is, to some degree, socially constructed.

©pathdoc/Shutterstock.com

Berger and Luckmann (1966) dive deeper into social construction when they explore the nature of symbols. Symbols are, of course, socially constructed. Someone had to tell us that "green means go" or that holding your palm open but touching your forefinger to your thumb in a little circle means "okay." How do we know these things are socially constructed? We know that these things are socially constructed because we were not born with this knowledge about what these symbols mean. In fact, if we made the same "okay" **symbol** in certain other countries, the people would interpret our gesture as meaning something offensive—quite the opposite of the meaning we have assigned it. So, another property of social construction is that the meaning can be different depending on which culture that symbol is found in.

> **Symbol** Something that stands for something else.

©ArtFamily/Shutterstock.com

Words too are symbols. We were not born with the ability to read, write, and interpret words, yet words enable thought. Thoughts, that is, are just various strings of words . . . "I am hungry right now" or "I am bored out of my mind." The way we describe our feelings, the way we rehearse what we want to say to someone, and the way we interpret what we see ("Outside my office is a tree with pink blossoms")—all of these rely on socially constructed symbols—namely words.

As a result of all of this, Berger and Luckmann simply want us to recognize that our thoughts (and our knowledge, ideas, beliefs, and so on) all have a socially constructed element. It is as though we are born into a world of symbols that we must learn the meanings of, and then, we "borrow" those symbols in order to construct thoughts and then convey those thoughts through speech. Therefore, we construct a reality with other people who are doing the same things with their thoughts and symbols.

It is through our interactions with other people that we establish a mutually accepted, recognizable reality. In other words, the socially constructed has been **reified**—something that is socially constructed that is then taken for granted as being normal and natural. When we reify something, we transform a social construction into something that we treat as real. An example of reification is evident in racial categories. There is nothing genetic about race. Biologists have demonstrated this as a matter of scientific fact. Yet, we treat race like it is something natural—like there are physiological differences between Black people and White people that run deeper than the mere pigment of people's complexion. Just think about all of the laws that in the early 20th century segregated Whites from Blacks. People during that era reified race as something factual, when in reality, race is a social construction.

> **Reified** To confirm something to be true or exist.

©Daxiao Productions/Shutterstock.com

Knowing that there is nothing genetic to distinguish people on the basis of "race" might make it seem like reification only takes place when we have developed scientific evidence for proving something is socially constructed. But we actually engage in reification all of the time. Take, for instance, the typical college classroom. The reality of the college classroom is one that is socially constructed, yet, it seems quite natural. We assume that it is perfectly natural to step inside a blandly colored, walled room that contains chairs with some sort of shelves attached that we call desks. Then, an "expert" will come in and hand out some papers that tell us what we are going to read and what work we will need to complete in order to receive a number (i.e., a grade).

The "expert" is only an expert by dint of the fact that she or he has received a piece of paper that contains some letters such as "Ph.D." on it. In reality, the primary accomplishment of obtaining that piece of paper with those letters was likely due to her or him having read more books and taken more classes than you.

©Monkey Business Images/Shutterstock.com

Yet, we take that person's words so seriously that we spend hours upon hours coming back to that room and writing down much of what that so-called expert says. Then we take our notes, and we reread them and try and memorize them as though they were more important than magazines or blogs we also happen to be reading. At one or more points in the oddly compartmentalized period of time we refer to as a semester, we spend even more time rereading our notes. We might even find ourselves getting anxious or fearful, so much so that we have trouble sleeping because on an arbitrarily selected day during the semester, we have to sit down and recite some of the things we recall from our notes. Why? Because that "expert" is then going to judge us and write down a number or a letter on this thing we call a test. We do this over and over again—probably at least 20, or 30, or 40 times. It seems normal only because everyone else is doing the same exact thing.

At no point do we witness someone in the rooms where we re-enact these activities (e.g., note-taking, listening to lectures, and taking tests) stand up and say, "This is all an illusion and that so-called expert is really just a fraud; we've all been duped!" So we keep at it: struggling sometimes, getting worried other times, and even going into financial debt.

©Robert Kneschke/Shutterstock.com

Why? So we can someday get up on a stage in front of other people and shake someone's hand and collect a piece of paper with our name on it and some letters such as "B.A." or "B.S." But it's just a piece of paper, isn't it? Yet, some of us will put it in a frame and hang it on our wall. Mostly, we work for that piece of paper because everyone else is doing the same thing or because we think that it will enable us to get a better job. Still, hardly anyone in life will ever ask to see that piece of paper as some sort of proof. Mostly, though, people take your word for it when you tell them you have such a piece of paper.

It isn't just the people around you who believe that all of that matters . . . the note-taking, the worry, the debt, and the piece of paper. When you take out a loan or apply for a job or even meet new friends or romantic partners, people will ask if you have one of those pieces of paper. So, the institution of education is socially constructed and then reified by people in other institutions such as the workplace or financial organizations.

All of them, all of the emotions, behaviors, roles, and activities, are social constructions. They have not always looked this way, and in other places, they look a whole lot different.

The same can be said for the institution of religion. For example, many Catholics believe in the concept of transubstantiation wherein, during the ritual of communion, the wine and bread that are symbolic of the blood and body of Jesus Christ actually become blood and body in that moment. To sustain that belief takes a great deal of collective construction by people over a long period of time. Lest you think Catholics are somehow "strange" in this belief, it is no more extreme than many other beliefs and practices across religions. On a very micro level, these myriad social constructions, which make up the core activities and beliefs of religion in daily life, are translated over time into religious community and culture.

Furthermore, as a social construction, people's attitudes regarding its functions and its relative importance are subject to change. If we, collectively, make religion on a daily basis, then we, collectively, can change religion and religious structures and culture. Indeed, some have made the claim that religion has outlived its usefulness for society and that it is more important for people to take responsibility for their own spiritual development. So, we need to ask . . .

IS RELIGION IN DECLINE?

We ended Chapter 1 on a kind of ominous note when it comes to the state of religion. The religious nones, it would seem, are taking over. After all, we have seen an unprecedented rise in the number of people who do not identify with a religion. When we look at the data, religious nones tend to be younger (and conversely, most of the people who identify with a religion tend to be older). It would, therefore, be easy to conclude that as the older people become too old to take part in religion, religious institutions will shrink in membership and religion itself will begin to wither and fade away.

©Paul Vasarhelyi/Shutterstock.com

We have actually seen evidence of this taking place on a smaller scale—that is, on the level of churches. Some congregations have been unable to retain their youth. Perhaps their young people left for college or moved to another location for a job or simply became dissatisfied with their church. When those churches then are unable to attract new members who are in their 20s or 30s (i.e., people who are at the age of beginning a family), then the average age of the congregation will creep upward. Eventually, these churches become populated almost entirely of senior citizens. Eventually, without population replacement either by attracting new members or by current members having children, the congregation numbers will dwindle and the church will need to close its doors on a permanent basis.

So, since we have seen churches die out, is it, therefore, reasonable to predict that religion too will eventually begin to die out due to these same forces? If there are enough individual congregations who are incapable of appealing to younger people who themselves are less interested in identifying with religion, then is it possible that entire denominations and even religions will begin to fade away?

It is, of course, possible. However, we should keep in mind that every generation has its own list of naysayers and doomsday artists predicting the end of religion. In fact, some of the most brilliant and informed sociologists of religion have predicted the end of religion and, of course, have been proven wrong. Religion, as an institution, is highly resilient and highly adaptable. Nowhere is this more true than the United States, where the history of religion contains a number of innovations, revivals, and rebirths.

In the previous chapter, we touched on the work of one of the most influential sociologists of religion—Peter Berger. Earlier in his career, he was one of the people who argued that religion was on its way out. Society, he believed, was becoming less religious through the process of **secularization**. For our purposes, secular refers to that which is not conventionally considered to be religious. So, we might talk about the government as being a secular institution because it is not a religious one. Or, we might say that engaging in activities such as exercising, reading comics, and going to school are examples of secular activities. As you can see, the word secular can be quite broad, perhaps too broad. So, it is important to carefully consider what we mean when we talk about the process of secularization.

> **Secularization**
> The "dereligioning" of society; stems from the word "secular," which generally means anything that is not religious; the process by which sectors in society and culture are removed from the denomination of religious institutions (Berger).

©aga7ta/Shutterstock.com

Peter Berger defined secularization as "the process by which sectors in society and culture are removed from the domination of religious institutions" (1967: 107). Berger's definition is rather technical, so let us take a moment to unpack what he means by secularization. There are a couple of important facets to Berger's perspective.

First, if we line up all the various institutions that make up public life in society—such as government, education, family, and religion—then, according to Berger, religion would be viewed as less significant, less impactful, and less central to people's lives than these other institutions. Furthermore, when we examined the way one institution might influence another, then religion would be less influential than the other institutions. Consider, for example, capital punishment, the use of the death penalty that the justice system sometimes employs in cases of homicide. How does religion shape the legislation that states rely on when determining the legality of capital punishment? Or, consider education—is religious morality something that is taught in schools? Or, even the way the institution of medicine—do you think religion impacted how funding agencies support research into AIDS? According to Berger's theory of secularization, religion would over time begin to play less of a role in influencing the ways in which secular institutions are run and the ways people who have decision-making power regulate and operate secular institutions.

Additionally, Berger's definition of secularization would also predict that religion, as an institution, would be less important in the daily lives of people when compared to secular institutions. This leads us to the concept of **functional differentiation**. Functional differentiation refers to the process whereby individual institutions (religion as well as secular institutions) have an increasingly narrow specialization with regard to what each provides for people in everyday life.

> **Functional differentiation** Process whereby individual institutions have an increasingly narrow specialization with regard to what each provides for people in everyday life.

©Shebeko/Shutterstock.com

One way of thinking about functional differentiation is to compare it to the division of labor. If you have ever had a job in which you were assigned a specific task that you repeated over and over while your coworkers had their own different tasks that they performed over and over, then you know what this means. For example, in college, I worked at a small Mexican restaurant where my job was to build burritos. All day, I layered beans, lettuce, and cheese on tortillas while my coworkers did other things such as fill soft drink orders and staff the cash register. The division of labor is a way to make complex operations more efficient by having workers focus on one specific thing. The same thing can be said for society and its institutions: as society becomes more complex, its institutions develop their own sets of functions and purposes.

Secularization would predict that religion would become more and more differentiated and specialized in what it does or how it functions in people's lives. For instance, rather than seeking out a minister or a priest for counseling, we now go to professional psychologists. Rather than meeting a potential romantic partner at church, we can turn to companies that provide dating services. Rather than getting our education through a religious program, we attend public schools. In other words, functional differentiation as a characteristic of secularization would predict that we participate in religion for a narrow set of well-defined purposes: that is, to develop a sense of moral codes, to foster our spiritual nature, to hear lesson from a rabbi or priest, and so forth.

So, Peter Berger predicted that secularization would become more and more a factor in the world and that religion's importance in people's lives would dwindle. This also had ramifications for people in another way. According to Berger, because religion would become less important as a public institution and would become less important in comparison to other public institutions, it would also begin to become less visible. Think about it—if religion is less influential to making decisions in the political arena or if religion is something that is confined to serving a narrow set of purposes for individuals, then it makes sense that it might not be something that is covered in the media or something people have much need to talk about in everyday conversation. It begins to fade from the public consciousness and thus begins to be something that really only matters to me as an individual. In this view, it might lead us to think along the lines of "My religion is my own business." When people begin to have the perspective that religion is something that is only important to them as individuals rather than a public institution that is important and influential in civic life, then we say that religion has become **privatized**.

> **Privatized** When something becomes relevant to individuals on a personal level rather than to groups on an institutional level.

©g-stockstudio/Shutterstock.com

The privatization of religion would mean that religion becomes something very personal. Recall in our previous chapter that today's young adults are far more likely than previous generations to *not* belong to the religion in which they were raised. In the past generations, one's religious identity (e.g., "I am a Catholic," "I am an Orthodox Jew," and "I am a Presbyterian") was something **ascribed**. That is, one's religion tended to be something one was born into. Now, however, religious identity is something that is more likely to be **achieved**. It is something one may be born into but is frequently something one selects and chooses.

> **Ascribed** A social category one is born into.

Freed from the conventional religious path, people have increasingly been choosing not to affiliate at all or to claim an identity of "**spiritual but not religious**" (SBNR). SBNRs may still identify with a higher power and a sense of cosmic presence and the afterlife, but they reject the religious systems offered to them in the form of major world religions. That is, they do not identify as Muslims, Christians, Jewish, etc. They may borrow and adapt parts of those systems, but they create, in effect, their own religious life.

> **Achieved** Something one can be born into but is either solely or also chosen/selected by the individual.

So, why does an achieved religious identity relate to privatization more than an ascribed identity? Let us use an example . . . if you are like me, there are certain holidays during the year when I get together with my parents, siblings, cousins, aunts, and uncles. Thanksgiving is one example. In my family, my siblings, as well as most of my cousins, identify with a religion other than the one in which we were brought up. So, religion, as a conversational topic, is largely off the table, so to speak. Some relatives belong to a completely different religion than others, so no one wants to get into debating theological differences or arguing over whose religion is better than whose.

Even when the religions between two different people are similar, the two people don't belong to the same faith community, so even in those instances, there is no shared commonality regarding trivial matters such as: who the preacher is, or who got married to so-and-so, or what special events took place in the past week.

So you see, just in this simple example of a family get-together, one's religion is not something that is brought up as a matter of course. In our example, religion is something that is unique to each individual in the family. Religion becomes something that the individual herself or himself participates in and finds meaning in rather than an area of interest in which multiple people share commonly.

©Monkey Business Images/Shutterstock.com

Peter Berger felt that the increasing functional differentiation of religion would lessen its significance for society and would lead to increased privatization of religion. Berger believed that these things would lead more people to consign and compartmentalize religion to something rather minor and insignificant. He felt that people would begin to treat religion and the choices they make around religion to be a part of just another lifestyle choice among other lifestyle choices. So, religion would be something we pick and choose and change the way we pick and choose and change the brand of toothpaste we buy, the diet we decide to try, or the airline or credit card we use. People's lack of enduring commitment would lead ultimately to religion's decline and eventual demise.

As it turned out, just as had happened so many times in the past, predictions about a rise in secularization and the end of religion turned out to be inaccurate. While there are certainly more religious nones than ever before, religion continues to be a vital institution in our society and one that, at least in the present moment, the majority of Americans are taking part in.

To his great credit, Peter Berger, in later years, not only softened his claims regarding the increasing secularization of society but actually began reversing his earlier predictions in a variety of publications. You can read an article he wrote that discusses his current feelings on the matter here: http://www.firstthings.com/article/2008/02/002-secularization-falsified. As any good sociologist would, Berger let the data drive the conclusions about his hypothesis.

Since secularization has not completely prevailed and religion continues to be a central social institution, one that is essential to the lives of millions of people, let us now turn to addressing the issues of how and why people join religions.

RELIGIOUS SOCIALIZATION

Getting socialized into a religious tradition or community operates in ways that are very similar to the socialization processes for other groups. In order to understand exactly how this process works, let's refresh a few core concepts that you may remember from an introductory sociology class.

A **norm** is one of the most fundamental concepts in the field of sociology. A norm refers to a behavior or thought that is socially acceptable and generally socially expected. When you ride in an elevator, you face the front. You wear certain kinds of clothes to work and others to the beach. You try not and burp loudly when you are with large groups of people. All of these are behavioral norms. But norms also relate to our thoughts and feelings. You may find yourself so angry with your roommate that you give them the finger or call them a name but if you actually feel like you want to murder them and proceed to go about thinking of ways you can accomplish this, you are violating a norm. Social norms dictate that feeling angry is acceptable in certain circumstances, but planning a homicide is not.

Roles are personal identities that are characterized by a set of norms. Roles change from context to context. Your role as a student is separate from your role as a girlfriend or boyfriend. Each role has a different bundle of norms that guide your behavior and thoughts. In your role as a student, there are norms such as: coming to class on time, taking notes, and completing the assigned homework. As a girlfriend or boyfriend, the bundle of norms might include: texting or calling your significant other on a regular basis, remembering their birthday and your anniversary, and expressing appropriate affection, and so on.

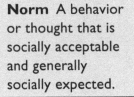

Norm A behavior or thought that is socially acceptable and generally socially expected.

Roles Personal identities that are characterized by a set of norms.

©Imageman/Shutterstock.com

Institutions are communities, organizations, or collectivities that are made up of bundles of roles. The institution of higher education then would include roles such as professors, deans, students, and janitors. Each of those roles, of course, contains its own bundles of norms that guide their actions within the institution.

Socialization is the process wherein an individual learns and internalizes the appropriate norms that allow them to fulfill their roles within an institution. Thus, we all must learn the social norms for going to college so that we can navigate our ways through the institution of the university and ultimately graduate with a degree. If we have done so, then we have been properly socialized within higher education. When

Institutions Communities, organizations, or collectivities that are made up of bundles of roles.

Socialization Process wherein an individual learns and internalizes the appropriate norms that allow them to fulfill their roles within an institution.

I graduated from high school, my best friends and I all decided to attend the same university. Rather than live in the dorms, we opted to share an apartment together and divide the rent. For whatever reason, one friend within our group was far more interested in going out to parties than showing up for class on a regular basis. After one semester, he was placed on academic probation because of his low grades. The second semester he actually flunked out, thus demonstrating that he had not internalized the values of the institution. He was not adequately socialized.

Socialization must take place within religion too. Proper socialization results in committed members with high levels of religiosity who know the norms and roles and are able to not only act them out on a daily basis but also to pass them along to new members. For example, most Americans were brought up in a religious household. Their parents essentially chose their religion, so they were raised in a specific tradition. In those cases, individuals do not so much convert as much as they reaffirm their faith. Thus, **reaffirmation** is the means by which a person chooses to adopt the religion in which they were raised.

But, how about when people decide to join a religion in which they were not raised? In order to understand this process, it is helpful to recognize that there are different processes depending on how quickly the shift into the new religion takes place. Some forms of conversion take place quite suddenly while others may take months or even years. Most conversions do not occur quickly but rather take place over a period of time and in a series of stages.

An individual's relationship with a religion can be likened to a relationship with another person. For example, you may have known someone or heard about someone who is in a committed romantic relationship or is currently married. When asked about the development of their relationship, the person said they "knew" right from the start that their significant other was the one for them. They may have even said something like they fell in love at first sight. But, how often do you hear people make those kinds of claims? I imagine that if your experience is like mine, those "love at first sight" stories are pretty rare.

More often than not, the relationship developed over a series of stages. Perhaps a friend of a friend introduced the couple, they became friends and only very slowly developed their relationship. This is because such relationships (whether they are romantic

Reaffirmation The means by which a person chooses to adopt the religion in which they were raised.

©Dragon Images/Shutterstock.com

or platonic) necessitate trust and vulnerability. Long conversations, talking about one's past, introducing the significant other to one's own network of friends and family members . . . all of these things take time. Particularly for couples in a romantic relationship, something else often happens too—at some point, the couple withdraws from their network of friends and loved ones to spend more and more time with their new partner. Think how often this has happened with a friend of yours who has fallen in love with someone and now wants to spend more time with them than with you. All of the stages we have just touched on that take place in romantic relationships between people also have a parallel equivalent for most people when they convert to a new religion.

While we discuss the ways sociologists understand the stages of religious conversion further, it is important to note again that most processes of conversion are slow and deliberate. **Social drift theory** is one prominent explanation for why people convert to a new religion. It suggests that there are both "push" factors and "pull" factors. People experience push factors when they suffer a setback or feel less than satisfied with their current state of existence. Feeling lonely, going through a difficult breakup, having lost a job, becoming seriously ill, all of these can be reasons why people can feel a "push" to seek some solace in religion. The very experience of emotional, psychological, or physical suffering can be a strong catalyst for people to look for meaning, a sense of belonging, and some contentment in a religious community.

Then there are the "pull" factors to account for why a person is pulled, drawn, or attracted to a particular religion or religious group. Social drift theory suggests that one very important pull factor is the people we know. If someone we respect, care for, admire, or love is participating in a particular religion, then we are more likely to view that religion as a reasonable option. However, according to social drift theory, conversion is a gradual process rather than an immediate one. Furthermore, it is a process in which the individual who is converting to the religion is an active participant who is thoughtfully and carefully considering the conversion process. When we hear about a religious group that we think is "extreme" or "crazy," we often want to think that their members have been "brainwashed." In fact, there is no evidence to support this notion. Instead, the sociological data points to a very active process wherein old ties are severed, often after a traumatic or stressful event, and new relationships are formed. One of the key components to these new relationships is a concept sometimes called "love-bombing" wherein potential new members are showered with genuine affection and attention. The result is that new bonds are formed and the convert is socialized into acting on behalf of the group.

While there is some nuance to the general theories about conversion, there is widespread agreement about the basic steps in the process. First, a stressful or traumatic event (e.g., divorce, moving, going to college) results in the loss of existing community. Next, new bonds are formed that encourage further distance from old ties and identities. After that, group norms and interactions become an increasing part of daily life, and finally, the new member acts as an active "recruiter" for other potential members.

When it is summed up this way, the process can seem very dispassionate and rationale, but in real life, none of these stages would feel unnatural or disingenuous. In part, this is because we go through similar processes all the time with regard to other groups. Can you think of any other groups or organizations that socialize new and potential members in this way? My students typically come up with athletic teams and

> **Social drift theory** A gradual process of changing religious ideas; suggests there are both "push" and "pull" factors that drive us away from a current religion or lack thereof and guide us to a new religion or lack thereof, in order to find meaning.

fraternities and sororities as examples. None of them think they were brainwashed into pledging for a particular sorority or had to be coerced into hanging out with their teammates. Instead, they tell a story of their socialization as an active process of increasing commitment to people and an organization they genuinely enjoy.

©solominviktor/Shutterstock.com

Additionally, one might compare the social drift theory of religious conversion to the development of a romantic relationship: there are push factors (e.g., feeling lonely, having gone through a breakup, and sensing the longing for companionship) and there are pull factors (e.g., meeting someone new and being physically attracted to a person). Just as it generally takes time to establish a strong, intimate, and trusting relationship with another human being, the same can be said for establishing a relationship with a new faith community. After all, it is little more intimate and personal than one's relationship to God or one's sense of spirituality. There is, then, a significant amount of trust that is needed in order to begin talking about those things in a genuine manner with other people.

John Lofland (1977) is among the most prominent sociologists of religion to conceptualize a model for the conversion process. For him, conversion into a religious group could be illustrated best like a funnel in which each step weeded out potential converts until only the most committed filtered through to the bottom and actually joined the religious group.

Proselytizing
When a religious group actively seeks out new members, attempting to convince people to convert to their religion via persuasion.

Some religious groups actively seek out new members and attempt to convince people to convert to their religion through **proselytizing**. However, most people join a religion through the influence of a friend or family member. Lofland argues that most converts first must be predisposed to conversion. They are generally dissatisfied with their current state of affairs or have experienced some challenge or setback that leads them to seek out a religious group that may hold the promise of greater satisfaction or an ease to their suffering (i.e., "push factors"). Two, they must believe that a religion can, in fact, be a feasible means of addressing their dissatisfaction or suffering ("pull factors").

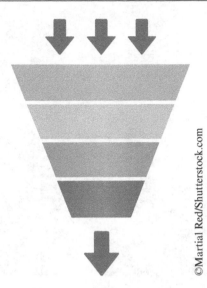

©Martial Red/Shutterstock.com

Perhaps a person has sought out comfort through her or his current network of friends, or tried psychological counseling, or turned to books or other media for answers. If those outlets prove ineffective, then she or he is more inclined to view religion as a reasonable pursuit. Lofland says that this initial state of tension makes people more open to the possibility of trying out a new religion.

©Photographee.eu/Shutterstock.com

Next, the individual actually visits a religious organization or some smaller group within a larger organization. She or he gains exposure to some of the basic tenets and values of that religion. Lofland states that in this initial period, an individual may begin developing emotional connections with members of the religious group. This stage of bonding with others is critical to the development of someone who is seeking to convert to a new religion. Without the friendships that one establishes in a new community, it is difficult to feel like the group is worthy of letting go of the barriers needed to foster an intimate and committed relationship with the newfound community.

©Rawpixel.com/Shutterstock.com

If one successfully creates emotional intimacy with a new religious group, then the individual is more likely to spend time with them and less time with others outside the group. Consider our previous example of the romantic couple . . . as their relationship grows, they seem to withdraw from participating in activities with their old friends. This is simply an artifact of the nature of time. We only have so much of it, and when we are falling in love with someone, we desire to spend more time with them and thus have less time to spend engaging in some of the activities we may have been accustomed to doing with our friends. The same process is relevant to the individual who is becoming closer to her or his new religious group members.

Religious socialization also requires that the group devote more attention to the newcomer or visitor. Slowly, the established sets of ideas and values that are at the core of the faith community are taught and instilled. The newcomer is welcomed to special events beyond merely a weekly worship service. She or he is also often asked to contribute some sort of service (e.g., joining the choir or working as a greeter). Social psychologically we know that whenever we invest our resources in something, we tend to justify that investment even after the fact. Thus, for instance, were I to agree to serve as an usher for a service, even after I have completed the task, I will most likely tell myself that my work was worth it with any variety of rationales. Maybe I would think about how it was a privilege to be asked or that I agreed to be an usher because I wanted to be more of a leader in the community, and this was a way to be more visible. Regardless of the justifications I created, I have, in the end, spent more time and energy in my new community and thus less time with people in my social networks outside the religious group.

So, in general, as the convert involves more of her or his time in the new religious setting, she or he spends less time in other areas. For the most part, this withdrawal from former relationships is gradual as is the development of stronger and stronger ties in the new setting.

Conversion also entails a reframing of one's perspective in a number of different areas. First and most importantly, if I am a potential convert who is considering adopting a new religion, then I need to be assured that the worldview, values, and rituals that are a part of that religion are sufficient to meeting my needs. I need to first trust that others around me are genuine in their participation and faith in the religion. If that trust is present, the actions of those other people create what is called a **plausibility structure**. A plausibility structure refers to the set of interactions and behaviors of a group of people that help to make a situation real.

©Andrey_Popov/Shutterstock.com

To understand the nature of plausibility structures, let us recall our discussion on reification in the classroom. Imagine that you are from another planet visiting your classroom for the first time, except that you do not know what a "classroom" is or what its purpose is. All you see are 30 or so people in chairs facing in one direction while a single individual stand facing the opposite direction from everyone else. That one individual seems to be talking on and on about seemingly trivial details regarding something called the sociology of religion. For some strange reason, one person is doing all of the talking while everyone else is writing down what is being said. You interrupt the situation to ask why everyone is noting what is being said and is told, "It is important to remember what is being said." Further inquiry leads you to be told that, eventually everyone, except the person who is doing the speaking, will be given a piece of paper with questions on it that

©Arejpa.It/Shutterstock.com

require them to remember what they had written down in the previous class sessions. Then, the speaker is going to assign a number or a letter based on what was written on that piece of paper. "Why is that important?" you ask. "Because we do this on hundreds of occasions so that eventually we will get another piece of paper that says 'Bachelor of Arts' or 'Bachelor of Science'." "So why is that important?" "Because it will help us to get a good job or a better one than we currently have."

In short, all of these activities that take place in the institution of higher learning are rather arbitrary and unnatural. The only reason why these processes exist is that society has created these activities. The ultimate reason why we participate in them is that since everyone else is, if we deviated from this norm, we might find ourselves on the bottom of the pile when it comes time to apply for a job.

Religion works the same way. It is a socially constructed institution that has meaning because others interact in ways that make it meaningful. That is not to say that just because religion is socially constructed, it is worthless—just the opposite. It is important because generations and generations of people have deemed it to be important. We chant, pray, sing songs, bow, do prostrations, tithe, and many other things besides. If we were to isolate those behaviors and somehow extract them from the context of religion, they would seem rather strange and even a little silly. Yet, because others are doing them and they are oftentimes doing them together, we accept them to be meaningful and even sacred.

Thus, it is crucial for individuals who convert to a new religion to accept the plausibility structures that have been established by other people. When we accept those plausibility structures, we begin to see the situation as something real and meaningful—it becomes reified. We interpret the behaviors and interactions in a particular way, and furthermore, we reinterpret our own identity in light of those plausibility structures. They are encouraged to see the world through a new set of eyes. They are also encouraged to reinterpret their past as one that creates a kind of story that leads them to where they are now. Thus, their biographies are reinterpreted. How often, for example, have you heard someone account for their conversion with something along the lines of . . . "God led me to this point in my life." In this way, converts begin to reinterpret their past as a connected series of events that brought them to the point where they could, in a manner of speaking, "see the light."

So, to further illustrate this process of reframing your past, consider the following question: "What led you to this moment in your life in which you are reading these words?" You might answer, "Nothing really important led me to this moment. Just a series of random events . . . I applied to college, got in, began taking classes. Then I decided to register for this one and the professor is requiring me to read this chapter."

Now, contrast that with a different kind of answer: "When I graduated from high school I wasn't quite sure what I wanted to do. My best friends at the time knew they were expected to go to college. To be honest, I did not want to be left behind—it would have felt lonely and a little sad. I enrolled in college not knowing exactly what I wanted to study but then took a class in sociology. The professor was awesome and the material just seemed to 'make sense' to me even though others seemed to struggle. From then on, I knew I was meant to be a sociologist." That kind of response is far different from the previous one. Religious conversion often works in a similar manner. Rather than being a kind of random series of events and happenstances, when someone converts

to a new religion, they frequently revise their past stories in light of their newfound religion. In fact, a prominent theme to some people's conversions is that they begin to feel as though they always were [Jewish, Buddhist, Catholic, etc.] but just needed the right circumstances to realize their identity as such (Johnston, 2013).

Finally, most traditions require a formal ritual to symbolize that the person is now a "member." Perhaps it is baptism or the person is asked to give a public testimonial of their faith. In some religious traditions, such as Buddhism, one is given a new name. This kind of ritual is what is called a **rite of passage** (Turner, 1969). A rite of passage refers to a ritual one undergoes that marks the transition from an old personal identity to a new one. Commencement is an example of a rite of passage since one goes from being a college student to a college graduate. At the university where I teach, commencement ceremonies typically involve several speeches including one

Rite of passage A ritual, often formal and required, that one undergoes marking the transition from an old personal identity to a new one.

from the university president and one from a minor celebrity or a prominent leader in the community. A group of musicians playing bagpipes and drums offer a ceremonial opening and closing to commencement. Parents, friends, and other loved ones take pictures of the graduating student shaking hands with the university chancellor as they receive their degree. At the end of commencement, there is a lot of joyous shouting and clapping on the part of the audience, and graduating students frequently hug one another and offer their congratulations.

©Prasit Rodphan/Shutterstock.com

Personally, I was reluctant to participate in my graduation ceremony but was convinced otherwise by my insistent parents. In hindsight, I was happy that I did attend. This is because one of the functions of rites of passage is to provide a sense of closure on one period of life as we anticipate and prepare for the next one. At commencement, you are told that you are now, officially, a college graduate. That is something meaningful, and society treats it as such since it affords opportunities that may not have been available to you had you not gone to college and graduated.

©oatawa/Shutterstock.com

Rites of passage also involve what the anthropologist Victor Turner (1969) called a **liminal period** of your identity. The liminal period refers to the stage between an old identity and the new identity. For instance, when you have completed your exams and you are awaiting formal commencement, you are in a liminal period. You are no longer really a college student since you have completed all of the required course-work and attained the necessary grade point average in order to graduate. Yet, the college or university has not yet formally recognized you as a graduate by conferring your degree. Turner's phrase is apt: you are "betwixt and between" important stages of life. Existing in a liminal period can make one quite anxious. One is confident that the old stage has ended, but it has not been made official yet. I know from experience, just how challenging it can be to try and be at ease during liminal periods and recall quite vividly the fearfulness I felt after graduating from school and then had to go about applying for jobs. I was constantly second-guessing myself and having thoughts such as: "Am I now really qualified to start an actual career?" Liminal periods reveal just how important rites of passage can be—they represent socially acceptable forms of reassurance and confirmation that you belong to a particular social group, whether that group is "college graduates," or "teachers," or "Baptists," or "Jews," or "Muslims."

> **liminal period** The stage between an old identity and the new identity.

THE RELIGIOUS ECONOMY

There are a variety of ways of studying religion from a sociological perspective. One prominent train of thought likens religion to the manner in which the financial economy operates. In short, the best description for thinking about this view is that the religious economy refers to "all of the religious activity going on in any society: a 'market' of current and potential adherents, a set of one or more organizations seeking to attract or maintain adherents, and the religious culture offered by the organization(s)" (Stark and Finke, 1992: 193). In other words, religion can be compared to a "product" that can be "sold" by faith communities, churches, synagogues, and temples and "bought" by lay people, congregation members, worshippers, or religious followers.

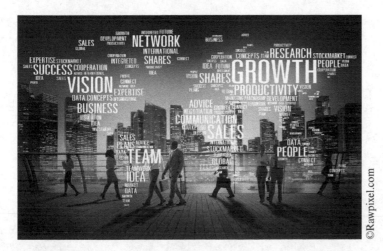

Just as there are producers and consumers that make up the financial economy, some sociologists believe that we can best understand religion as being made up of producers (i.e., religious leaders, founders of religions, clergy members, and so on) and consumers. "Consumers" include both people who attend or participate in religious services and rituals and people who do not. People who do not identify as religious are also considered to be potential consumers because they too are faced with a market of religious products of which they can either opt in or out. For example, my neighbor who identifies as agnostic and who does not attend or participate in any faith community works from home. About once a month, he tells me that a representative from one of a variety of religious groups knocks on his door and asks him if he might be interested in taking part in a religious group or event. He politely informs the proselytizer "no" and goes on about his day. The person who goes from door to door can be said to be selling a religious "product." The product in this instance is typically membership in a religious organization. Last month, a group of Jehovah's Witnesses were going door to door to talk about their beliefs with those who would listen. If my neighbor were to suddenly be convinced by the individuals' message, they would have successfully "sold" their "product," which, in that instance, was the core set of beliefs and values produced by Jehovah's Witnesses.

"Economistic perspective," View that all religious organizations can be interpreted as religious "producers" and they compete for a limited number of consumers.

Thus, all religious organizations can be interpreted as religious "producers," and they compete for a limited number of consumers. This is a zero-sum game since there are only so many consumers to go around. Therefore, within a given religious economy, sociologists who adhere to this view, which we call the "**economistic perspective**," also argue that the laws of supply and demand are operating.

Religious pluralism There are a wide variety of religions that are available to people.

In a religious monopoly, one religion predominates and people lack many options. In the United States, we have a long history in which the government and religion are kept separate, and therefore, we have what is considered to be a religious free market. Here, an abundance of religions are in competition with one another. We refer to this as **religious pluralism**: there are a wide variety of religions that are available to people.

©alphaspirit/Shutterstock.com

Religious pluralism can have both negative and positive consequences. If there are too many religions in a given society, each with its own set of values and claims on what is true, then people can become more uncertain regarding their own religion. In other words, when there are different groups, all of which assert that theirs is the true way to salvation, we can easily begin to take a **relativistic** point of view. A relativistic point of view means that we believe that there is no single version of truth or single path to salvation. Rather, we begin to believe that each group is true "in its own way."

> **Relativistic** Point of view that there is no single version of the truth or single path to salvation; each group is true "in its own way".

©Diego Schtutman/Shutterstock.com

Some sociologists believe that religious pluralism is a good thing for society because, just like in a capitalist economy, the more suppliers of a product there are, the more competition there will be between those suppliers. Thus, religious pluralism will force religious organizations to continue to adapt to society's needs and the religions that fail to provide what people want will eventually die out. Having said that, let us turn to addressing how people "buy" religion. In order to do so, we must address the issue of "cost" or how much effort one has to put into a religion. Here, we can think about cost in terms of how strict or demanding a religious organization is.

©1000 Words/Shutterstock.com

Strictness is measured by a variety of characteristics. Strict churches tend to expect more work on the part of their consumers. What kind of work? My grandparents attended a church where they were expected to not only show up for Sunday services but also be regular attendees at a Wednesday evening service. If they weren't teaching Sunday school, they were certainly expected to be participating regularly. Members were also expected to regularly go out and "witness" to nonmembers. Tithing money weekly was also the norm as was participation or leadership in a variety of other ways such as choir, or serving as an elder or a greeter. Consumers at strict churches might also be expected be a member on a committee such as the one my grandmother was always involved in which she was in charge of visiting the "shut-ins" each week. Of course, members were also expected to engage in individual rituals and behaviors too: regular prayer, Bible readings, and keeping the commandments. When they did read the Bible, the norm was to interpret it as the literal and inerrant word of God. That is, for them, the Bible is timeless and universal and can be applied the same way no matter the era or culture of which one is a part.

On the other hand, my neighbor's grandparents attended a church where the rules were much less rigid. First of all, the Bible was viewed as something inspired by God but written by humans. While it was perceived to be beneficial, if people were regularly investing time and money in the church, no one would have minded if the members only showed up to Sunday service once a month. In fact, no one batted an eye when it came to "Chreasters," people who attended church only on Christmas Eve and Easter.

©Edward Lara/Shutterstock.com

Generally speaking, if we were to only consider Christian churches in the United States, we would characterize "evangelical" churches as being more strict and "mainline" churches as being less so. If we were to divide denominations into evangelical and mainline style churches, we would classify denominations as Baptists, Pentecostals, Church of Christ, and Assemblies of God, as being more evangelical. On the mainline side of things, we find Presbyterians, Episcopalians, Lutherans, and Methodists, to give some examples. Also, you might notice that not only evangelical churches are more strict and more likely to view the Bible as being more literal than mainlines, but also evangelicals tend to be more conservative on the political spectrum. Mainlines, on the other hand, tend toward the center or even progressive side of the spectrum.

Sociologists who draw on the economistic perspective of the sociology of religion assert that strict churches cost more since they expect more out of their members as we noted earlier. Mainline churches, then, cost less. Now, if I were to point out that in the past few decades in the United States, one group (either mainline or evangelical) has grown in terms of the numbers of people participating while the other one has fallen drastically, which would you imagine has grown and which has shrunk?

Interestingly, and somewhat counterintuitively, evangelical churches, which cost more, have grown while mainline churches have seen a decline among their ranks. So, why would that be? It seems, on the surface, that people would opt to participate in a religion that does not place high demands on their time, money, behaviors, and beliefs. Sociologists though point out a number of reasons for this trend.

First of all, the reason is psychological. The more something costs, the more one perceives something to be valuable (Finke and Stark, 1992). Relatedly, the more one participates in a group and its activities, the more one becomes mentally and emotionally invested (which is in itself a reward) (Iannoccone, 1997). Also, the more one participates, the more likely one is to be on the receiving end of others' goodwill (Iannoccone, 1994). So, while the initial "costs" for becoming involved in a costly religion can be high, the rewards will be higher as well. So, rewards include not only being seen as a "good person" but also an increase in social capital that is realized through business or job networking opportunities or romantic relationships (Stark and Bainbridge, 1985).

Further underscoring this point is the concept of "free riders" (Iannoccone, 1994). Free riders are people in any organization who reap the benefits of the products created by the group without investing any time, energy, or other resources. Surely, you are familiar with this dynamic from doing group work in various classes. Frequently, students complain about a group member who is not doing any of the work but still gets the same final grade. This same dynamic exists in religion.

Of course, churches do not offer "grades" in exchange for work or even other tangible rewards. As Finke and Stark point out, the only thing religious groups truly have to offer is a sense of cosmic reward, often in the afterlife. Religious economists call these thing **supernatural compensators**. The basic exchange formula works something like this: in exchange for good behavior and belief in this life, you will be rewarded in the afterlife.

However, imagine a church or religious group that demands very little from its members in terms of adhering to strict morals, contributing financially or volunteering

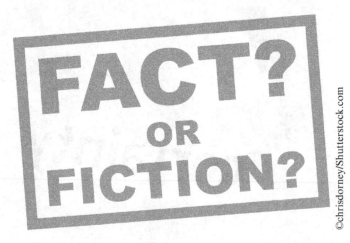

©chrisdorney/Shutterstock.com

time, but guarantees the same supernatural compensators (e.g., eternal salvation) for all. How do you think the members who work hard on behalf of the organization and devote time, money, and energy would feel about people who do nothing for the same reward? It is reasonable to think that they would be attracted to a different kind of church where their work is more valued and rewarded.

Another reason why strict churches have seen an increase in membership has to do with the way our contemporary culture works. In today's society, we are bombarded with media, politicians, religious leaders, and even scientists who often seem to advocate for competing and sometimes contradictory "truths." Just take into consideration the way there seems to be a new diet for good health emerges every couple of years. Each time, we are told that the most accurate scientific evidence backs this or that diet. If we decide to follow it, we are assured to find good health. Yet, it seems like each new diet tells us to rely on a completely different combination of food: eat raw food only, we are told, or just protein, and don't mind the fat, or eat "paleo" . . . on and on it goes.

Thus, in our world, it is fairly easy to fall under the perspective we discussed earlier called relativism. We might throw our hands up in the air and just concede that all truth is relative and that all of these competing claims on what is good and bad and what is right and wrong merely depend on where you are coming from. That is the relativistic point of view—there is no one "Truth," only a bunch of differing versions.

For many people, relativism is very uncomfortable. They want some assurances in life, particularly when it comes to spiritual, emotional, and moral matters. As it turns out, costlier religions tend to offer more concrete answers to our existential questions, and they avoid devolving into relativistic perspectives (Kelley, 1996). They present the world in black and white terms and avoid the gray fuzziness of relativism. So, while mainline churches offer rewards such as a sense of community and recreational activities, evangelical religions focus on the reward of eternal salvation (Ibid.). Knowing with certainty what is good and bad, right and wrong, and knowing that by doing things such as repenting or being baptized will guarantee them everlasting life is a source of great comfort: so much comfort, in fact, that the extra costs are worth it.

CHURCH AND SECTS

Similar to the division between evangelical and mainline churches, sociologists have developed a model for thinking about the growth and decline of religious organizations. This is the sect-church model developed by Ernst Troelsch. Here, the term "church" does not refer to a physical building or congregation but has a technical meaning. In this model, a "sect" is a religious organization whose values and beliefs are in stark contrast to the community or society in which it exists. A "church," on the other hand, has values and beliefs that are closely aligned with the community or society in which it exists. Now, there really are no "perfect" instances of either a sect or a church. They merely represent two poles along a continuum. Thus, we say that an organization can be more "sect-like" or more "church-like."

sect-like   church-like

©Kendall Hunt Publishing Company

Let us say, for example, that we are talking about a religious organization that believes in reincarnation, regularly performs animal sacrifices, and believes in sorcery and magical spells. You most certainly would say that that organization is sect-like. Yet, if we were to go back in time several hundred years to pre-Christian Ireland, such a group, a Druid one, would be considered quite normative and acceptable. We would not consider it to be sect-like but in fact church-like. Therefore, it is important to note that the characterization of organizations into either more or less sect-like or more or less church-like can vary depending on the cultural context.

Today, many consider religious groups such as Scientology or the rare Mormon groups that accept polygamy to be quite sect-like. Religious organizations that center around the Bible as a sacred text, believe in a higher power, and acknowledge the importance of Jesus are, on the other hand, considered more church-like.

Typically, religious organizations begin life on the sect-like end of the spectrum. Sects are typically small, avoid professionalized clergy, and focus on supernatural matters such as eternal salvation, hell, and heaven. Worldly concerns are seen as secondary. Thus, sects tend to be more ascetic—that is, they emphasized the value of denying oneself bodily pleasures in favor of a more strict form of self-discipline and self-control.

©JHershPhoto/Shutterstock.com

However, if a religious group remains on the sect-like side, then they tend to dissolve as members die out. In fact, the vast, vast majority of sects simply fade away. This is because in order to grow beyond a certain point, they need to attract more members, and if the general population perceives the group to be nonnormative or just plain odd or weird, no one will want to be a part of the group. The group can only grow when they temper their beliefs and align their values to be more in accord with the larger society. Sect-like groups reject the dominant secular society (e.g., attending public schools, going to the movies, and hanging out in malls). So, while sect-like organizations, on the one hand, tend to try and insulate and protect members from the larger society, church-like organizations tend to allow their members to participate in all forms of secular society (Johnson, 1963).

This model helps us to understand how religious groups grow or die out and how they evolve over time. The model also helps explain the emergence of new religious organizations since there is a corollary to this: as groups become more church-like, some individuals in the group will take issue with the softening of the beliefs and feel as though the group has not remained true to their original, core set of values. "True believers" begin to see the more church-like organization as having strayed from the more pure and authentic form of the original organization (i.e., the sect-like group). Thus, the sect-church model predicts that while religious groups begin on the sect end of the continuum and move toward the church end, some members will opt out of this movement and start a new group on the sect end, thereby beginning a new cycle along the continuum.

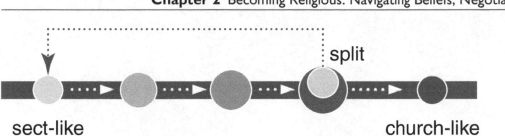

split

sect-like   church-like

©Kendall Hunt Publishing Company

It can be very disconcerting to have religious conversion, belief, and commitment broken down into these kinds of sociological constructs. Our own experiences with religion often feel so much more organic, authentic, and honest than these rationalized explanations offered by the theories in this chapter. It is important to keep in mind, however, that these theories are not offered in place of personal experience but alongside our personal experiences. Many of the theorists cited in this chapter are, themselves, religious. Understanding the systems that constrain and structure our religious choices does not mean abandoning the personal, autobiographical experiences that make religion such a profound force in many people's lives. In fact, one could not truly adopt a sociological perspective about religious belief and conversion without holding both the personal and structural aspects in mind at the same time.

DISCUSSION QUESTIONS

1. Define what being "religious" means to Americans, according to the chapter, and then to yourself. How can this term be problematic?
2. What are the five dimensions of religiosity, according to sociologist Charles Glock? Give an example of each.
3. Explain secularization. What did Berger predict according to this concept? Was his prediction correct (so far)?
4. What is functional differentiation? Give a concrete example of how this works in your own life.
5. According to the chapter, why has religion become more privatized? What does this mean? Compare and contrast being ascribed into and achieving a religion in your answer.
6. According to Lofland, what makes people more open to the possibility of trying out a new religion? Explain his process of people converting.
7. Give an example of a liminal period in your own life. Who coined this term? What are these periods typically a part of?
8. What is religious economy? Give three examples of its potential components.
9. What does it mean to hold a relativistic point of view about religion?
10. According to the chapter, why do sociologists say that participation in evangelical religions has grown recently, while participation in more mainline religions has dropped?
11. Compare and contrast "church" and "sect."

CHAPTER 3

RELIGION AND ECONOMICS AND THE WORLDS BETWEEN THEM

What's money got do with religion?

KEY TERMS

- Alienation
- Bureaucracy
- Commodity fetishization
- Conspicuous consumption
- Consumerism
- False consciousness
- Rationalization

OBJECTIVES:

- Develop a basic understanding of conflict theory and the insights of Karl Marx to sociology and the sociology of religion.
- Examine how the economy intersects with the institution of religion.
- Appreciate the complexities entailed by Max Weber's analysis of Protestantism and modern capitalism.
- Begin to look at ways in which consumer culture impacts the religious commitment and religious affiliation.

SOCIAL STRATIFICATION

Whenever I teach Introductory Sociology, I kiddingly suggest that sociology is obsessed with the number 3, since traditionally much of sociology has been comprised of the following three areas:

1. The primary topics for consideration are these three things: race, class, and gender.
2. The three major theoretical paradigms are: conflict theory, functionalism, and symbolic interactionism.
3. The three founding figures of the discipline are generally thought to be: Karl Marx, Emile Durkheim, and Max Weber.

In sum, there are nine areas—all of which intersect with religion in a variety of ways and all of which we address throughout this textbook. In this chapter, we are going to discuss socioeconomic class as it relates to religion and highlight the ideas of Karl Marx and Max Weber. Often, when sociologists address the matter of class and discuss Marx and Weber, they do so by drawing on the ideas and concepts developed in conflict theory.

©InesBazdar/Shutterstock.com

Conflict theory provides us with a kind of lens through which to interpret and understand society. In conflict theory, one of the major assumptions is that humans must compete for a limited quantity of resources they need to get by. We call this state "zero-sum" since there is only so much of something to go around, and thus, if there are winners, then there are going to be losers. Take a natural resource such as oil—there is only so much oil that is available for us to extract from the earth, so some people worry that when the wells begin to dry up, societies will erupt in conflict to compete for the remainder. Money is something else that is often thought to be zero-sum. While the government can print more money, introducing substantial sums of money into circulation can have negative economic consequences. Therefore, the government closely monitors how much money is in circulation at a given time. So, in this regard, money is a zero-sum resource. If some people have too much of it, then it is likely that others will not have enough. When this takes place, we have economic inequality.

©Roman Bodnarchuk/Shutterstock.com

In the United States, we have very high levels of economic inequality. There are a few people who have a great deal of wealth, but there are many, many more who live in poverty. About 15% of Americans (approximately 45 million people) live in poverty according to the U.S. Census. Furthermore, there are statistical methods for measuring how much inequality exists in a society. The GINI coefficient is a popular measure that tells us how wide the gap is between the most and the least wealthy. Current GINI coefficients suggest that the gap between the "haves" and the "have-nots" has grown wider in the past couple of decades.

Conflict theory is a perspective on society that says inequality is wrong and unfair because the people at the top will develop policies, laws, and other means that benefit their interests while making it much more difficult for those at the bottom to get ahead. In turn, this will create divisions between economic classes and will result in people feeling more competitive and less unified than they would otherwise be. Conflict theory suggests that our current economic system is more likely to produce conflict between individuals than amiability and agreement. Individuals must not only compete for a limited resource such as money, which is needed for survival, but also grapple with issues such as fairness and justice. Is it fair that, in the past decade, about 95% of the growth in people's income went to the people who were in the top 1% of income earners or that the wealthiest 10% of people control more than 75% of the nation's wealth?

©durantelallera/Shutterstock.com

Some social scientists believe that our economic system is set up to be unfairly advantageous to those who already earn the highest incomes and/or own the most wealth. Such scientists often look to the insights of Karl Marx in order to better understand how the current state of capitalism contributes to inequality. (Note that I wrote "current state of capitalism": this is because capitalism, as an economic system, has looked very different depending on the historical era or the nation that relies on it.)

©Everett Historical/Shutterstock.com

Marx believed that capitalism pits people against one another—thus producing conflict (hence, the name "conflict theory").

Capitalism is a system that is intrinsically based on competition. Because there is only so much money to go around, the system requires that businesses seek out profit in order to survive. The positive outcome of competition for businesses that are forced into competing with one another is that businesses are often obliged to innovate and constantly develop new goods and services that putatively aid the consumer. On the other hand, as Marx points out, while some businesses might create new and better products in order to realize profits, unless they charge more for those products, the primary means for realizing profit is to keep the wages of their employees as low as possible. Marx saw this as the main contributor to the creation of economic classes—there are those who own businesses or are large shareholders in companies, and then there are those who must sell their labor in order to make a living.

©waewkid/Shutterstock.com

"So what does all of this have to do with religion?" you might be asking. One of Marx's most famous lines is: "Religion is the opium of the masses." Notice that he chose opium as the drug to which he compared religion. Opium is a painkiller that soothes physical suffering. On an emotional and psychological level, Marx believed that religion was created to serve the same purpose. Whenever people feel dissatisfied with their lot in life, they can simply turn to religion as a kind of crutch. Rather than try and overcome the structural barriers that prevent people from getting ahead, religion, Marx felt, allowed people to tell themselves that even though this life is less than satisfactory, there is always the next one.

For Marx, religion contributed to what he called **false consciousness,** which is the state of mind that takes place when people who are being exploited and oppressed do not realize they are being exploited or oppressed. Religion contributes to false consciousness by distracting people from taking a stand and working to end systems of oppression such as poverty, sexism, and racism. Marx felt that religion was a crutch that often promoted complacency and inaction. However, Marx was not universally critical of religion. While he generally expressed skepticism about the possibility that religion could be a force for social change, one should be aware that Marx also suggested that religion could promote justice and equality. This was because religion, by its social nature, was well equipped to mobilize people toward revolution. Religion has the capacity to bring people together in solidarity and, as such, can foster unity among a diverse group of people.

> **False consciousness**
> The state of mind in which people do not see their own oppression and exploitation.

However, for Marx, most religion served as a palliative institution that mollified more than it agitated. Religion contributed to narrowing people's views of their world by requiring that people expend more time working on their own salvation and less time exploring the interdependencies between individuals—particularly among others in working classes. He worried that religion would become so important for people that they would ignore things such as economic inequality and even oppressions such as sexism and racism. Religion, in those instances, would become something like a fetish.

Often when people use the term "fetish," they use it to refer to something they really like or as a synonym for an "obsession." A friend of mine, for instance, says he has a "guitar fetish." He owns around 20. He seems to be constantly reading about guitars or watching online videos posted by guitar collectors showing off their collections.

©Pop Tika/Shutterstock.com

When he attends shows and concerts, he focuses on the guitar players. When he hears about someone selling a guitar, he would like to add to his collection; he has demonstrated that he is perfectly willing to drive more than eight hours away to meet with the seller. For my friend, guitars are a kind of fetish.

Now I love this friend; he is a really terrific human being. But he can be a little "crazy" when it comes to his guitars. For instance, he keeps his guitars in an area of his house that is relatively climate-controlled. When he has visitors, he likes to show off his collection but is very reluctant to allow anyone to actually pick one of the guitars up much less play it. He does not have children, but he refers to his guitars as his "babies."

Perhaps you have someone in your life that is like that with something they collect. They might be kind and generous people, but when it comes to their "fetish," it is almost as if you feel like if something awful were to happen like their home caught fire that they would make sure their collection was safe before they made sure you were safe. It reminds me of the part in the movie "Ferris Bueller's Day Off" where the protagonist, Ferris Bueller, is trying to convince his best friend to borrow his dad's fancy sports car—a collectible, antique Ferrari. Ferris's best friend tells him no way. He says: "Ferris, my father loves this car more than life itself."

©mekcar/Shutterstock.com

Commodity fetishism When, as a result of the global capitalist economic system, people begin to value goods over human beings and begin to treat human beings as though they were things.

Marx says that when we put our commodities above our value for human beings or when we treat human beings like they are commodities, then we are engaging in **commodity fetishism**. Now, you might think that only people who get a little obsessive about their collections or hobbies, like my friend who collects guitars, are engaging in commodity fetishism. Marx says that in fact we are all to some degree guilty of commodity fetishism because of the way our capitalist system works in a globalized world.

If you are like me, when you look at most of the tags on your clothes, you will find that many of them were made in places such as Bangladesh. According to the New York Times, more than 500 people have died in fires in garment factories there since 2006 (http://www.nytimes.com/2012/11/26/world/asia/bangladesh-fire-kills-more-than-100-and-injures-many). Just a little exploration will lead you to discover that many of the popular clothing brands you and I wear have been made in one of the unsafe factories in Bangladesh. Most of the employees are women who make about $35 a month.

One of the biggest reasons our clothes are so affordable is due to the fact that so many garment companies outsource the manufacturing to other countries where there is high levels of poverty and, thus, people are willing to work for very low wages. Additionally, the cost of manufacturing in those countries is also highly reduced by the fact that there is little government oversight ensuring the safety of workers. So, the people who make most of our clothes are not only paid very poorly, but they also work incredibly long hours in generally unsafe environments.

I own an iPhone (which I love). However, in 2010, the factory in China where most iPhones were being made at the time suffered a rash of suicides by workers who were exhausted and overwhelmed by the poor working conditions inside the factory (http://www.bbc.com/news/business-30532463).

These are just a couple of examples that illustrate how I am guilty of commodity fetishism. Many of us are, and in fact, it is difficult in our global economy to avoid, falling prey to commodity fetishism. When we buy and use products that were created by someone who is put in harm's way as a direct result of their work, we are complicit because we are disregarding the human life that goes into the final product. We are essentially valuing the product more than we are valuing the lives of those who

Alienation The separation caused by modern capitalism that takes place between people and within individuals that keeps people at odds with one another and even with their own inherent nature.

make the product. The people who make the product are "lost" in the system and are basically just like cogs in a great big machine.

Commodity fetishism results in **alienation**. For Marx, alienation describes the process wherein we become separated from ourselves and one another when we participate in a global economic system that exploits people for low wages, creates high levels of economic inequality in which there is a wide disparity between the haves and the have-nots, and causes us to engage in commodity fetishism. For Marx, alienation took place on a variety of levels. For instance, we become alienated from one another when we fail to recognize the value of the people whose hands made our clothes or our iPhones (or any number of other commodities we regularly consume). We begin to think of people working in sweatshops in developing countries as being somehow less worthy of our attention, our concern, or our compassion. "After all," we say, "they are on the other side of the globe so what can one person possibly do?"

©alphaspirit/Shutterstock.com

Capitalism also produces another form of alienation too since it creates division within each of us as individuals. Marx felt that capitalism had the potential to create a split self. On the one hand, people tend to equate success and happiness with monetary success. On the other hand, Marx felt that true fulfillment and satisfaction were actually the product of our ability to connect with other people. He believed that humans are inextricably tied with other human beings. Since each of us depends on the ability of other people to provide for our enormous variety of needs, our very survival depends on these other people. Just think about how many people are interconnected just to provide for simple things such as your mail, the gas in your car, and the groceries in your fridge. Marx said that capitalism makes it easy to ignore all the actual human lives that form the vast web of connections that make each of our lives possible. For him, our true happiness is derived from a state in which others around us are healthy and happy.

The irony here is that many religions promote the kind of genuine understanding and compassion that, Marx says, are undermined by capitalism. So, while he was critical of religion as an institution, we can see some of the ideas and values espoused by many religions implicit within Marx's own work. When we get caught up in a system that equates monetary gain with success, fulfillment, and happiness, we lose sight of what Marx believed was our inherent interdependency. Rather than recognizing how interconnected we are with one another, we can become increasingly self-interested and selfish. As a result, we become alienated from our fundamental human nature—and for Marx, religion held great potential to remedy this egregious malady of human spirit. Unfortunately, at least according to him, most religions uphold such forces of alienation rather than work to dissolve them.

In Marx's work, religion as a social institution is secondary to what Marx felt was far more important when it comes to having an impact on society. The economic system, according to Marx, anyway, was the primary driver and the foundation in any given society. He felt that the way a society extracted natural resources for survival and the mechanism a society used to exchange those resources served as the foundation for all of the other social institutions. Economic determinism is the idea that it is a society's economic system that will influence and give shape to other social institutions. The economic system is the "base" of society and, in this model, the other social institutions, including religion, constitute the "superstructure."

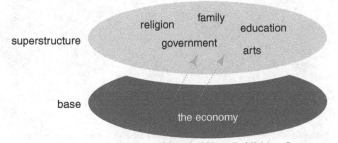

©Kendall Hunt Publishing Company

According to this model, when something changes in the base, those changes ripple out and cause changes in the superstructure too. While we will examine some of the large-scale ways in which our economic system has influenced religion as an institution in subsequent chapters, we might easily consider a more mundane example of how this works. You may recall that back in 2008, the United States and much of the rest of the world sunk into what has been called "The Great Recession." Many Americans faced losing their homes to foreclosures, unemployment rose, and stock markets around the world lost significant value. Merely on a psychological level, we can imagine what concerns and worries filled prayers, talks, sermons, and liturgies. This is not to mention the way many faith communities responded to the increased number of people in need who suddenly faced homelessness and hunger.

So, while Marx believed that the economic system was the base of society and everything else was affected by it, other early sociologists challenged that view. Some even felt that the institution of religion had the power to shape other institutions, including a society's economic system. One of them is the German sociologist Max Weber, to whose ideas we now turn.

RATIONALIZATION

When I think about times in my life when I have experienced an emotional "high," I recall a night spent at my cousin's house. We both were 10 or 11 years old at the time, and he and I pitched a tent in his backyard and pretended that we were camping in the great outdoors. Even though his parents had come outside to tell us it was time to go to sleep at 10 pm, we were wide awake well past midnight.

At one point I remember, we both were lying on our backs staring into the sky and pondering how many stars there might be in the galaxy and how many galaxies there might be in the universe. My cousin reported that based on a television show he had watched, there were billions of stars in our galaxy alone and that there were more stars in the universe than there were grains of sand on all the beaches on all the continents on planet Earth. We began imagining how long it would take to count to a million and then a billion and then a trillion and concluded that we would likely be dead long before we reached that point. Then we began debating whether the universe was infinite, and if it was, did that mean that no matter how many lifetimes we spent counting, we would never ever reach the end?

©AstroStar/Shutterstock.com

My cousin then told me that he had heard somewhere that the universe started with a big bang and that the universe was not infinite. So, then I asked, "Well, if the universe is not infinite, then it must have an end, right? So what is at the end? A wall? What is past the wall, if there is a wall? Is that another universe or just nothing at all? Is that where God lives?" There seemed to be so much to unpack that we stayed up until dawn just looking up at all the stars until finally the sun began to rise and its light took over the night sky.

I think the reason why I remember that night so well was that I am pretty sure it was the first time I was overcome with a sense of awe. The immensity of the cosmos combined with the possibility of a divinity that was somehow a part of all of it was humbling, wondrous, captivating, befuddling, mysterious, terrifying, and yet somehow reassuring all at the same time. Since then, I have had similar moments. Sometimes, they have not been as powerful as that one, and other times, even more so. Friends have shared events in their lives that made them feel a similar sense of awe. Some have described moments when they were in nature, taking in a view of a mountain-filled landscape or standing before crashing waves as they look out and imagine the vastness of the oceans. Some people felt it when they witnessed something miraculous take place, such as one friend whose spouse was diagnosed with terminal cancer one month and then discovered a complete absence of cancer the following month. Many people who have given birth felt a sense of awe and inspiration when they first held their newborn.

©Anneka/Shutterstock.com

Quite a few of those stories ended with the person telling me that their experience was so powerful that they felt that whatever it was that so moved them (whether it was the face of a newborn baby or the wide-eyed wonder of an expansive view of a mountain range) was evidence of a God. Imagine how powerful that kind of experience must be in order for someone to say something like that!

When we think about those sorts of experiences of awe, we might use another word to help describe what it must feel like—a word like "enchantment." Enchantment has come to have an old-fashioned tinge nowadays. We are more likely to hear it in a TV show or movie that is a period piece such as when one actor says, "It's a pleasure to meet you," and the other replies, "Enchanted, I'm sure."

The word also used to refer to those initial "butterflies in the stomach"—a stage of having a crush on someone. We can find ourselves "enchanted" by another. But when we develop romantic feelings for someone, are we not in a kind of "awe?" If you have ever been in love, then you know the feeling . . . you are in awe of that other person. They seem somehow magical, inspiring, mysterious, intriguing, appealing, and awesome, right? You may find yourself so attracted to that person that you feel like you could spend all day and night just listening to them or spending time next to them.

But what often happens after some time has passed? Do you continue to feel so smitten, so enraptured, so *enchanted*? Probably not. The chemicals responsible for those initial feelings begin to loosen their hold on our physiology, we begin to grow accustomed to our beloved's flaws and foibles, and routine life settles in. We might even find ourselves feeling a little . . . uninterested, humdrum, or just plain bored. In other words, we have become *disenchanted*.

Max Weber (1864–1920) felt that disenchantment was the curse of modern life. To paraphrase one of his most famous statements . . . Our world has been deserted by the gods—we have chased them away. The "gods" here can be understood as a metaphor for a premodern life; a life in which we did not fully grasp the mechanisms of the universe and when humans turned more to magic, rituals, and charms in order to make sense of the mysteries of life and the cosmos we inhabit. There is also a hint of disappointment and grief in his statement because even though we have gained a better understanding of our world, we have lost the sense of awe that comes with not fully comprehending the reality in which we live.

©maxriesgo/Shutterstock.com

Rationalization
The process wherein society becomes increasingly ordered and structured according to rules and regulations.

Contributing to our current state of disenchantment, Weber believed that the processes wherein we have created so much order, so many daily regimens, so many rules, policies, and laws, and so many structures have also added to our disenchantment with life. He called this **rationalization**. Rationalization refers to the ways in which life has become so structured and ordered that we no longer have to do much thinking on our own in order to get through life. Everything is pretty much laid out for us. We know what is expected of us, and we know that as we traverse through life's stages; if we do not know all the answers, there is certainly someone or something out there that can tell us. It is as though life were a big factory assembly line in which we have been dropped. Thus, we need to merely follow along and go through the motions as we are molded by the factory that is our society.

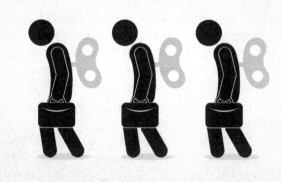

©iluistrator/Shutterstock.com

Processes of rationalization are pertinent to the sociology of religion in a number of ways. First of all, Weber predicted that rationalization was an ongoing process that would slowly infiltrate all aspects of society, including religion. Weber argued that rationalization would begin to remove the mystery, the sense of the unknown, and the miraculous in religion. Since so much of religion revolves around the supernatural (such as divinities, angels, heaven, and so forth), this would prove detrimental to religion. If religion were to become too rationalized, all that would be left would be a community in which people socialized and argued about ethical principles. These are important activities, to be sure, but Weber would lament the absence of emotional experiences and the sense of awe that is associated with religious experiences.

Furthermore, rationalization would mean that religious leaders would need to rely less on their charismatic personalities in order to successfully grow their groups of followers and persuade people to act according to religious principles. Rationalization, instead, would mean that religious groups would rely on policies, regulations, and codes for precepts and moral guidelines.

©Nirat.pix/Shutterstock.com

Some of those developments can be quite beneficial. It is, after all, helpful to know that when problems arise or questionable events take place, there is a resource for addressing those problems and issues. On the other hand, according to Weber's theory of rationalization, religious groups would also need to develop the kind of organizational structures we have in other nonreligious institutions: bureaucracies. A **bureaucracy** is an organization that has developed specialized subgroups or departments in which each of those departments has a unique function.

Consider your university or college. There are likely very many academic departments, administrative offices, deans' offices, athletic programs, etc. The result of bureaucracies is that they are not the most responsive when it comes to individual problems or unforeseen circumstances. Committees need to be formed, new policies written, forms to be signed, and experts to be consulted. Some people who are concerned about the rise of bureaucracies in religion worry that their organizations will lose sight of their original mission (e.g., providing spiritual guidance or helping out those in need). Such bureaucratic organizations often require that members or participants invest a great deal of time doing bureaucratic things such as filling out paperwork or holding meetings, things that take time away from interacting with others on a more genuine, emotional level.

Bureaucracy The kind of organization in which groups are compartmentalized according to specific purposes, activities, and functions.

©alphaspirit/Shutterstock.com

While Weber was a little pessimistic in his outlook regarding rationalization (which he saw as inevitable), he may have been too pessimistic. As we shall see in other areas of this book, some religious organizations have been quite strategic in their efforts to re-enchant the lives of their members or have been very careful to avoid the deleterious effects of bureaucracies. Many in religion know far too well the importance of an enchanted spiritual life.

WEBER'S THESIS

As we have already seen, the institution of religion does not exist in a vacuum. The institution of religion is malleable and is affected by other cultural factors. Take race, for example, as Martin Luther King, Jr., once pointed out—the single most segregated time of the week is on Sunday morning. Today, in many congregations, one finds either mostly White people or mostly persons of color in the seats. One can only wonder what religion would be like if the United States did not have the long and shameful legacy of racism. Conversely, we also know that people used religion to justify their racist beliefs in the past and that undoubtedly contributed to sustaining race relations in this country. Because race relations impacted the institution of religion and religion impacted race relations, the two (race and religion) can be said to a more or less degree "mutually constitutive." Each one helped shape the other, and the socially constructed reality of one cannot be understood without understanding the other.

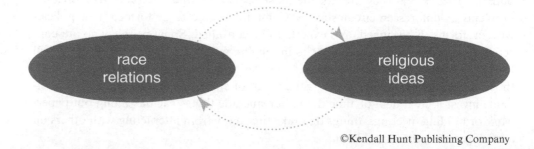

©Kendall Hunt Publishing Company

One of the earliest sociologists who wrote on the institution of religion as it is mutually constituted alongside other institutions happened to be Max Weber. In the first years of the 20th century, Weber sat down and produced one of the most influential texts in all of sociology: *The Protestant Ethic and the Spirit of Capitalism.* In it, Weber demonstrated the way religion and economic relations can be seen to be mutually constitutive. More specifically, he revealed the way Protestantism and modern capitalism shared what he called an "elective affinity." His phrase "elective affinity" meant that one did not cause the other, but rather Protestantism and modern capitalism each helped one another's development, spread, and rise in popularity in Western Europe.

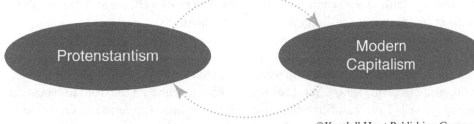

©Kendall Hunt Publishing Company

The book is highly influential, and Weber's argument is highly compelling. He basically sets out to answer the following question: Is it merely coincidental that Protestantism and modern capitalism appeared to emerge and gain widespread acceptance at the same time? As you might suspect, Weber concludes that it is not a coincidence. So, he lays out a historical outline to support his conclusion.

To begin with, Weber points out, Catholicism had a kind of religious monopoly over much of Europe until the early 1500s. While there were earlier schisms, the split with Catholicism that was initiated by Martin Luther is considered to be the most significant. At the time, Luther, increasingly outraged by the corruption in the Catholic Church, decided to publicly condemn the Church by posting his 95 Theses on the door of the church at Wittenburg, Germany in 1517. The primary focus of Luther's attack was the selling of indulgences (in which people of means could essentially purchase a ticket into heaven). But the theses also included attacks against the way clerical offices were appointed either through nepotism or bribery.

©photoilike/Shutterstock.com

Not surprisingly, Luther was excommunicated for his actions but that did not stop him from another significant contribution to the emergence of Protestantism. Luther proceeded to translate the Bible into German and make it more widely available to others since most people had to otherwise rely on the clergy (who, of course, were seen as corrupt) for interpretation of biblical messages.

This new translation, called the Luther Bible, had two major effects on people's understanding of Christianity. The first was the emphasis this bible placed on faith as the means for salvation. This was in opposition to the way many had to rely on clergy members in the Catholic Church to tell them whether or not they were going to heaven. Specifically, Luther added the word "alone" to a verse in Romans that says that "through faith alone" could one gain entry into heaven (Romans 3:28). So, faith now took on enormous centrality in the lives of Christians.

The second major impact had to do with the Luther's translation of the way God called the chosen into heaven. Here, Luther translated "call" into the German word *beruf*. So, in other words, those who were designated for eternal salvation were called (again, using the word *beruf*). Yet, Luther also chose to translate the word for vocation as *beruf* as well. Thus, *beruf* had two distinctive meanings. It referred to God calling people into heaven and to one's work or vocation.

©Marzolino/Shutterstock.com

Also, during the 1500s, the theologian John Calvin introduced another important contribution to Weber's thesis that modern capitalism and Protestantism share an elective affinity: predestination. Predestination is the notion that regardless of what one does, God knows (even before you were born) whether or not you are going to go to Heaven or Hell. The reason: God is omniscient or all-knowing. Therefore, it would be silly to think that God didn't know your destiny. Even worse, it would be heretical and blasphemous to think that anything you actually did in life, such as pay off a priest, could convince God to change God's mind. Thus, people are predestined, and only God knows how things will turn out for you.

Predestination was such a radical concept and one that created much anxiety, Weber tells us, in people trying to wrestle with religion outside the Roman Catholic doctrine. On the one hand, they believe that only through faith can they get into heaven, and on the other hand, how can they possibly know for certain since they were predestined? Faith is powerful, but everyone has doubts, right? Everyone questions their faith once in a while, right?

Well, this is where we return to the German word *beruf*. Remember that *beruf* had two meanings. The first was that God called people into heaven. So, here, Weber wants us to reflect on what it must have been like for people who are exposed to the new theology of Luther and Calvin. Before, one could be certain that one was getting into heaven because a priest said so. Think for a moment how comforting and reassuring that must have been. We are, after all, talking about one's everlasting, eternal life.

On the other hand, after Luther and Calvin introduced their ideas, you were forced to simply have faith that you were among the called. Well, if you have ever had faith in anything, then you know that faith is just that: an optimistic belief, but a belief that lacks 100% absolute certainty. Faith can waiver. At times, one's faith in something can be quite strong while at other times, it can weaken. Doubt can creep in, and with doubt, you can experience a whole host of emotions: worry, fear, anxiety, and even a sense of panic.

Yet, early Protestants simply had to rely on faith and faith alone that they were saved and that they were not damned to eternity in hell. Making matters worse, since you were already predestined, there were no actions you might take to alter your fate. It is as though you were confined to a life in limbo, always lacking a complete guarantee as to where you will spend your life everlasting. Weber said that this created so much internal cognitive dissonance and psychological discomfort that people would eventually need to come up with a way to allay their fears and anxieties. So, what did people do to ease their doubts, concerns, and worries over whether or not they were one of the chosen?

Weber tells us that people bolstered their faith and eased some of their worries through work. Why work? Because remember that *beruf* refers to both a call and a vocation. So, people saw it as a sign that when they were successful at their vocation (their *beruf*), they were one of the people who had been called (a *beruf*) by God. In other words, the two separate meanings of *beruf* were transformed into something new: a *beruf* was a vocation that reflected God's calling.

To use an example, let us imagine that someone starts a business selling fruit. Selling fruit is how that person makes their living; thus, it is their vocation (*beruf*). Now, say that the fruit seller begins working longer hours to collect more fruit and sell even more fruit. The person will then have more money than they did before. Since the perspective at the time was to see money as something merely to satisfy only what you needed to survive (rather than as a means to buy things that satisfy a desire or a want), the fruit seller has more money than she or he needs. It is a surplus. So, they use that money to buy more land to grow more fruit trees, and they buy bigger fruit stands to sell all the additional fruit they are growing.

The fruit seller is, of course, a product of their time and so, like everyone else, is facing the same dilemma regarding predestination and the need to simply have faith that one is going to heaven. According to Weber, the fruit seller, because she or he has been so successful at their vocation (their *beruf*), will see that as a sign that she or he has been called (again, a *beruf*) by God. In other words, success at work is evidence that one is clearly part of God's call because one is fulfilling one's vocation.

Weber says that many people start to view work this way: doing a good job is a reflection that one is chosen by God. In fact, so many people begin viewing work as a divine calling , this gave birth to modern capitalism. People across Europe begin working longer hours and earning more money than they need to subsist. So, they begin reinvesting their money in order to build bigger businesses, which will allow them to make even more money. People begin acquiring more money than they know what to do with, so they begin saving it, investing it in other people's businesses, or even loaning it out. This approach becomes increasingly popular, and as it spreads, capitalism spreads.

This idea persists to this day though we do not overtly and explicitly tend to equate monetary success with being one of the people God has chosen to go to heaven. However, think about how of our lives center around work. We go to school for over 12 years so that we can proceed to college so that we can earn a degree that will allow us to get a job. Our job then becomes part of our core identity, so much so that one of the first questions we ask when meeting someone new is, "What do you do?" The reply is not something like, "I work as a college professor," or, "I spend at least 40 hours a week engaged in professorial work." Instead, it is, "I *am* a professor."

©Rawpixel.com/Shutterstock.com

Then we work very hard in order to get a raise and a promotion to a new position that oftentimes entails even more responsibility and more work. For many people, work is the center of their social life since most of their colleagues are also their friends. We increasingly take work home with us, and even when we don't, we are often thinking about or worrying about work when we are with our families and friends. Sometimes, we will even work on vacations.

Many people work to the point that they make more money than they actually need to survive. So, we do things such as buy bigger houses, newer cars, and the latest computer, iPhone, television, etc. We will work and work and work until we can pay for our kids to go to college so that they can work just like we do and so that their lives will revolve largely around their work just like many of ours did.

Furthermore, we have attached extra significance to the word "vocation." It means something more than merely just a "job." Many of us directly appeal to its earlier meaning and say that what we do for a living is a calling. In fact, when I talk with students, many of them tell me that they are *meant* to be a social worker or *destined* to be an attorney. So, even when they do not attribute a supernatural force or a divinity

©xtock/Shutterstock.com

that designates different people with different career paths, their words subtly suggest that there is an external force that influences their fate.

Also, when you think about applying for jobs, you might say something to an interviewer or write on your resume that you have a "good work ethic." Just think about what that means: you work hard; you appreciate the value of delayed gratification; and you show strong self-discipline. All of these are characteristics of individuals who were trying to cope with the anxiety and uncertainty brought about by the concepts introduced by Martin Luther and John Calvin.

So, when did work become so important? Weber said that we have Protestantism to thank for that. Yet, the link between hard work and Protestant theology is largely invisible today. The association between the two does, however, make an appearance in a couple of ways—one that is subtle, and the other that is less so. The subtler way that Protestant theology and modern capitalism get revealed is the way we sometimes hear celebrities or professional athletes attribute their success to God. Statements such as, "God has blessed me with this talent," reflect precisely what Weber wanted us to realize. People, still to this day, will sometimes view their occupational success as a sign that they are one of God's chosen. It is as though they are implicitly stating: "God chose me and not you and that is why I am so good at this." Think about how different that is from attributing one's success to genetics, luck, inherent skill, chance, practice, trial and error, or any number of other things.

©rangizzz/Shutterstock.com

The second way in which we can see the association or, to use Weber's term, the elective affinity between Protestant theology and modern capitalism is in what is often called the "prosperity gospel." Some people refer to this as the "health and wealth gospel." Here, the underlying theology is that if one has the right amount of faith and is ostensibly a "good person," then God will bless that person with health, happiness, and even financial prosperity. Preachers who are commonly associated with the prosperity gospel include: Joel Osteen, Creflo Dollar, Kenneth Copeland, and Oral Roberts.

©Kaspars Grinvalds/Shutterstock.com

The prosperity gospel has not been without its critics, and many people express skepticism and even disapprobation when it comes to Christian preachers very openly displaying signs of their wealth. Yet, for the most part, preachers who adhere to the prosperity gospel are unfazed. They unabashedly and unapologetically discuss the fact that they live in lavish mansions, fly in private jets, or drive Rolls Royce automobiles. Their ostentation is evidence, they claim, of their faith in an all-powerful God. In their view, if God wants to bless his faithful with monetary success, then we should not question that action. To paraphrase Weber: those who have been successful are not just satisfied with that fact. Those who are successful desire the psychological reassurance that they in fact deserve their success. In other words, people who are wealthy want to believe and want others to believe that their wealth is a product of their own efforts rather than the consequence of chance or good luck.

So, in this regard, the prosperity gospel supports what the sociologist Thorstein Veblen referred to as **conspicuous consumption**. Conspicuous consumption is the way in which people purchase things that symbolize a high social status . . . such as driving a fancy car or wearing certain brands. Cars and clothes are necessities for many people, but many of us go out of our way to not merely buy things we need but, instead, buy things that communicate to others that we have a certain status. While we recognize that many products that are made by different manufacturers are very similar in nature, the label on the product communicates that one is familiar with the cultural cachet of the brand and that one's identity can be linked in some way to that brand. For example, think about the ways some people consistently drive one make of car. I might be a "Dodge person," and you might be a Ford driver. Someone might choose to wear a certain model of Nikes or carry a Kate Spade bag. There are Pepsi drinkers, and then there are Coke drinkers.

Conspicuous consumption The purchasing of ostentatious items that are meant to show off one's wealth to others.

©Bloomua/Shutterstock.com

So, what we consume, whether we do so consciously and deliberately, often communicates an aspect of our identity. Conspicuous consumption though only refers to the act of using, driving, consuming, or wearing something that is associated with higher socioeconomic classes (i.e., the wealthy) and is something that is obvious and apparent to others who can recognize its value. In sum, we can begin to see that religion intersects with how we fulfill our roles not only as workers but also as consumers. In fact, sociologists who study consumers and consumers' behaviors have interesting insights that contribute to our understanding of religion. So, in our final section of this chapter, we will look at some theories that have been developed by one of the foremost present-day sociologists who studies the area of consumerism.

CONSUMERISM AND "LIQUID RELIGION"

Zygmunt Bauman is a British sociologist who made a name for himself for his conceptualization of "liquid modernity." For Bauman, "liquid" is a highly flexible metaphor that described not only an era of time that some people also refer to as postmodernity but also life, love, consumption, identity, and many other areas including, you guessed it, religion.

When you think of different ideas, phrases, and words that are associated with the word liquid, you could probably generate quite a list: fluid, flowing, not solid, takes the shape of whatever its container is, unfixed, temporary, waves, expansive, and others besides. So, when we describe areas of life as being liquid, we mean that things are always in flux, that there is no definite fixed meaning, and that whatever it is that we are describing as "liquid" is open to change and interpretation.

Bauman's central concept of liquid is relevant to religion in two important and related ways. First, in liquid modernity, **consumerism**, which refers to the way in which the purchasing of goods and services is considered to be a valuable and even prioritized activity for the maintenance of the economy, heavily influences how people understand themselves and the institutions in which they are a part of. The second way Bauman's liquid concept is relevant to religion has to do with our understanding of how we are connected to other people and our commitments and involvement in their lives. Let us first address the matter consumerism . . .

> **Consumerism**
> The belief in modern society that the purchasing of goods and services is a valuable activity in support of a capitalist economy.

Throughout much of the 20th century, the manufacture of goods played a prominent role in the country's economy. We lived in an industrial economy in which a significant portion of the workforce was employed in plants and factories that made goods that were exported around the world. Some economists refer to this period of American history as the era of Fordism, named after the automobile industrialist, Henry Ford. Ford not only famously established the factory assembly line as an efficient way to produce large quantities of goods but also paid his workers relatively well. In fact, his aim was to pay his workers enough money that they could actually afford to buy the very automobiles they were hired to help build. This approach helped contribute to a strong American economy and established the country as a central provider of goods and services to the rest of the world.

In the 1970s, the American economy began to move toward being driven more by consumption than production. We began importing more and more goods, and large companies began closing their manufacturing sites in the United States and establishing them overseas in places where labor was cheaper. Today, more people are employed in service industries and tech-driven "knowledge industries." Individual consumption is valued as an activity that helps to promote a strong U.S. economy, and thus, consumerism is normative and quite acceptable.

With consumerism, Bauman argues that individuals increasingly begin to equate their personal identity with the things they consume. Thus, we strongly identify with commodities (e.g., I am a Mustang driver, I am a Trader Joe's shopper, or I am a Levis wearer). Bauman also points out that equating one's identity with the things one purchases carries over into the lifestyles in which we engage. So, for instance, because I consume (i.e., eat) vegetarian food, I'm a vegetarian. Because I purchase mountain bikes and I also consume (i.e., watch) mountain biking competitions on TV and consume (i.e., read) mountain biking magazines, I am a mountain biker.

Religion too is something we consume. That is, by attending particular worship services, reading particular sacred texts, purchasing items related to a particular religion, I am a consumer of my religion. A religion, then, is a kind of "product," and my consumption of that religion allows individuals to associate their identities with that religion (e.g., I am a Baptist, I am a Muslim, or I am a Catholic). Because there are so many religious communities available to us at any given time, religion is a kind of marketplace from which we can pick and choose. Just as we are bombarded today with an abundance of choices when it comes to products (just think about how many different kinds of toothpaste there are), we are also bombarded with a seemingly unlimited supply of different religious choices.

©oneinchpunch/Shutterstock.com

As we shall see, liquid religion has different meanings. As it relates to consumerism, liquid religion refers to the ways in which individuals treat religion as something we can pick and choose from. For example, I have on many occasions heard someone who is not a member of a faith community but who is considering joining one say something like, "I am church shopping," or "I am shopping for the right spiritual home." In fact, because we often think about religion in terms of consumerism, more and more people engage in "cocktail spirituality" (Wuthnow, 1998). That is, some people mix and match different elements from different religious traditions and combine them into their own, individualized religion. In this sense, liquid religion refers to the way that some people do not see individual religion as being walled-off and separate from one another. Rather, the borders between different religions are more porous, and different religious ideas flow into one another.

The fact that we now have access to mass media from across the globe, religious traditions themselves become quite liquid in their movement between national borders. The average person can much more easily learn about religions that were previously viewed as distant and foreign. Americans, for example, can easily turn to the Internet to familiarize themselves with Theravada Buddhism or Sunni Islam even when they do not personally know anyone who subscribes to that tradition. This in turn makes it easier for people in a consumer society to value and incorporate different ideas from different religions into a more personalized version of faith. This approach is a type of liquid religion because a variety of religious ideas, rituals, and beliefs get "stirred" together and blend into something that is different from their historical roots.

LIQUID RELIGION AND COMMITMENT

As I just stated, one area of life that could be described as "liquid" for many people is religion. So, liquid religion can have a variety of meanings. It can mean that the ways in which we define religion have become less tied to a concrete meaning and that religion means different things for different people. It can also refer to the way that people's religion changes throughout their life. In fact, we know, for example, that younger generations of Americans are more likely than at any previous time in history to choose not to be in the religion that their parents raised them in.

Hand-in-hand with the notion of liquid religion (and liquid life and liquid society more generally) are two additional important concepts that Bauman develops in his sociology: serial and episodic. These terms can easily be understood by thinking about how serial and episodic apply to television. There are television shows that are difficult to pick up in the middle of a season. Instead, you really need to start at the beginning to fully appreciate the development of the characters and the story as it unfolds gradually from one show to the next. These are "serial" programs.

On the other hand, there are television programs in which you can easily sit down and watch one episode and the full story unfolds in that one sitting. One show is not necessarily tied narratively to the next. In this instance, I always think of the animated show "South Park" that aired on Comedy Central for a long time. For a while there was a running joke that in each episode, one of the central characters "Kenny" would get killed off in some absurd fashion, prompting Kenny's friends to scream "They killed Kenny!" Of course, in each of the subsequent episodes, Kenny is alive and well (of course, until he is predictably killed off yet again). These shows are episodic. The stories rely on the same characters, but each show is self-contained and the narrative is not really weaved with the previous episodes or later ones.

©Andrey_Kuzmin/Shutterstock.com

Bauman suggested that life is lived either serially or episodically, and this depends a great deal on the society in which we find ourselves. Bauman's argument is that the previous generations lived life more serially, while today, we tend to live life more episodically. These are not hard and fast distinctions but rather ideal types. What Bauman was trying to convey is that there have been significant shifts in the ways our lifestyles become naturalized and seem perfectly acceptable. Yet, at the same time, our beliefs reflect social constructions. For instance, when your grandparents wanted to buy a car, they likely scrimped and saved for years until they had enough money that they could take to go and buy a car outright. You and I are much more likely to perhaps save a little money for a down payment but finance most of the cost of the vehicle through the bank. We don't think twice about going into debt, and it's very likely that you yourself have taken out loans to pay for your college tuition. (I know I did, and I'm still paying off my loans!) Credit card debt too would seem as perfectly reasonable, but your grandparents probably looked on financial debt with an eye to the future—they did not want to be beholden to a financial institution for years to come. Bauman would argue that this is due to the difference in perspectives. Our grandparents thought about their lives "serially." The present was linked inextricably with the future. We, on the other hand, think about our lives episodically. Today is today, and there's no sense in being too concerned about the future. We see our life more or less in self-contained compartments. One compartment, or stage in life, is sealed from the other ones. Thus, we think that what takes place in the here and now will not have as much of an effect on later "episodes" of life as, say, our grandparents might think about it.

This can apply to other areas of social life. When our grandparents married, they tended to stay married more often than we do today. They tended to remain in one career for much of their lives unlike people today who often change careers.

The running thread behind the shift from serial to episodic life, as Bauman described it, is commitment or the lack thereof. Obviously, in a serial form of existence, long-term commitment was taken for granted. If Bauman is correct in his assertion that everyday life is presently dominated by a more episodic perspective, then the corollary presumption is that people are also less committed. Because divorce rates are so high, we might conclude that people are less committed to the institution of marriage. Because people switch careers as frequently as they do, they may be less committed to a particular company or firm. Because people switch the religious identification more than ever before, one might conclude that people are less committed to their faith.

That is one perspective and one that is frequently taken up by older generations. But I would argue that the belief that younger Americans are less committed to a particular religious organization is pessimistic and not unlike the way a parent or grandparent who bemuses "What went wrong with kids today?" or nostalgically pines for the "better days of yore."

On the one hand, one might argue that the more institutions someone can identify with, as in the case of someone who changes religions throughout their life course, the more diffuse, diluted, or watered-down the identification with any specific religion is. On the other hand, we might say that the opposite is true: the more religions one can identify with, the more expansive the potential for one's personal identity. A parallel example might be the way people today are much more mobile than they had been in the past, wherein people tended more often to remain in the same regions in which they were raised. People are increasingly likely to live in places other than the one in which they grew up. Do the people who move around a lot lack commitment to any particular place? Do they lack commitment to their family of origin? Not necessarily.

Commitment is not necessarily zero-sum. That is, when we assume that religious switchers lack commitment, we are also assuming that individuals have only so much commitment on which they can rely as a resource. But that would be like saying that a parent has only so much love to offer their children and that the more children a parent has, the less love any given child is likely to receive. While that may be true for a cognitive skill such as the capacity for attention, it is not true with a quality of attention such as love. I would argue that commitment too is a quality of attention and not something that is of limited supply.

DISCUSSION QUESTIONS

1. What is meant when we say that someone can be alienated from one's own self?
2. How do you see religious groups today work against economic inequality? How might some religious groups actually perpetuate and reinforce economic inequality?

3. What is the prosperity gospel? Can you identify examples of the prosperity gospel beyond the ones we mentioned in this textbook?

4. How does consumer society impact religion? What are examples of religious services and goods that people can buy?

5. Do you agree with Bauman's claim that people today tend to view their lives episodically more than serially? How do you see this reflected in the way people view religion?

6. What is "cocktail spirituality," and why do you think it is more prevalent today?

7. What are some ways religious leaders work to re-enchant people who belong to their religious groups?

8. What is rationalization, and how has religion become increasingly rationalized?

CHAPTER 4

RELIGION AND EQUALITY FOR ALL: AFRICAN AMERICAN ACTIVISM

If we really live in a "postracial" society, how come there are still so many Black churches and White churches?

KEY TERMS

- **Agency**
- **Color-blind racism**
- **Double Consciousness**
- **Institutionalized racism**

OBJECTIVES:

- Think about religion broadly and as a social construct.
- Consider what role social structures play in people's lives, and how they influence their thoughts, beliefs, and actions.
- Understand agency, and how this varies both with social groups and with individual persons.
- Understand race as a social construct, as well as something that others have used both historically and currently as an excuse to discriminate against and oppress Black people.
- Understand the paired role of religion and social justice for many African Americans.

INTRODUCTION

Martin Luther King, Jr., famously pointed out that the most segregated hour in America was Sunday morning. One of the reasons his observation is so powerful is because it is ironic. On the one hand, we have religion's values—after all, religion is the social institution that is most responsible for promoting kindness, love, and compassion for one's neighbor. On the other hand, it appears as though the institution is not practicing what it is preaching.

You might think that things have really changed since King made that pronouncement over 50 years ago. They haven't; at least not much. Roof and McKinney (1987) say that race continues to be the most enduring distinction between Protestant denominations. In other words, when we look at where Americans go to church, the most significant factor that contributes to where they go to church is race.

Emerson et al. (2011) found that less than 10% of congregations in America are mixed racially. Protestant Christian churches, they found, were the least likely to be mixed. Furthermore, when they looked at individual congregations to see how segregated religious organizations are, and then compared them to nearby public schools and their surrounding neighborhoods, they found that the congregations were far more likely to be segregated by race. In other words, the churches themselves were *more* segregated than the neighborhoods in which they were located!

The ways in which race and religion are interconnected are incredibly complex. Our country's shameful history with slavery, Jim Crow laws, segregation, and new and ongoing forms of racism are in themselves the focus of thousands of sociological studies. Understanding how religion contributes to that mix, and conversely, how race impacts religious organizations and belief systems, is one of our goals for this chapter. Also, we will examine the significance of religion in generating social movements and activism, with an emphasis on African American protestant Christianity.

So, while this chapter examines the role African American churches had to play in bringing about greater social justice, it is also a chapter about the place of the individual person in society. What can one do to make a difference? Anything? Or, does it take groups of people who come together? What things limit what we can do? So, let us begin there. . . with a discussion on the sociology of the individual and her or his role in religion and social change.

©Ucleroo/Shutterstock.com

Certainly, it must be said at the outset, religion can be a source of positive social change. . . whether it is fighting poverty or fighting racism. Religion can be a tool for justice, providing a common bond of solidarity, and it can be a source of inspiration to make the world a better place. All of these things can be accomplished but only when people, individuals, come together and work toward a goal. It does, however, begin with the individual. She or he must feel inspired, empowered, and be able to make a change. In other words, she or he must feel that she or he has a sense of agency. So, our discussion begins with how sociology makes sense of individuals by asking—What are we free to do and think, and what limits what we do and think?

AGENCY AND STRUCTURE

You are likely familiar with the "nature versus nurture" debate. Scientists have long been interested in answering questions about what kinds of things cause us to act in certain ways. There are some good arguments to account for both. Genetics may predispose us to behave in ways, for example, that resemble the behaviors of our parents. There is no denying that nature has a role to play in making us who we are.

Sociologists, though, focus on the "nurture" side of the debate. Most tend to believe that our environment shapes our behaviors, thoughts, values, and beliefs to a great degree. While sociologists recognize that biology is also a factor, we are discovering more and more ways all the time about how our social contexts make us who we are. Since we are sociologists and not biologists, we focus on social factors and leave the biological factors to the experts in that field.

©Rawpixel.com/Shutterstock.com

However, sociologists do take into account the biological factors since we know that even things that are biological can have social ramifications. Simply consider the color of one's skin—something largely inherited from your parents. In the United States, we have a long legacy of treating people differently depending on the color of their skin. So, while nature endows us with different characteristics, nurture can have an enduring, ongoing impact on one's life.

The ways sociologists think about the role of nurture are encapsulated in the concept of "structure." Social structures are the abstract forces in everyday life that shape, limit, constrain, guide, and direct our thoughts and actions (or what we call an individual's "**agency**"). While structure, in this regard, refers to something abstract, one can easily understand how something that does not exist in any tangible, concrete manner works by simply thinking about physical structures.

> **"Agency"**
> Individual's ability to act on her or his own accord.

©MOSO IMAGE/Shutterstock.com

So, take a moment to think about where you are sitting as you read this. If, like me, you are inside a building, then you are readily aware of the walls that separate you from the outside environment. The physical structure of my office acts as a constraint on my actions (i.e., if I want to go outside, I'll need to exit through the door, walk down a hallway, etc.). So, structures, whether they are tangible structures such as concrete walls or social structures such as institutions, for example, the government, constrain what we can and cannot do. That makes it sound like structure is a negative thing. It contains us, blocks us, constrains us, and controls what we can and cannot do.

©Robin Fritzson/Shutterstock.com

©KieferPix/Shutterstock.com

However, structures can be understood in a positive sense too. Structures guide us and give us direction. For instance, the physical structure of my office also works to inform me on how to act. That is, in my office, I have a desk, a shelf of books, and a computer. Thus, the physical structure of the office tells me that this is my workspace, so when I am there, I generally try and be productive. At home, I have a room just for my guitars and amps, and of course, there I get little "real" work done. (Okay, I get absolutely no work done in that room). The fact that one room is located on my university campus and one is in the basement of my house serves to guide my actions.

Social structures work in the same way as the physical structures of buildings. They constrain our actions and thoughts by defining what the limits of possibility are, or at least, the limits of probability. At the same time, they shape and guide our actions and thoughts by providing us with a history and a sense of identity.

Allow me to share a personal story to help illustrate how social structures impinge on our behaviors as well as our thoughts and beliefs about the world around us. Imagine that you probably have at least one friend who you grew up with but who, unlike you, is not in college and will likely never go to college. My oldest friend in the world is like that. His parents survived paycheck to paycheck. When he was quite young, the company his parents worked for closed its doors and they were laid off. The economy, at the time, was in poor shape.

My friend's family often had to rely on "food stamps" to pay for their groceries. If you know anything about government assistance to the poor, then you know that, in spite of what some people tend to believe, welfare benefits are truly scant. In fact, it is probably not a coincidence that he was most often hanging out at my house around dinnertime so that my mom would invite him to stay and eat with us. In high school, he worked two part-time jobs to help out at home. During the school days, he could barely keep his eyes open in class. His GPA suffered. When it was time to apply for college, completing applications was barely on his radar, and even if he had the time or money, his poor academic record would have been an impediment.

©wavebreakmedia/Shutterstock.com

What is important to take away from the example of my friend is that not only did social structures such as his family environment, the economy, and social services limit what he was likely to do and not do (his personal sense of agency), the same social structures also shaped his outlook on life, his values, and how he thought about himself.

So, social structure shapes not only what we are able to do in life (our agency) but also shapes how we think about ourselves, our lives, and the world around us. Social structures can be anything from prominent belief systems (such as racism) to laws and policies established by governments and to social institutions such as religion. Each of these is social structure because they both constrain and guide our actions, and they shape people's sense of themselves and their view of the world around them. In other words, structures *structure* individual agency. Social structures enable us to both act and limit our actions simultaneously.

This is perhaps more true in the field of religion than anywhere else because religion is where personal agency and structure come together to form a particular worldview. For example, Josh had a student who grew up in a religious household with a very conservative theology. His student could not even conceptualize what gender equality truly looked like, despite numerous sociology courses, until his theology changed. His belief system that privileged patriarchy was the result of the religious structure into which he was socialized. Once that structure changed, as a result of a new religious experience in college, he was able to reframe his personal choices and beliefs.

In the following discussions, it will be helpful to think about how social structures change over time. The social structures include but are not limited to: government policy, the institution of slavery, how people think about race, religious communities, and activist organizations. It is also useful to keep in mind that all of these things have an impact on individuals' agency—that is, what they can and cannot do. Finally, it is important to note that some social structures can limit people's agency, but others can actually increase their agency.

RACIAL EQUALITY

Religion has played an important role in the struggle against racism throughout U.S. history. For instance, Frederick Douglass, Harriet Beecher Stowe, and John Brown all employed religious rhetoric to fight for the abolition of slavery. Of course, Martin Luther King, Jr., very unequivocally drew on his religion to try and end Jim Crow laws and segregation.

But when it comes to eradicating racism, religion has not always been used to promote justice and freedom. For instance, White, Christian slave owners often justified their actions with their religion. Because many slaves were not Christians, slave owners viewed them as heathen, unworthy of dignity and freedom.

Even today, religion is used to justify racism among some people. The Christian Identity Movement, for instance, believes that Adam and Eve were White. Since according to the Book of Genesis, Adam and Eve were created in God's image, White people must be favored in God's eyes. Sadly, the Ku Klux Klan, which originated around the time of the Civil War, is still alive today. The KKK has, from its start, claimed to be abiding by Christian moral virtues, and thus, their members too draw on religion to justify their actions.

©Everett Historical/Shutterstock.com

Now, before we go any further with our discussion on religion and the fight for racial equality, we should note something very important: race is not real. That is a scientific fact. That is, there are no biological or genetic differences between, say, White people and Black people, save for some different levels of pigmentation in our skin. In fact, when geneticists tried to see if there were differences between what we generally consider to be racial groups, they instead found that there was more variation within each of those "racial" groups than between them.

©Rawpixel.com/Shutterstock.com

So, if race is not real, then why talk about it? If we were anthropologists and the book you were reading was called *The Anthropology of Religion*, the fact is that we would not be talking about race (anthropologists do, however, talk about ethnicity). Sociologists recognize that race is a social construction and has no natural or genetic basis underlying it. But sociologists are interested in social constructions, and race is a social construction. In other words, most people think that race is real, and because they think it is real, they act in ways that reinforce their perceptions.

This idea is called the "Thomas Theorem," which comes from the sociologist W. I. Thomas (1928). The Thomas Theorem basically says that if people view something as real, then it is real in its consequences. When we apply the Thomas Theorem to race, we can definitely see the consequences. In the United States, we have a long history of believing that racial differences are real and then acting on those beliefs through hundreds of years' worth of enslavement, discrimination, and oppression of many kinds.

In other words, the beliefs Whites had with respect to Blacks helped to structure their thinking and their behavior. Of course, our system of laws and legal codes are also social structures, and when racial segregation was the rule of law, that too affected people's thinking and behavior.

But let us pause for a moment and look at structure and agency more closely. Remember that social structures give a kind of shape to one's agency. Because social structures guide our thoughts and actions, social structures determine not only our options for action but also our options for how to think about the world around us. Josh's student, discussed earlier, illustrates this dynamic perfectly. His structure literally constrained the available ways that he could even conceptualize the world around him, and this, in turn, severely restricted his options for action.

So, when we speak of agency, individuals can have less of it or more of it depending on the circumstance. Clearly, when we think about how much agency someone has, when it comes to the institution of slavery, Whites had more agency than Blacks did.

When examining people's actions, it is always valuable to ask: What are the social structures guiding their thoughts and actions? To what degree is their agency either limited or strengthened? When we said that religion has been used to both justify racist attitudes and defeat racist systems, we saw that a social structure, religion, shaped individuals' agency in different ways. What we will be focusing on next is how religion empowers people to fight for greater social justice and equality. So, the question you might keep in the back of your mind is: How do social structures work to constrain people's agency, and how does the institution of religion work to augment people's agency?

AFTER SLAVERY

As we already noted, slaveholders would sometimes use religion to justify their position. If their slaves were *not* Christians, as was the case early on in the period of slavery, then many slave owners believed their slaves to be ungodly, primitive, and less than human. That is, White slaveholders who felt their slaves' African roots were blasphemous accounted for their positions as slaveholders since African religions were considered heathen. Interestingly enough though, 10–20% of slaves brought to the United States from Africa were Muslims (Johnson, 2011).

©CHOATphotographer/Shutterstock.com

Of course, some slaves converted to Christianity. When that was the case, slave owners also used religion to maintain the status quo and perpetuate the institution of slavery. They would do this by telling their slaves that the only way they would get to Heaven was to remain obedient and to not try and break free from their ordained position in this life as slaves.

This idea that dominant religions (of all kinds) are inherently ideological systems used to keep the powerful in their privileged positions by legitimating oppression and placating lower classes with the promise of future rewards is at the heart of Karl Marx's perspective on religion. He famously declared that religion is the "opiate of the people" (Marx, 1977:131). By this, he meant that religion is used to deaden the masses to realities of injustice that are being perpetrated by the rich and powerful. This perspective on religion is at the heart of a conflict theory approach to understanding the role of religious institutions in modern society.

However, religion is not always utilized in that way. We can think of Catholic peasants mobilizing in Central America during the 1900s, the development of Sikhism as more egalitarian alternative to the other major religion in India at the time, and Jewish resistance against Nazis in Germany and other parts Europe.

Even with regard to slavery, religion played a positive force as it was also used as a reason to abolish slavery. Immediately following the emancipation of slaves, both White and Black missionaries proselytized freed slaves. As we shall see, religion, particularly Christianity, was an important part of African American lives in the period we call Reconstruction (the approximately two decades following the end of the Civil War), and many oppressed people have utilized religion of all kinds to sustain them through struggle for equality and justice and mobilize those around them to fight for their human rights.

While many freed women and men were exposed to Christianity prior to being free, and many more were exposed to Christianity through missionaries, a large portion of African Americans first encountered Christianity at religious revivals. Such gatherings included energetic and emotionally expressive worship services. Thus, some believe that is the reason so many Black churches continue to this day to be more revivalist in nature with expressive and enthusiastic worship styles (Baer, 1984).

©Gong To/Shutterstock.com

An important figure in the Black church who drew on the strategy of revivals in order win people to Christianity was William Seymour. Seymour, an African American minister whose parents were slaves, opened a church in Los Angeles, and his charismatic style of preaching, his espousal of speaking in tongues, and his insistence on a racially inclusive faith community attracted an abundance of African American, Latino, and White followers. The popularity of his services blossomed into a full series of revivals, now called the Asuza Street Revival that lasted from 1903 to 1907. The flamboyant style of worship so engaged followers that others were inspired to begin what became known as Pentecostal churches across the country.

To this day, Pentecostalism remains as one of the largest Christian movements for African Americans. It helped pave the way for the two leading and most influential majority of African American denominations: the African Methodist Episcopal Church, which was founded in the early 1800s, and the National Baptist Convention, founded around 100 years later.

During this period in the early 20th century, W. E. B. Du Bois (1868–1963) rose to prominence within the field of sociology. Du Bois, himself an African American, was a brilliant sociologist who authored a number of works that highlighted not only issues of race but also economics, social movements, and, very importantly, religion. A contemporary of the famous Booker T. Washington, Du Bois was a strong advocate for racial integration and racial equality.

©Everett Historical/Shutterstock.com

When Booker T. Washington presented southern politicians with the Atlanta Compromise (that basically said that African Americans would accept segregation and discrimination so long as government leaders would ensure that African Americans have access to educational opportunities and fair treatment in legal and criminal justice institutions), Du Bois argued that no compromise should be brokered. He felt strongly that Black leaders and activists should not accommodate their demands to the expectations of the dominant White society. Instead, he argued that equal rights in *all* areas of life were a necessity.

In 1903, Du Bois published *The Souls of Black Folk*, a major sociological work that remains significant and relevant today. One of the important concepts he developed in the book was that of "**double consciousness**." What he meant with that idea was that an African American in White-dominated society is forced to maintain two different perspectives simultaneously. If one is African American, then you are raised with a certain view of the world—particularly, a view that is shaped by being a victim

"Double consciousness" Term, coined by W.E. B. Du Bois, referring to how certain groups of individuals are forced to maintain two different perspectives simultaneously; for example, African Americans historically were forced to view themselves not only as their own community of African Americans does, but also how White society views them.

of oppression and prejudice. But in order to navigate a White-dominated world, Blacks, he said, had to also adopt the point of view of Whites. So, African Americans had two views or a double consciousness.

For a specific example of double consciousness, we need to only note the position of Black church leaders. Since Whites owned many of the buildings where African Americans worshipped, the minister was in the position of communicating with not only his church's members but also with the White owners (Roberts and Yamane, 2016). But Du Bois said that double consciousness was a fact of life for all African Americans. They were forced to live outside of the dominant culture, giving rise to one kind of consciousness. At the same time, they had to be aware of Whites' perceptions and expectations of them, thus creating the second layer of consciousness.

Prior to writing The Souls of Black Folk, Du Bois published another great volume of work, *The Philadelphia Negro* (1899). This book was one of the first major sociological studies that combined statistical analysis (through collecting numerical data) and ethnographic interviews with people in his study. In this work, Du Bois revealed the central role the church played in the lives of African American citizens. To be sure, the Black church served as a "meta-institution." In other words, the church was one institution, but it incorporated the functions of other institutions.

Du Bois writes: "[The] church is, to be sure, a social institution first, and religious afterwards, but nevertheless, its religious activity is wide and sincere. . .The Negro Church is not simply an organism for the propagation of religion; it is the center of social, intellectual and religious life of an organized group of individuals. It provides social intercourse, it provides amusements of various kinds, it serves as a newspaper and intelligence bureau, it supplants the theater, it directs the picnic and excursion, it furnishes the music, it introduces the stranger to the community, it serves as a lyceum, library and lecture bureau."

©Anna Omelchenko/Shutterstock.com

Thus, the meta-institution that was the Black church at the time provided for multiple needs: people shared news about their communities, educated the young people, acted as a setting for the development of romantic and marital relations, and provided a venue for people to learn leadership skills. Because the church was a focal point in Black communities, African American clergy were not only leaders within their churches; they tended to be leaders in the Black community even outside of church (Lippy, 2000). Black leadership became a critically important way to mobilize African American communities to work toward a more just and equal society. Because even with the abolishment of slavery, there proved to be many more battles ahead—as we shall see in the following section.

INSTITUTIONALIZED RACISM

In the early and middle parts of the 20th century, millions of African Americans moved from the south to industrial cities in the north in a process known as The Great Migration. It entailed both push factors and pull factors. African Americans were, in a sense, "pushed" out of the south by systemic Jim Crow laws and explicit forms of racism. In being pushed out, they moved to the regions of the country that were perceived to be more tolerant (I say here "perceived" because as we will see next, Blacks encountered new forms of racism in the north). African Americans were "pulled" to the north due to a booming industrial economy. Factories, such as automobile plants, were in need of additional labor, and though Blacks were often hired at pay, that was substantially lower than that for their fellow White workers, and there was still more opportunity for gainful wages than could be found in southern states.

©TTstudio/Shutterstock.com

Between the years of 1910 and 1970, millions of African Americans had moved to large mid-western and northeastern cities. By and large, Blacks moved to inner city areas since housing was more affordable. Often located near factories

"Institutionalized racism." policies, laws, or regulations that either intentionally or unintentionally help members of one racial group while preventing members of another racial group from accessing valuable resources.

themselves, such housing was less desirable than what could be found in residential areas that were further away from polluting, congested, and noisy industrial areas of the city.

As more African Americans moved into cities, Whites moved out of cities. Social scientists refer to this as "White flight." Due to oftentimes unspoken racist attitudes and beliefs, Whites were fearful of their Black neighbors and also believed that the value of their homes would see a sharp reduction.

Now, one might reasonably ask, "Why didn't Blacks move to suburbs or other parts of the city that were seen as more desirable?" There are a number of reasons for this, and most are linked to what sociologists call "**institutionalized racism**." Institutionalized racism refers to policies that sometimes unintentionally and sometimes *quite intentionally* helped Whites at the expense of Blacks and other persons of color.

©Junk Culture/Shutterstock.com

For instance, the G.I. Bill that was signed into law in 1944 was designed to assist returning soldiers from World War II with housing and education. Low-interest mortgages were made available to servicemen who had been honorably discharged. Even though many veterans were African Americans, only a tiny fraction of those mortgages were given to Blacks.

In part, this was due to the fact that the bill was facilitated by the all-White organizations American Legion and the Veterans of Foreign Wars. Furthermore, the individuals on the ground who were responsible for working with applicants were almost entirely White. So, while tens of thousands of Whites were aided by the G.I. Bill through housing subsidies, hardly any African Americans were. Thus, a housing boom that mainly took place in suburban areas led to almost all-White communities. African Americans though mostly continued to reside in the inner cities.

©Marko Marcello/Shutterstock.com

Another form of institutionalized racism was endemic at the time called "redlining." The term comes from the way in which bankers and mortgage brokers drew red lines around certain areas on a map. The lines indicated where they would and would not offer loans to Black applicants. If, for instance, an African American wanted to apply for a home loan that would permit them to live in a majority of White neighborhood, the loan officer would either not grant the applicant the loan or would otherwise charge exorbitant (and prohibitively high) interest rates.

©Nicku/Shutterstock.com

Restrictive covenants were written into housing deeds too saying things such as: "No person or persons of Negro ancestry or lineage, shall be allowed to occupy any part of this property." Thus, White owners were prohibited from selling their houses to anyone who was not White. Furthermore, real-estate agents enforced this with their own form of restrictive covenants: "Until 1956, brokers were expected to follow the code of ethics set forth by the National Association of Real Estate Boards: Don't try to sell houses in White neighborhoods to Black homebuyers" (Capps, 2015).

Sundown towns were more manifest forms of racism, and many towns had charters and posted signs warning African Americans that they could commute and do business in a White community only during sunlight hours. If African Americans were found in these sundown towns at night, they were subject to arrest or physical attacks.

©Jakkrit Orrasri/Shutterstock.com

Additionally, there was the practice of "blockbusting." Blockbusting describes the practice in which real-estate agents would go into White neighborhoods and tell residents that African Americans were beginning to move into their neighborhood. Their goal was to frighten Whites by implying that their real-estate value would drop drastically when Blacks moved in. Then the real-estate agents would offer to buy the White persons' homes, albeit at a much-reduced price than what the homes were really worth. Next, the same agents would sell to African Americans at a much higher price than what they had just paid for those same houses. The practice of blockbusting also contributed to widespread segregation.

All of these forms of institutionalized racism were pervasive throughout the north, the consequences of which have been enormous. First of all, it has led to highly segregated cities in which there are majority of White communities and majority of Black communities. Second, in many large cities, it has had a huge impact on the economic well-being of both the cities and the citizens who live there. Because Whites had higher incomes and accumulated more wealth than Blacks did on average, when they left cities and moved to suburbs, that money, or tax base, also shifted. Whites now paid their taxes in suburban communities and Blacks in more urban areas. This meant that many cities had less money coming in from taxes to pay for things such as police, social services, and school districts.

Many cities faced (and continue to face) financial hardships and are unable to properly provide for services that many Whites take for granted. I live outside the city of Detroit. There, for instance, a number of public schools have recently had to close, teachers have taken enormous pay cuts, and children have fewer options when it comes to just getting to school. One part of the city literally could not afford to keep the streetlights on, and when children walked to school each morning in the winter, they did so in the dark and through crime-ridden neighborhoods, because policing suffers too when cities face revenue shortfalls.

Institutionalized racism combined with what we might call "traditional racism" (the belief that one race is superior to another), led many in Black communities to rally against discrimination and disenfranchisement, and fight for greater economic opportunities. Religion, not surprisingly, played an important part in mobilizing activists' causes that promoted equal rights for African Americans. Thus, we now turn to what is termed the Civil Rights Era.

THE 1950s AND BEYOND

In 1954, the National Association for the Advancement of Colored People (NAACP), a civil rights organization that W. E. B. Du Bois helped found, recruited a group of people to take on the Board of Education, Kansas, in court. This culminated in the landmark Supreme Court decision known as Brown v. Board of Education. The issue at stake was related to an earlier Supreme Court decision that said segregation was legal so long as both groups had equal access to opportunities and resources. The "separate but equal" concept underlying segregation had proven to be incredibly weak since institutions that were designated for Blacks were far less functional than those intended for Whites—and this was especially true when it came to schools. In the end, the Court ruled unanimously that schools had to desegregate. Despite the court-mandated order, many schools in the South in particular avoided the issue, claiming that it would result in violent attacks between Blacks and Whites.

©Joseph Sohm/Shutterstock.com

Also, many other public institutions enforced racial segregation. One of those was the Montgomery, Alabama, bus system. In 1955, Rosa Parks, a member of the NAACP, refused to take a seat in the back of the bus in the section designated for non-Whites. This event helped spark the Montgomery bus boycott that lasted through 1956. On the night of her arrest, a group of African American women created and distributed flyers asking other African Americans to engage in a boycott of the bus system to protest the arrest. Martin Luther King, Jr., convened a meeting at a local church the following day in support of the boycott and thus began one of the seminal events of the Civil Rights movement: the Montgomery Bus boycotts.

The development of the Southern Christian Leadership Conference (SCLC), of which Martin Luther King, Jr., was the first president, began in 1957. The existence of the SCLC and its future successes in advancing the Civil Rights movement were in large part made possible by the ability of Black churches to work together in solidarity (Morris, 1996). What should be obvious is that religion, and in particular, Black Christian churches were at the forefront of a great deal of activism during this period. Indeed, church was a setting in which African Americans were free to strengthen their agency as individual actors in the Civil Rights movement. Black churches then were literally "sanctuaries" or safe spaces where people felt empowered to act without succumbing to White oppression and racism. Furthermore, Black ministers created enduring relationships with other ministers and felt free to explore issues related to race and economic justice (Morris, 1996). Ministers often leveraged religious rhetoric to motivate themselves and others to action drawing heavily on the Old Testament stories describing the Hebrews' escape from Egyptian oppression.

©Forty3Zero/Shutterstock.com

With White flight, many inner city communities were left predominantly African American. Because of this, ministers of Black churches had more visibility and clout in their communities. Political candidates who in earlier eras were running for office would therefore have to work with preachers to gain favor among residents: "The result was an almost entirely African American voting district that unintentionally became a point of leverage with white politicians" (Johnson, 2011: 457). This, Johnson writes, is why so many White and Black politicians even today ask to attend and speak to Black congregations during worship services.

BLACK POWER

If African American churches in the south were greatly responsible for instilling people with the sense of personal agency needed to bring about radical change in the repressive social structures, a different movement was taking shape in many large cities in the north. Elijah Muhammad was born in the rural south but, in the 1930s, converted to Islam and joined the Nation of Islam in Detroit.

After serving time in prison, Malcolm Little, who corresponded over mail with Elijah Muhammad, was released in 1952. He joined the Nation of Islam and became Malcolm X. Throughout the 1950s and early 1960s, Malcolm X was a highly significant leader with the Nation of Islam, and he worked tirelessly for social justice in Black communities.

Malcolm X was part of a broader religious movement both in American Islam and in Black churches in northern cities that focused on empowering oneself within one's own African American community. If what was taking place in the south was an effort to build solidarity with Whites, Malcolm X and others were less concerned with desegregation and more with creating sustainable, autonomous Black communities that had little need or desire to be accepted, welcomed, or even simply tolerated by Whites. Theirs was a revolutionary movement that sought to give African Americans a sense of self-worth through discipline, a strong moral code, abstinence from intoxicants, and an ethic that sought to bring about social justice by increasing the economic viability and well-being of Black communities through entrepreneurship and hard work.

©GongTo/Shutterstock.com

The Nation of Islam was not the only religion to espouse values of self-empowerment combined with a refusal to accommodate or compromise with the dominant White society. Christian groups too preached a gospel of self-worth and Black empowerment. One's means of accomplishing this was by reclaiming the racial characteristics of Jesus. As Albert Cleage, an inner-city Detroit minister stated in one of his sermons in the 1960s: "For nearly 500 years. . . the illusion that Jesus was white dominated the world only because Europeans dominated the world. Now with the emergence of the nationalist movements of the world's colored majority, the historical truth is finally beginning to emerge—that Jesus was the non-white leader of a non-white people, struggling for national liberation against the rule of a white nation, Rome. . . Jesus was a revolutionary black leader, a zealot, seeking to lead a black nation to freedom" (in Allitt, 2003: 112). Similarly, James Cone, the author of *A Black Theology of Liberation* stated in his book, *Black Theology and Black Power*, "Where does Christ lead his people? Where indeed if not in the ghetto. . .Christ is black, baby, with all the features which are so detestable to white society" (in Allitt, 2003: 114).

©Attila JANDI/Shutterstock.com

Both Cleage and Cone represented a growing movement called Black liberation theology. Black liberation theology describes the religious movement developed by African American theologians and ministers who interpreted Christ's message as one that highlights the need to work toward social justice—including economic justice such as the eradication of poverty. They also viewed racism as being bound up with economic inequality since so much of racism was due to Whites working to exclude Blacks from educational and job opportunities—opportunities that would enable African Americans to grow their incomes and attain some degree of wealth.

In fact, following the assassination of Martin Luther King, Jr., a number of Black ministers began highlighting the fact that theirs was not merely a fight for racial equality. Instead, they saw racial inequality as tied up inextricably with economic inequality. The publication of "The Black Manifesto" in 1969 by James Forman outlined a demand for reparations of $500 million for damages wrought by slavery. Forman interrupted the mostly White Riverside Church in New York City where the Rockefellers attended in order to publicly state those demands. He opened up by saying, "Our fight is against racism, capitalism, and imperialism" (Allitt, 2003: 113), thus clearly aligning himself with a Marxist view that working against economic injustice must be a primary goal for the Civil Rights movement.

THE SOCIAL GOSPEL

Historically, there have been many notable progressive social movements that were explicitly religious. Significant among them is the Catholic Worker Movement, which was begun by Dorothy Day in the 1930s. Day was a pacifist who began the newspaper the *Catholic Worker,* and she advocated for the rights of the working poor and strove to alleviate homelessness and poverty. Because she identified with anarchist movements and wrote for socialist papers in her early years, she is often characterized as a socialist. However, Day herself purported to seek a third way between capitalism and communism. Her interpretation of the gospel was one that understood Jesus to be active in alleviating the plight of the oppressed, so Day was an ardent social activist and crusader for justice.

The "Social Gospel" is a progressive religious movement that began about 100 years ago by Christians who interpreted Jesus's message as one in which people were meant to redress social ills. Jesus's teachings were not perceived solely as a moral guide for the individual but rather a call to action to work for increased social justice and equality. Proponents of the Social Gospel then see the religious person's mission as one in which she or he gets involved in causes to eradicate inequality, poverty, hunger, homelessness, racism, sexism, and xenophobia. The Social Gospel was highly influential in the work by Dr. King and other leaders of the Civil Rights movement.

Today, we see evidence of the Social Gospel in many different areas of religion. One such area where we see it at work is in the thought of Cornel West, a philosopher primarily but also an activist, actor, artist, and public intellectual. West frequently relies on his religious background (his father was a Baptist minister) in developing his philosophy and social commentary. West has taught at a number of high-profile universities, appeared in the Matrix movie series, and has been a guest on countless television talk shows and news programs. His charismatic and energetic manner of speaking is engaging, and it is well worth anyone's time to watch and hear him speak.

One of the problems with talking about race today is that many people believe racism is now a thing of the past. Some might point to the fact that the country elected its first Black President. Some people might honestly say that they do not know anyone who is "out-and-out" racist. That is, they don't know people who are racist in the old-fashioned sense of the word (someone who believes that one race is superior to another). While it is true that the old-fashioned form of racism has become less apparent, we are faced with what one sociologist refers to as "**color-blind racism**" (Bonilla-Silva, 2013).

Color-blind racism The belief that racism no longer exists, which ignores how race continues to play a role in ongoing inequalities.

Color-blind racism takes place when we ignore the long legacy and consequences that "old-fashioned" racism and institutionalized racism have left us with. Because of the decades and decades of these forms of racism, we still live in a highly segregated society and one that is plagued with economic inequality that has had an enormous impact on Black Americans. For instance, in cities where there is a majority Black population, we find a huge disparity in school funding when we compare Black school districts with White ones (Kozol, 2012).

©a katz/Shutterstock.com

Thus, today, there is a need to combat color-blind racism by first acknowledging that, just like the title of one of Cornel West's books: *Race Matters* (1994). In *Race Matters*, West, among other things, talks about the role of the Black church in working to establish strong Black leaders. West claims that African Americans need to put on what he calls "Black cultural armor." He uses the image of "Black cultural armor" to allude to a biblical verse—specifically Ephesians 6:13. What West fears is that more and more young African Americans see the continued economic and racial challenges before them, and those challenges can seem so overwhelming that they simply give up in defeat. What is needed, he states, is a renewed sense of compassion and the desire to make others' lives better.

West, like Martin Luther King, Jr., and others to be sure, sees the importance of the Black church in promoting social and economic justice. Indeed, West relies on Karl Marx's insights regarding class inequality. While West is aware of the plight and despair wrought by our country's long history of racism and violence, his messages are inspirational. He is also well aware of the color-blind racism that helps reinforce inequality and discrimination, yet he "preaches" hope. It is a specific kind of hope though, for West makes the distinction between hope and optimism.

Optimism is about the actual circumstances, and if we are realistic, it can seem sometimes like there is little use for optimism. In those times, it is easy to give into despair. Hope, he says, is a form of faith. Hope relies on love for others and a desire to intervene in the world in order to make it a better place. Hope, for West and others who work from the perspective of the Social Gospel, always wins when there is little cause for optimism.

©PopTika/Shutterstock.com

So, where are we with race and religion today? Well, it seems that we see the same dynamics today that we have always seen. Religion is sometimes a force for dramatic integration, pushing for social change and equality, especially as the United States becomes increasingly more racially diverse.

That being said, religion also continues to present its own challenges with regard to racial equality. Even with a professed desire and belief system that excludes racism from mainstream teachings, individual congregations often struggle with diversity. Gerardo Marti's research, for example, reveals the importance of the worship gathering itself in promoting and fostering diversity. However, he demonstrates as well that even in those interactions, old stereotypes and challenges are reinforced, often unconsciously. The fact remains that race continues to have a complex relationship with religion as our religious structures struggle to change and adapt adequately to an ever-changing social world.

DISCUSSION QUESTIONS

1. Explain agency, and how social structures affect people's sense of it.
2. What role does religion play in your life? Consider family, friends, ethics, politics, and your ability to decide what is right and what is wrong. Does this affect your personal sense of agency?
3. How can religion be a social construct?
4. What is social justice? With that in mind, how is social justice connected to religion? Give some examples from the chapter.
5. Consider the role of social justice in your own life, and whether or not it could have any religious ties, as well as why it does or does not.
   a. Does this have anything to do with your perceived race, gender, class, or sexual orientation? Consider this compared to your own religiosity, or lack thereof, as well as that of those discussed in this chapter and others in your social circle.
6. Why were so many social justice movements discussed in this chapter connected to religion for African Americans? Does this pattern still exist today? Why or why not?
7. Compare and contrast "redlining" and "blockbusting." Explain how these practices affected African Americans.
8. Why did African Americans separate themselves from Christianity? Later, how were some African Americans able to then identify again with Christianity? Is this different from any Christians you know or your understanding of Christians/Christianity today?
9. Explain "double consciousness." Who coined this term?

CHAPTER 5

THE RELIGIOUS RIGHT

*Why do conservative religious voices, which make a minority of the religious population,
get so much of the attention in our culture?*

KEY TERMS

- **American exceptionalism**
- **Biblical inerrancy**
- **Complementarianism**
- **Dispensationalism**
- **Neoliberalism**

OBJECTIVES:

- Understand the similarities and differences between Evangelical Christianity and Christian Fundamentalism, as well as how they are connected to the religious right.
- Understand the key role that religion has played, and continues to play, in American politics, and how this affects the general public.
- Understand how the religious right uses conservative ideology to implement their religious beliefs into politics and, thus, the everyday life of all Americans.

INTRODUCTION

As we have read in other chapters, religion as an institution can never be understood in isolation from other social institutions. The messiness and complexity of the real world mean that religion both impacts how other institutions, such as the family, and the economy work and, as we have seen, is impacted by these institutions. How is religion shaped? At different points in history, the importance we place on religious ideas, the importance of particular religions, the ways in which we interpret sacred texts and make use of them, the significance of special rituals . . . all of these things have changed from time to time and from culture to culture. Thus, we know that not only religion contributes to how we act and view the world around us, but the world outside of religion also contributes to how we act and view our own religion.

In particular, we have seen in the United States an increasingly visible intertwining of religion and politics. Each has helped to shape the other. Most notably, this has occurred on the conservative end of the religious and political spectrum. Of course, religion has long been a part of politics in this country, but it has recently taken on unprecedented significance. This allows us, as sociologists, an opportunity to examine this phenomenon, so we can better understand the forces that bring religion and politics together, under what circumstances, and to what effect.

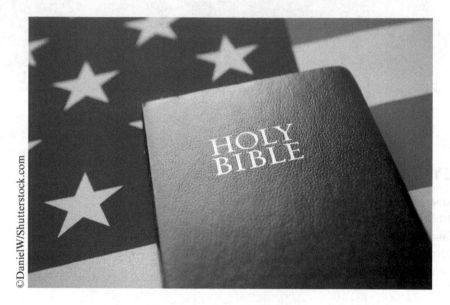

©DanielW/Shutterstock.com

There is no doubt that the combination of both evangelical and fundamentalist Christianity and conservative politics has been a force to be reckoned with in shaping our world today. But conservatism in the government and conservatism in religious institutions have not always been so bound up with one another. This is a recent phenomenon. We might tend to assume that they have always shared a significant amount of overlap with one another as they do now, but in fact, it has only been in the past 30 to 40 years that the two have become as tightly woven together as we see them today.

Evangelical Christians   Political Conservatives

©Kendall Hunt Publishing Company

It is during this period (the recent past) that we see the emergence of what we now call the Christian Right. The Christian Right refers to the large group of people, from ordinary church members to professional lobbyists, media personalities, and congressional leaders, who actively promote a conservative Christian agenda in the halls of government. Further, we describe some of the ways the Christian Right works to accomplish their goals as well as, of course, discussing what some of those specific goals include. But first, we begin with a little history. . .

CHRISTIAN EVANGELICALISM AND CHRISTIAN FUNDAMENTALISM: SOME BASICS

In order to understand the ways the Christian Right developed, it is helpful to understand the evolution of conservative Christianity that can be described as either evangelical or fundamentalist. The two terms, evangelical and fundamentalist, describe a similar strain of Protestant Christianity, but they are not exactly the same.

Evangelicalism describes the brand of Christianity that is more conservative theologically and politically than the brand of Christianity we call the mainline. Two of the most important theological characteristics of evangelicalism are:

> They believe in **biblical inerrancy**, which means that the Bible is the true word of God and is without any errors.
>
> In order to receive everlasting life, one must repent of one's sins and accept the Lord Jesus Christ as one's savior. Personal salvation is critical, and one must be "born-again." The experience of being born-again is oftentimes a central point in an evangelical Christians' biography and sense of personal identity. Because of the requirement to be born-again, evangelical Christians also emphasize the importance of proselytizing or spreading the word in order to convert people who have not been "saved."

> **Biblical inerrancy** The idea that the Bible is the literal word of God, is completely factual, and contains no errors

©Dream Perfection/Shutterstock.com

Additionally, evangelicals tend to hold onto traditional views of family. Fathers and husbands are expected to be leaders in the household, decision-makers, and breadwinners. Wives and mothers are expected to be nurturing and care-giving supporters of their family, community, and their churches. Children are expected to be obedient.

Complementarianism The view that women and men are essentially different and thus have separate but equal and necessary roles to play.

Their view of gender relations is called **complementarianism**. That is, drawing from Biblical justification, they argue that women and men complement each other but are not the same as one another in terms of the roles God has in mind for each of them. Feminists, mainline Christians, and other groups point out that this complementarianism viewpoint is misleading in part because women are never afforded a "role" that accords them any substantial institutional or social power.

Evangelical Christians also maintain a strict sexual ethic. They view homosexuality as unequivocally sinful, so same-sex relationships are forbidden. Premarital sex is frowned upon, divorce is highly discouraged, and "no-fault" divorce is not an option in some communities.

These beliefs are coupled with actions that encourage significant community investment and religious devotion and study. Social life tends to revolve around one's church, and one is expected to pray and read the Bible on a regular, if not daily, basis.

Earlier, we said that Christian evangelicalism and Christian fundamentalism are similar but not the same. That is because Christian fundamentalism can be understood as a kind of subset of Christian evangelicalism. Remember that evangelicalism when compared to beliefs and practices of mainline Christians is more conservative. We might place the two on a continuum.

Evangelical Christians · Mainline Christians

more conservative · more moderate

©Kendall Hunt Publishing Company

Christian fundamentalists believe in similar values and ideas as evangelicals but are even stricter and more conservative. But if we were to make a Venn diagram on how fundamentalism and evangelicalism are related, it might look like this:

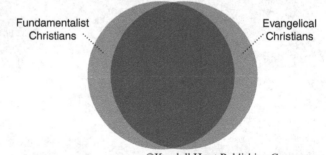

Fundamentalist Christians · · · · Evangelical Christians

©Kendall Hunt Publishing Company

You will notice that there is a great deal of overlap between fundamentalism and evangelicalism, but there is an area where the two do not overlap. Where they overlap, fundamentalism and evangelicalism share a conservative and traditional view of people's roles and the importance of being born-again.

However, where they do not overlap, where they differ, is primarily in two areas. First, fundamentalists believe in Biblical inerrancy, but they also believe that the Bible is not metaphorical but rather can be read in a very literal manner. This, in fact, is what describes fundamentalists in any religion. Second, fundamentalists have a specific belief about the final book in the Bible—the Book of Revelation, something we will discuss next. Before we get to that, however, let us look at the sociocultural roots of American Christian fundamentalism.

HISTORICAL BACKGROUND ON FUNDAMENTALISM

Christian fundamentalism can be traced back to German Biblical scholars who, in the 19th century, began asserting that the Bible was a product of human authors. These scholars took a historical approach to studying the origins of the Bible. In short, through careful historical and archaeological investigation, the Bible had multiple authors. The discovery of ancient texts revealed that there are multiple early translations of both the Old Testament and the New Testament, and depending on the source, some books were included and others were left out.

These scholars concluded that humans intervened at all stages of the process in creating the Bible as most Christians know it today. In other words, multiple recorded passages from different origins would end up in today's Bible. Other people had to

©Swellphotography/Shutterstock.com

translate those passages into Hebrew and Greek. Then other people had to edit the passages and decide what to include and what not to include. Then still other people had to take those passages and combine them in order to create whole books in the Bible. Finally, still other people had to decide what books would make up the Old Testament and the New Testament.

The scholars that examined these stages in the making of the Bible concluded that the Bible is a human product and not one that emerged from a divine source.

Therefore, the way people should read and interpret the Bible ought to be read as a human created story. The scholars were by and large not arguing that the Bible was not a sacred text, only that it could not be understood as the literal "word of God."

As you might imagine, calling into question the divine provenance of the Bible caused a furor for some people. Some American Protestants expressed their concern that people would begin to question the divinity of Jesus, for instance, or the importance of the Israelites in God's plan. This growing number of people in the United States who emphatically denied the interpretation of the Bible as human-made would eventually coalesce into the group we now refer to as Christian Fundamentalists.

They were not called fundamentalists until the early 1900s though. What solidified the movement and helped give its name was the publication of a series of pamphlets calls "The Fundamentals: A Testimony of the Truth" that appeared beginning in 1910. These publications asserted that the Bible was of divine origin, that Jesus was "God-made man," that prayer could bring about real-life changes, as well as quite a few other claims. Among those other claims is an idea that is vital for anyone wanting to fully understand the motivations and values of Christian fundamentalists, and that is the topic of our next section.

MILLENARIANISM

Millenarianism is the belief that significant, history-changing events take place every 1,000 years. It is important to note that millenarianism is not unique to Christian fundamentalism and that there are quite a few groups who adhere to various kinds of millenarianism. However, what is unique to Christian fundamentalism is the kinds of millenarianism that support their belief system.

The millenarianism that is used in Christian fundamentalism is rooted in the final book of the Bible: Revelation (with a special emphasis on chapter 20). The book reveals a prophetic vision on the part of the author ("John") who richly describes numerous evocative and frightening events. Characters such as the Whores of Babylon, the Beast, the Archangel, and the False Prophet are depicted in places such as the Lake of Fire and a scorched earth. Numerology is also an aspect of the book. For instance, you likely know about the number of the Beast being 666. The number 7 is ubiquitous

throughout the book. Just to name a very few of the examples, there are seven seals to be broken, seven trumpets that announce the seven bowls poured on the earth, and a seven-horned lamb with seven eyes.

At some point, following multiple battles, plagues, and all assortments of trials and tribulations, the dragon is cast into a bottomless pit, Christian martyrs are resurrected from the dead, and Jesus Christ would reign for 1,000 years.

Given the allegorical nature of the stories in the Book of Revelation, it is not surprising that there have been countless different interpretations of all of the book's characters, events, and locations. Christian fundamentalists view the book as a prediction for how the world will end and when Jesus will return. Many fundamentalist (as well as evangelical) Christians believe that the world is in a heightened state of disorder and turmoil, and this indicates that we are nearing the apocalyptic end of the world. In general, the present state of the world in their eyes is such that they wish to hasten its end in order to also hasten the return of Christ and return to a peaceful world order.

©Sabphoto/Shutterstock.com

Dispensationalism
The idea that God has divided history into well-defined eras of time.

Related to Christian fundamentalists' interpretation of the Book of Revelation is their belief that history can be divided up into epochs or long periods of time called dispensations. **Dispensationalism**, then, describes the belief that history is divided into various dispensations. According to one interpretation by fundamentalist Christians, we are in the final dispensation prior to Christ's return. Some fundamentalists have even argued that there is evidence for this even in the first book of the Bible: Genesis. They interpret the story of God's creation of the world as taking place in millennial dispensations. According to Genesis, God created the world in six days and on the seventh, he rested. Some fundamentalists popularized the idea that if one day in God's perspective is 1,000 years from a human perspective, then we can date the beginning of the world to a little before 4,000 BCE (Aldridge, 2013: 121). The day God rested? Well, in this view, it is right around the corner.

As we said, the Book of Revelation is an important feature that contributes to fundamentalist Christians' ideas about the world and their place in it. There is another popular interpretation of the book that sees the world in a state of chaos, turmoil, and sin, but in order for the dispensation to end (signaling Christ's return), it is necessary to establish a more Godly state of the world. So, some believe that Christ will return only after a millennium in which a Christian-dominated society has "paved the way." These fundamentalist Christians, therefore, are motivated to establish a world that matches their Christian moral values and belief system. One means of accomplishing this is through political action, and their aim is to establish the United States as a solidly Christian nation, which we will discuss as follows. However, before we do that, let us discuss some of the sociological characteristics of fundamentalist Christians.

FUNDAMENTALISM IN THE 20TH CENTURY

If you do not identify as a Christian fundamentalist, the word "fundamentalist" might bring to your mind a number of different images or associations. Some people automatically think of fundamentalists as being extremists. Some might have other stereotypes that come to mind. Interestingly, contrary to some generalizations that portray fundamentalists as uneducated, southern, and rural, the fundamentalists in the first half of the 20th century were highly educated and lived in big cities in the northeast and midwest (Bendroth, 2012). They included many intellectuals and scholars who offered an opposite account of what their opponents were saying.

During the early part of the 20th century, Christian fundamentalists were not as stigmatized as they are in many social circles today. They merely represented a sizable group of people who shared particular viewpoints and religious ideas. Neither

©StockLite/Shutterstock.com

disparaged nor placed on a pedestal, theirs was just more or less accepted along the continuum of religious perspectives and beliefs. That changed, however, with an important court case that captured the widespread attention of Americans.

©MSSA/Shutterstock.com

In 1925, the Scopes Trial, sometimes referred to as the Scopes Monkey Trial, a teacher in Tennessee was sanctioned for teaching evolution (which was against the law to do so in public schools there at the time). Christian fundamentalists were particularly strident against the teaching of evolution. The court case drew media frenzy, and fundamentalists were pilloried in national press as simple-minded. Such widespread derision contributed to the weakening of the visibility and prominence of Christian fundamentalism for a number of years. Fundamentalism was seen as antiscience and antimodernity.

While fundamentalism waned, mainline American religious participation was quite high. The United States saw a rise in church membership and financial giving. In fact, some historians called this post-World War II increase in religious involvement as the second great religious revival.

So even though the First Amendment in the Constitution protects freedom of religion ("Congress shall make no law respecting an establishment of religion . . . [nor] prohibiting the free exercise thereof"), many Americans did not balk when the separation of church and state grew a little less separate. In the middle of the 20th century, "In God we trust" was a phrase that was added to money. Additionally, the Pledge of Allegiance was established (which, of course, included the phrase "under God").

Still, Christian fundamentalism had taken backseat for many years following the Scopes trial but began to emerge again as a popular movement in the 1960s and 1970s. This was due in part to what some believed was a corruption of American society and a flagging interest in biblical teachings. The "pill" was approved as a form of contraception in 1960. For many people, the introduction of the pill foretold a period of immorality and lasciviousness since it freed women up to having more control over their bodies and their sexual behavior. In 1962, the Supreme Court ruled that prayer in public schools was unconstitutional. In 1963, *Time Magazine* featured a prominent cover that merely contained the phrase: "Is God Dead?" and this fueled fears that America was "losing its way" as more people were questioning their religious beliefs. Also, in 1963, John F. Kennedy was assassinated.

Throughout the 1960s, civil unrest was a ubiquitous sign of the times given the fight to end segregation and racist Jim Crow laws. The U.S. military escalated its involvement in Vietnam throughout the early part of that decade. In the mid-1960s, the hippie was popularized. The Black Panther Party formed in 1966. In 1968, both Martin Luther King, Jr., and Robert Kennedy were assassinated. In 1967 and 1968, there were numerous riots in large urban cities that resulted in millions of dollars of damage and destruction and not a few human casualties. In 1969, the Stonewall Riots took place, an event that served as the impetus for the gay rights movement.

The Manson murders took place also in 1969. In the late 1960s and early 1970s, the Equal Rights Amendment (ERA) was high on everyone's radar. In 1973, the Supreme Court legalized abortion (Roe v. Wade). In 1974, President Nixon, facing impeachment at the time, resigned from office.

This period was a tumultuous one for America, no matter how you look at it. It was a time of tragic loss, but it was also a pivotal time for a renewed drive toward equality and social justice. For fundamentalist Christians, it served as a call for action and thus began a resurgence in fundamentalism.

FUNDAMENTALISM AS IT IS LIVED TODAY

Nancy Ammerman is probably the best-known sociologist to explore Christian fundamentalism. In her book *Bible Believer: Fundamentalists in the Modern World* (1987), she outlines some characteristics of fundamentalists today. The most central factor that distinguishes fundamentalists from other forms of religious traditionalism or conservatism is the belief in the Bible as inerrant. This means that they believe the Bible was not merely inspired by God but the Bible represents God's word. Thus, the Bible does not contain any errors and is not open to interpretation. Equally important, the Bible is to be understood literally.

Additionally, fundamentalists tend to see the world in very "black-and-white" terms and have a low tolerance for uncertainty. In fact, Ammerman notes, religious fundamentalism grows when there are events or occurrences in society that threaten people's sense of stability and security. Her observation of this is evident when we look back to the times when the popularity of Christian fundamentalism surges. You will recall from earlier in this chapter that the first time is when Biblical scholars question the belief that the Bible is the divine word of God and instead assert that it is a human creation. The second time fundamentalism saw an increase in growth was following the tumultuous 1960s and early 1970s.

Fundamentalists believe God has a plan for everyone and that people can relate to God as though their relationship is contractual. In other words, fundamentalists believe that, for example, "If I do this, God will do that" (Ibid., p. 41). Thus, when fundamentalists sin, they believe they will be appropriately disciplined, and when they repent, they will be forgiven. If one believes in Christ as their savior, God will grant them eternal life. This last belief, that repenting of one's sins and taking the Lord as one's savior, is imperative. Thus, evangelizing is an important activity, and it emphasizes the importance of witnessing to others and working to convince others to accept Jesus as their savior.

While the inerrancy of the Bible and the view that it should be taken literally are vital to Christian fundamentalists today, a second central aspect has to do with the view of the "end times." Specifically, many fundamentalists subscribe to what is called "dispensational premillenialism." Recall that a dispensation refers to a certain period of time and we are, it is believed, in the final dispensation prior to Christ's reign. Because this is thought to be the final dispensation, many fundamentalist Christians feel an urgency to convert as many nonbelievers as they can.

This view of the end of the world is evident in the popularity of the *Left Behind* book series by the authors Tim LaHaye and Jerry Jenkins. In it, the authors describe how the end times unfold. First, the rapture takes place when Christians, both those still alive and those who are deceased, are brought up to Heaven. The eponymous "left behind" are forced to live in a world of disorder and disarray. Some of those left behind choose to repent and be born-again Christians, and they become the protagonists of the 16 book series in which they try and take down a world leader who is in fact the Antichrist.

Because the Book of Revelation is so important, the interpretations different groups of evangelicals and fundamentalists have of Revelation also have pertinent sociological effects. For instance, among those who argue that we should understand the Bible in a literal manner, some see the story of Adam and Eve as evidence for women's subservient role to men in society. According to the book of Genesis, Adam was created first and Eve was made out of a rib from Adam. Adam the first of the male species, therefore, from the very beginning has a kind priority and status. Strengthening this view regarding sex and gender, you may be familiar with the story detailing how it was Eve who first ate from the forbidden tree of knowledge. She then passed the fruit of the tree to Adam and thus gave rise to the "fall of man" or the "original sin." According to the story, this is the reason why women suffer pain during childbirth.

Remember that some fundamentalist Christians interpret the stories in Revelation as suggesting that Christ will return only after the present world has been transformed into one that has been morally purified. If one adheres to that view, that too will influence one's view on sex and gender. Eve (who symbolizes the more general category of "women") is ultimately responsible for the original sin. Many Christians believe, therefore, that we are born into sin and thus must repent of our sins and be saved. While we will discuss this in more depth in Chapter 7, in this view, men are implied to be rational and reasoning. Women are emotional and impulsive and a temptation to men. Subsequently, men should generally be the ones in control and are better suited to the work of leadership and guidance.

Another consequence of according centrality to the Book of Revelation and interpreting the present era as one in which we are closing in on the end times is also reflected in international politics. The state of Israel has a special role to play in the end times, so the Christian Right advocates that the United States do what it can to support Israel (even at the expense of Palestinians' struggle for equality and independence). As one sociologist writes: "[D]espite their widespread anti-Semitism, dispensationalists have raised much money to help right-wing Jewish extremists reclaim the Temple Mount in Jerusalem from the Muslims who have their holiest, centuries-old shrines on the site" (McGuire, 1992: 48).

©Alexandra Lande/Shutterstock.com

Similarly, for those who believe that we are in the final dispensation, Christians must work to prepare the way for Jesus's second coming. That means that more Christians ought to be represented in the halls of power. The Christian Right, then, should actively work toward electing fundamentalist and evangelical Christians to public office. Further, we will discuss how the Christian Right has been able to coalesce into an identifiable social movement that has quite a bit of power when it comes to shaping the U.S. government and its policies and legislation.

THE RISE OF TELEVANGELISM

Certainly, one of the major contributors to Christian fundamentalism's popularity has to do with religious leaders' ability to convey their messages to a wide audience. Television served that function well, though, as we shall see, not without some significant complications. So, let us begin here by discussing what made the rise of televangelism possible in the first place.

The Federal Communications Commission (FCC) oversees the rules that regulate television stations and their broadcasts. Early on, the FCC mandated that television channels must include programming that bolstered the "public interest." Networks frequently offered free programming to mainline Protestants, Catholics, and Jews. However, in 1960, the FCC ruled that television stations could use paid programming that would still count toward their expectation that channels include public interest programming, more conservative and evangelical religious organizations began broadcasting their own shows.

©Anthony Correia/Shutterstock.com

Among the early "adopters" was the evangelical preacher Billy Graham, whose preaching would eventually reach prime time on the major networks. Later, the advent of cable television was an important contributor to the rise of televangelism—most notably when Pat Robertson developed his own network, the Christian Broadcasting Network, which with cable could be broadcast nationwide. Similarly, another evangelical station, the Trinity Broadcasting Network, began airing its shows in 1973.

These developments opened the door for a whole host of charismatic preachers. Jim and Tamme Faye Bakker, Pat Robertson, Jerry Falwell, Jimmy Swaggart, and Oral Roberts took on heightened visibility because of their television shows, and taken as a whole, they represent the origins of the phenomenon of televangelism that took place in the 1970s and 1980s. While estimates regarding how many people tuned in to this programming on a regular basis to these televangelists, conservative numbers counted viewers in the millions. Recall that prior to this period, most religious television shows were produced by Catholics and mainline Protestants. However, in the 1980s, 90% of religious television shows were evangelical and fundamentalist (Allitt, 2003). Evangelical and fundamentalist Christians clearly leveraged their newly granted access to the airwaves to their advantage.

While televangelists proved to be quite effective at spreading their messages to millions of people, some of them bore the brunt of increasing scrutiny by a growing public. This is because many of the television shows included extensive pleas for donations from viewers. However, the use of the millions of dollars that flowed into these shows was at times misused, mismanaged, and even exploitative. The scandals involving Jim and Tammy Faye Bakker make this fact apparent.

The Bakkers were notorious for the way they sought financial contributions from TV viewers. "Tammy had the gift of being able to weep at will and sometimes, appearing to be emotionally transported by her interviews with born-again guests, let the tears flow freely. Her mascara was so heavy that it mixed with the tears flowing down her cheeks, creating a Gothic web of black tracks. Nothing made her weep more than a falling-off and donations, and nothing seems so well calculated to bring forth more cash than another bout of sobbing" (Allitt, 2003: 192). So, Tammy Faye was very successful at increasing her program's revenue from contributions by the show's viewers. However, it was later discovered that many of the donations coming in were being used to support a lavish lifestyle of Rolls Royce cars, fur coats, yachts, and mansions. It was also discovered that Tammy Faye had sought professional treatment for drug addiction and her husband had been carrying on a long sexual affair with a secretary and had been photographed with prostitutes. Jim Bakker was later accused of fraud and served a six-year prison sentence.

In a similar scandal, Oral Roberts, who had his own television ministry, told viewers in 1987 that unless his viewers donated $8,000,000 to his ministry, God would "call him home." In other words, he pronounced that God would end his life unless that money flowed in from his viewers. As a result of his plea, his ministry received over $9,100,000.

TV BECOMES POLITICAL

Televangelist became synonymous for "scoundrel" to many Americans following these scandals. However, at the same time, the medium of television also helped religious leaders to mobilize a significant portion of the American population around conservative religious issues.

Jerry Falwell, for instance, began his political group the Moral Majority in 1979. Pat Robertson formed the Christian Coalition 10 years later. They, alongside other "born-again" politicians, preachers, and lobbyists of the Christian Right, began aligning themselves with very conservative-minded Republicans—the first one being Ronald Reagan. In part, this was due to Regan's designation of the Communist USSR as the "Evil Empire," which had connotations that tied the country to the book of Revelation's discussion of the Antichrist. This resonated strongly with conservative Christians who believed the Soviet Union to be "godless" since Communism and religion were incompatible.

Pat Robertson, the televangelist from the show *The 700 Club*, went on to run for president of the United States on the Republican ticket. While he did well in early primaries leading up to the Republican convention, in the end, he did not receive enough support to get the official nod as the Republican nominee. That position went to George Bush, Sr., himself a self-identified born-again Christian.

©Zastolskiy Victor/Shutterstock.com

Television also helped coalesce religious viewers around specific issues. Abortion was and continues to be an important issue for the Christian Right. Yet, following the Supreme Court's decision on Roe v. Wade, most of the activists crusading to have the decision overturned were Catholics and not evangelicals and fundamentalist Protestants. It was only when the matter got publicized on fundamentalist Christian television programs (notably, Jim Bakker and Tammy Faye Bakker's show *Praise the Lord (PTL)* and Pat Robertson's *The 700 Club*) in the 1980s that abortion became more widely associated with the Christian Right (Allitt, 2003). Operation Rescue was founded in 1987 as a formal activist and lobbying movement that was established by the Christian Right to try and abolish abortion. Operation Rescue successfully bridged Catholics with conservative Protestants to create a coalition that staged many well-attended protests and marches.

The fact that abortion is inherently related to a woman's body contributed to deliberations over women's agency and control as well as over women's roles with regard to the family and home. Thus, the ERA of 1972, which was supposed to guarantee the women's equality, also came into question by fundamentalist Christians who saw the ERA as contributing to upsetting the "natural" place of women as homemakers, mothers, and dependents (on their husbands). Phyllis Schlafly was a conservative Catholic who espoused reversing ERA. Her work resonated with many in the Christian Right who favored the biblical teaching, "Wives be subject to your husbands" (Ephesians 4:22). Schlafly helped contribute to the fact that the ERA failed to make it through all of the necessary channels in order for it to become a law.

The Christian Right also began mobilizing around other issues as well in the political arena, notably the teaching of creationism in schools and the inclusion of public prayer in schools. Since fundamentalists argue that the Bible is inerrant and literal, the first book in the Bible, Genesis, should be read as factual and scientific. Advocates lobbied school administrators and state legislators and successfully have been able to get creationism included in some states' school curriculum so that evolution and creationism are presented as competing theories.

The desire to teach creationism rather than evolution, combined with the Supreme Court's rulings against Bible reading and school prayer in public schools, has led to two major trends in K-12 education. First of all, there has been a significant rise in the number of private schools founded by and managed by evangelical and fundamentalist Christians. The historian Patrick Allitt estimated that during the 1960s and 1970s, there were, on average, two new such schools created each day (2003). However, more recently, fundamentalist and evangelical Christians have been at the forefront of the homeschooling trend and now comprise the majority of those households in which homeschooling can be found.

©Daria Filimonova/Shutterstock.com

The organizations Focus on the Family and The Family Research Council are also products of the Christian Right. Both had fought hard against the legalization of same-sex marriage in the more recent past. They also support traditional gender roles (something we discuss more fully in Chapter 7).

The Christian Right has proven quite effective at placing issues of morality at the center of political dialogue. What used to fall squarely in the domain of religious institutions (e.g., values pertaining to sexuality and the role of the family) are increasingly becoming part of our political institutions. This has created a strong divide in American politics.

The sociologist James Davidson Hunter famously describes this in his book: The Culture Wars: The Struggle to Define America (1991). He has convincingly argued that there are now basically two dominant political views: on one side, people whose religion is used to support and legitimize their perspectives and beliefs. They are conservative and traditional-minded. On the one side, he posited, are people who are largely reactionary and the other progressive. Therefore, with respect to voting habits, political ideology, and political participation, "[T]here are two Americas: those for whom religion is highly salient, and those for whom it is not" (Olson, 2007: 442).

Some credit this idea of two Americas being fodder for extremism on both sides. There have been a number of acts of violence committed by fundamentalist Christians (who drew on religious rhetoric or otherwise justified their actions through their religious fundamentalism): Branch Davidians, members of the racist and militia-like Christian Identity movement, as well as members or former members of the antiabortion groups Army of God and Operation Rescue who assassinated physicians providing abortions.

With regard to the separation of church and state, many in the Christian Right believe that America is a Christian nation, one that is blessed by God. President Ronald Reagan is generally beloved by those on that side of the religious and political spectrum not because he professed to be a born-again Christian as Presidents Carter and both Bushs did. Rather, Reagan's anti-Communist rhetoric, his support for a strong and independent state of Israel, and his belief that America was a "city on a hill," a phrase borrowed from Jesus's Sermon on the Mount, meant to indicate the special status of the United States in God's order.

The Christian Right's view that the United States is especially blessed by God, or is his "Chosen Nation," is part of what we call **American exceptionalism**. Just as the phrase implies, it is the belief that the United States is special, unique, and somehow better than other countries, usually for some inherent or divine reason. This kind of exceptionalism also works to help some in the Christian Right make sense of tragic events. For instance, both Jerry Falwell and James Dobson argued that 9/11 was a punishment for America's sins—most prominently among those "sins" included the legalization of abortion and the increasing tolerance of Americans of persons who identify along the LGBTQ spectrum.

American exceptionalism
The belief that the United States is unique, special, and blessed by God.

©Matej Hudovernik/Shutterstock.com

As we have seen, Christian Right organizations have proven to be highly instrumental when it comes to who is elected into political office. Indeed, they were crucial in George W. Bush's back-to-back presidential electoral wins given their endorsement of him. Thus, the Christian Right not only has grassroots, or ground-level influence, but also their influence reaches to Washington, DC, and beyond. What this reveals is that not only religions have the power to shape people's entire belief systems, behaviors, and morality, but they also can affect politics, legislation, and the economy. Ironically though, members of the Christian Right are strong advocates of small government, a topic to which we now turn.

NEOLIBERALISM

> **Neoliberalism** The ideology that values laissez-faire-style government and emphasizes individual agency.

Neoliberalism refers to the current dominant economic ideology. While "liberal" is at the root of the word "neoliberal," it does not refer to a progressive economic agenda. "Liberal" in neoliberal is not synonymous with the Democratic political party. Liberal, in this usage, refers to the liberalism of the 1700s during which Adam Smith and other political economists advocated for a laissez-faire style of government in which the state played little role in the lives of citizens. Thus, one can easily see the ideas of conservative politicians today who are proponents of small government. While many Democrats are proponents of a neoliberal society, it has largely been the domain of Republicans who see "big government" as a problem and who work toward fewer restrictions and regulations on the free market: for example, lowering restrictions on trade barriers and making it possible for American companies to relocate to other countries where it is cheaper to operate and employ labor.

There is an additional characteristic of neoliberalism though that impacts the ways in which citizens view themselves and others. In a neoliberal era, emphasis is placed on the freedom of the individual. Citizens are encouraged to think of themselves as completely free to map out the futures of their lives. The ability and wherewithal of individuals to bear the fruits of hard work and realize the American Dream are exaggerated. Many people, as a result, believe that anyone can pull themselves up by their "bootstraps" and become wealthy or successful. Indeed, studies demonstrate that Americans still believe this and the consequences can be dire—for instance, think how often the poor are blamed for their poverty while the wealthy are seen as moral, disciplined, and hard working. Such perceptions overlook the role of social structures that limit certain people while giving a leg up to others.

©Roman Bodnarchuk/Shutterstock.com

Neoliberalism, because it is an economic ideology that emphasizes laissez-faire, or reduced governmental presence in individuals' lives, has also led to another phenom-enon that is relevant to the sociology of religion. Because of widespread support for a reduction in the kinds of provisions and subsidies that have provided assistance to our most vulnerable people in society, religious institutions have had to increasingly step in. Indeed, President George W. Bush passed a series of domestic policies that reduced government aid to the impoverished and offered incentives to religious organizations to take over the role the government had previously played with respect to that aid. These "faith-based initiatives" created some controversy over the separation of church and state at the time, but some form of this policy continues to the present. Faith-based initiatives have really taken to the fore in neoliberal era in which people believe that the government is too large and that "local congregations could do a better job than welfare bureaucrats" and in which the morality of the local churches could draw on that to provide social support and social services (Farnsley, 2007).

It is important that sociologists untangle these intersections between religion and other social institutions, in this case, politics, from time to time. It is not the case that we need to be able to see the "corrupting" influence of one on the other, as so many people would be inclined to see. Rather, it is important because understanding these connections is a vital part of the sociological project.

It is true that the institution of religion does not exist in a vacuum, but it is just as true that the forces that shape religion do not occur randomly. In fact, we find that the very same *types* of processes that led to an intersection among conservative religion

©wavebreakmedia/Shutterstock.com

and conservative politics in the United States in the latter part of the 20th century are the same *types* of processes that are always at work when we see these two institutions come together.

Periods of high social tension and turmoil, an increase of diversity, and a mistrust in dominant social institutions are recipes, in other words, for the emergence of a conservative religious ethic that creates a similar set of politics. There is nothing inherently Christian about this process in general. Other cultures, with other dominant religious systems, experience much the same dynamics with different specific religious justifications.

DISCUSSION QUESTIONS

1. Compare and contrast Evangelical Christianity and Christian Fundamentalism. Give at least two examples for each from the chapter.
2. How does the religious right view gender roles? Does this have an effect on Americans who do not share the same values? How?
3. What does the religious right believe about homosexuality? How has this belief penetrated American Politics and thus the lives of all Americans?
4. Explain Millenarianism. How do Fundamentalists, and some Evangelicals, use this ideology to promote furthering religious doctrine? (think social structures)
5. Consider Fundamentalism. What generally comes to mind when you see/hear that term? According to the chapter, what is one surprising historical fact about Fundamentalism?
6. Explain the difference between creationism and evolution.
7. What was the political role of televangelism?
8. Is Neoliberalism an ideology in alignment with "liberal" politics? Why or why not?

CHAPTER 6

SEXED AND SEXUAL SOULS

Why do women traditionally have higher rates of religious adherence when religious systems have systematically oppressed them?

KEY TERMS

- **Essentialism**
- **Gender**
- **Normal**
- **Queer**
- **Sex**

OBJECTIVES:

- Understand the deeply rooted connection between gender and religion.
- Consider the ways religion privileges men over women; this includes the roles men and women generally occupy, the way women are spoken to and about, as well as the fact that religious leadership positions are typically held by men, i.e. "God the Father," "Jesus the Son," etc.
- Understand how sexual expression, especially that considered LGBTQ, and most other progressive topics are viewed within religion as discussed in this text.

WOMEN IN THE WORLD

You are probably familiar with the basic sociological patterns of gender inequality from other sociology courses. The vast majority of Wall Street executives are men. The vast majority of CEOs are men. Men have always comprised the majority of Congressional membership. In general, women put in more time working to take care of their relatives and their households. In the media, women are far more likely to be objectified and sexualized than men. Women are more likely to be judged on the basis of their appearance than men. Women are more likely to experience eating disorders than men. Women are more likely to experience negative emotions regarding their bodies when compared to men. Women are more likely to suffer from our society's double standard, which celebrates men's expressions of sexuality, yet shames women who engage in sexual behavior.

On average, for every $1.00 a woman makes, a man makes $1.25. Wage disparities exist . . . even when we compare the differences between women and men's pay within a specific occupation such as nursing or teaching; even when we compare how much women and men make in a specific company; and even when we control for variables such as how much education or work experience a woman versus a man has.

Women are more likely to be the victims of domestic assault. They are more likely to be subject to everyday harassment. They are far more likely to be the victims of a sexual assault. Over the course of her lifetime, the most conservative estimates suggest that one in six women will be the victims of sexual assault.

We see this same pattern of male domination in religion as in other parts of society. Men, by and large, control religious organizations. What makes this situation unique and interesting to explore sociologically, is that despite the power inequities in religion, women actually attend church more often and have higher rates of religiosity than men.

Aside from working for reform, women have very few options in many of these institutions. One cannot, for example, simply opt out of government. Religion, however, is a different story. There are myriad religious options, including the option to have no religion. So why would women continue to disproportionately support an institution that often relegates them to second-class status both structurally and ideologically?

The answer to this question relies in first understanding the system of patriarchy. A patriarchy is a society in which men have more power than women, hold more leadership positions than women, experience fewer barriers to getting ahead in life than women, and are generally more socially privileged than women. We live in a patriarchal society. The empirical evidence supporting that fact is unequivocal.

In order to counter the inequality that is such a big part of a patriarchal society a system of beliefs based around the equality of genders has developed. This ideological system is, of course, feminism. Sadly, in our society, when some people hear the words "feminism" or "feminist" they conjure negative associations. Some think that a feminist is a woman who hates men. Others think that feminism is the idea that women are better than men. And a few people think that feminists want to emasculate men by forcing them to relinquish any trait that bears an imprint of masculinity. None of these characterizations are accurate.

©Sunny studio/Shutterstock.com

Feminism is the belief that women ought to have the same opportunities as men and the same access to resources as men. A feminist then is someone who is an advocate of greater equality and who is committed to seeing girls and women given the opportunities, privileges, and rights that boys and men enjoy. Men therefore can be feminists. In fact, we both identify as feminists (and we are men).

In order to understand the role that **gender** plays in religion, it is important that we are able to understand it as both a mechanism that is used to support patriarchy while simultaneously being a site of resistance for many feminists and others who want to challenge prevailing gender norms.

RELIGION AND WOMEN

Religion has an undeniable role in perpetuating patriarchy. Far more often than not, men are found in leadership positions within religious groups. In religions' sacred texts, men are more prominently featured and women more frequently assume subservient roles. Divinities are far more frequently represented in male form compared to female forms, as are the major prophets and historical figures. For instance, we talk about "God the Father" and when God is referred to by a pronoun, typically it is "He" and "Him" that are used.

So religion by and large privileges men while women are more or less consigned to secondary roles. Because religion is such a dominant force in our society and more people are religious than are not, religious values and beliefs are bound to have an impact on the values and beliefs expressed by a culture. Thus, the patriarchal values

Gender Socially constructed understanding of one's masculinity or femininity, generally understood as one of two categories, woman or man; more recently many terms describing people who do identify somewhere else or nowhere on a "gender spectrum" have emerged.

©Renata Sedmakova/Shutterstock.com

found in the major religions allow people to justify the patriarchal values in society more broadly. In other words, if a person trusts what their religion deems to be worthwhile and acceptable, then by that same token, when the larger society finds the same things to be worthwhile and acceptable, the person is then more likely to be satisfied with the current state of affairs.

> **"Sex"** Biological understanding of oneself as either male or female; with the exception of intersex (ambiguous genitalia).

GENDER AND SEX

Sociologists have a specific way of talking about women and men. "Sex" refers to the perceived biological differences in the anatomy and physiology. To be blunt, genitalia are generally considered the most salient defining characteristics distinguishing women from men. However, we should also be aware that biological sex differences

©FMStox/Shutterstock.com

can themselves be fuzzy. Many people who identify as transgender may have genitals that do not accord with what those persons consider their *actual* sex or gender identity.

Additionally, persons who are intersex may have ambiguous genitalia or chromosomes that do not easily fall into one of two categories. Many people in the general public think intersex conditions are extremely rare and are often surprised to learn that it is more common than they originally believed. According to one of the foremost leading scientists on intersex, the frequency of intersex persons is roughly the same as persons who have red hair (Fausto-Sterling, 2000).

Also complicating our biological understanding of the differences between women and men is this fact: one's social context also has an influence on levels of hormones that we typically believe are exclusive to either women or men. That is, one's environment can influence how much testosterone our bodies produce or how much estrogen can be detected in the bloodstream.

Why is it important to note that the biological distinctions that distinguish between women and men can be fuzzy? Because as sociologists, we know that society often tends to treat women and men as being essentially different. We think that since there seem to be essential biological differences, then there must also be essential social differences too and that women and men therefore behave differently and think differently. This view—that there are essential differences between women and men—is called **essentialism** and it is a view that is scientifically inaccurate.

> **Essentialism** The belief that men and women are essentially, or "naturally," different based solely on biological characteristics.

WITCHCRAFT AT SALEM VILLAGE.

©Everett Historical/Shutterstock.com

Yet even before we had conceptualized essentialism, there is a long historical precedence suggesting that humans have thought women and men were akin to different species. In other words, societies have long believed that women were one way and men were another. Consider just one example that is relevant to religious studies: the Salem witch trials in Puritan New England. Women were the majority of those accused of witchcraft and it was because women were believed to have one set of traits and men another. The period reflected a double standard since "The very characteristics that made souls fitting brides of Christ—submission, passivity, humility—made female bodies more vulnerable to the devil's corporeal [bodily] attack than male bodies were"

(Johnson, 2010: 155). Thus women, even during this period were cast as docile, weak, and complacent (as opposed to men who were viewed as independent, instrumental, and assertive).

There is abundant empirical evidence that illustrates that *gender* differences are socially constructed. This becomes apparent when one examines the ways masculinity and femininity have changed over time. Indeed, one need not go back in time to appreciate the ways gender is socially constructed but merely look at the ways masculinity and femininity differ from culture to culture or nation to nation. We refer to gender, then, as something that is historically specific and culturally specific. When the historical context changes or when the cultural context changes, our ideas about gender also change.

©Tracy Whiteside/Shutterstock.com

Furthermore, because gender is not something permanent, universal, and unchanging, sociologists state that gender is "performed." In other words, we "do gender." We learn very early on from our parents and friends how to properly perform our gender. Media reinforce those ideas. Collectively, all of these ideas about how to properly perform our gender can be thought of as "social scripts." Like an actor recites lines in order to memorize and internalize a script as she or he prepares for a performance, you and I are socialized into certain social scripts. They get reinforced in us very early in our lives and so we do not even need to worry about memorizing them. We get corrected when we do not perform our lines well and praised when we do perform them well. If you have ever been told something like, "That's not how girls act," or "You should try and act more like a man," then you know what it feels like when you have not adequately performed the social script that goes along with your gender.

But performing our gender according to these social scripts is a lifelong project. For example, before going to work this morning, my wife applied some make-up and put on a dress. On the other hand, I applied some deodorant that was specifically marketed to men (in spite of the fact that the ingredients in the deodorant were identical to that which is sold to women) and wore shoes that did not have high heels. Had I mimicked my wife and shown up to work in a dress, high heels, and makeup, I would have felt the immediate impact of social shame through stares or even laughter. That is because we all are familiar with these social scripts. They are engrained in us.

©Cheryl Casey/Shutterstock.com

©Annette Shaff/Shutterstock.com

Thus, society reinforces particular forms of femininity and masculinity and in our society we make a big deal about having two social scripts for gender: masculine and feminine. My best friend recently had a baby and we went to shop for her newborn child and found very stereotypical messages: clothing, cribs, strollers, and toys were all clearly marketed for either girls or boys. It was frankly almost impossible to buy just about anything that wasn't in some way "coded" for either girls or boys. That is, hardly anything was available that was gender neutral.

These social scripts not only tell us how to act and dress, they also tell us what is appropriate and not appropriate in terms of how we think, feel, and how we are embodied. For instance, yesterday I went to the gym to exercise, and I focused on lifting weights. I held the door open for a woman as I left the gym.

All of these behaviors are part of the social script that says this is what a man "does" in order to properly perform his gender. But then something else happened. After the gym I went to work but encountered a lengthy delay on the interstate and arrived late. As a result I missed a couple of appointments and from that point on I could not seem to shake my foul mood. At home when my wife asked me how my day was I grumbled "fine" but did not go into much detail about how I was feeling nor did I discuss the latest gossip about one of my colleagues who'd had an argument with someone else. I did not even feel like I needed to talk about how I was feeling or about the socializing I had engaged in earlier in the day. Why? Because again I was performing my gender and norms dictate that men limit their emotional expressions and avoid talking about certain topics in conversation.

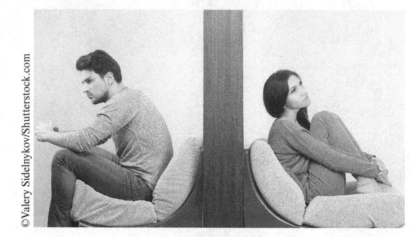

©Valery Sidelnykov/Shutterstock.com

"Normal"
Something/someone that is generally perceived as good and/or healthy; can also be understood as average or plain.

The important point to this is that we all perform our gender. We do it in the way we act, walk, talk, and even think and feel. The other important point is that the ways in which we perform our gender are socially constructed. There is nothing biologically imperative that says that women must be interested in sharing their feelings or that men are not good at being sensitive or capable of being nurturing. These are all based off of social scripts that tell us that the "**normal**" way of being a woman and the normal way of being a man is to follow certain guidelines. In fact, those guidelines, those social scripts, can be very limiting since they do not allow us the freedom to explore our full human-ness and potential. At worst, they can force us into harmful little boxes that lead us to denigrate others who don't fit into boxes or even contribute to making us feel that we ourselves are inadequate, unworthy, or unlovable because we do not fit into what society deems to be "proper" and "normal."

As we think about gender as a social construction it is important to keep in mind that what society says is the norm or what is accepted to be normal is completely made up by society. If you encountered someone talking to God you might call it prayer if you were in a church but if you encountered someone doing it in your classroom in the middle of a lecture you might suspect the person of being mentally ill. "Normal" is just a category. Being abnormal does not necessarily make something unnatural, wrong, or bad. We must always take social context into consideration and be mindful of the many ways we behave according to socially constructed scripts.

RELIGION AND GENDER

You may have heard of the proverbial "glass ceiling," a concept that refers to the ways in which women are oftentimes only able to advance in a career only to a certain point. While we generally expect that over the course of a career, one is able to continuously climb the ladder within a company (at the same time taking on more responsibility, gaining more expertise, and benefitting from periodic wage increases), many women reach a certain point before they are no longer promoted. Some attribute this to organizational homophily, which describes the social psychological phenomenon in which people seek to spend more of their time with others who are similar. In other words, birds of a feather flock together. Thus, if most of a company's top executives are men, they may be more likely to hire men at these top ranks. Regardless of the reason, the glass ceiling is an actual sociological occurrence that helps to explain why men disproportionately comprise the highest levels of a given field.

©Jef Thompson/Shutterstock.com

There is a similar phenomenon in religious organizations. Some sociologists have taken to calling it a "stained glass ceiling." Women, in spite of constituting the majority of religious followers or religious participants are underrepresented in religious leadership. While generally that holds true for most religions, there are a few exceptions.

©Anton Petrus/Shutterstock.com

The intersection between gender and religion is complicated and difficult to unravel. For instance, one of the most popular questions students ask me in my sociology of religion class is this: Why are men so frequently in leadership roles when it comes to religion? After all, religion is an institution that frequently espouses the dignity and value of all individuals and equality is accepted as virtuous.

To be frank, when it comes to religion, women have often been relegated to the role of second-class citizens. That is, their participation in religious communities has very often been subordinate to that of men. There are, not surprisingly, a number of reasons for this and we could not possibly exhaust them all here. However, one significant reason is due to the historical nature of patriarchy itself. The United States is obviously not the first instance of a patriarchal society. Indeed, many societies during many eras have been far less egalitarian when it comes to the treatment of women versus that of men. This was certainly the case for the societies in which the authors of the Torah and the New Testament were working. Thus, it should be fairly evident that sacred texts produced during a particular cultural and social context will in some ways reflect the values and worldview of those societies. In other words, sacred texts have a cultural and historical specificity to them.

©Frank Gaertner/Shutterstock.com

Therefore it should not be surprising that this is precisely what we find in the majority of religions' sacred texts: women are subordinate to men. Even when those texts are read and interpreted in other epochs, the sacred nature of those texts is such that its overall importance often overrides the texts' historical nature and their authorship. In other words, we tend to ignore the historical and cultural specificity of sacred texts.

But let us still return to our original question, asking why it is that women are so rarely the leaders of religious organizations? The question becomes even more urgent when students learn that religion, at least in the United States, is what sociologists call "feminized." The feminization of religion refers to the trend that more women than men participate in religious institutions and they perform the behind-the-scenes work required to sustain religious organizations (work that is most of the time unpaid). In spite of this, more men continue to be leaders. Men are more likely than women to not identify with a religion. More atheists and agnostics are men. This means that more women than men have a religious affiliation (Pew Research 2007). The same research also shows that women are more likely to engage in religious practices and rituals such as prayer than men. In fact, women have been the majority of religious members since the Colonial era in most Christian denominations (Morrill, 2010).

So what happens when we look at these sacred texts that serve as the foundational guidelines for our ethical and moral behavior? When we examine them closely we find a lot of differing and sometime contradictory perspectives regarding women and men. For instance, take the book of Genesis. In Hebrew there are two different words that have both been translated into a generic word in English as "man." *'Adham* is Hebrew for "humanity" (what in English used to be called "mankind." *'Ish* is Hebrew for biological males. So in Genesis when the Bible in English says that God created man, the original Hebrew is more specifically that God created humankind. Nevertheless, much of the Old Testament was written for a male audience. Consider, for example, that in the 10 Commandments thou should not covet thy neighbor's wife. On the other hand, there are some instances of powerful and wise women—particularly Esther and Ruth.

©Everett Historical/Shutterstock.com

In the New Testament, the letters of Paul can be quite sexist and demeaning for women. Women, he asserted, ought to obey their husbands. While Paul was no doubt a product of his time, his theological assertions were nevertheless problematic since he believed that original sin was due to Eve. Jesus, on the other hand, would have certainly been considered progressive by the same standards since he allowed women to accompany him and participate in his ministry.

Additionally, there is the matter of sexuality. Men's sexuality is often viewed as something "natural" and, as such, men's sexuality is seen as being a kind of biological imperative or uncontrollable force. Women then are viewed as threats to men's "proper" sexual behavior. Merely consider the way that some people in our society see women as being temptations to men—thus there is a need to make women more modest. Such views rely on the assumption that men want sex and women largely do not. Clearly this is a flawed construction of both men and women's sexuality since we now know that women enjoy sex.

All of this has led to what Rosemary Reuther conceptualized as "hierarchical dualism." This refers to the kind of way in which some people like to see the world, in black and white, concrete terms, and where much of reality can be divided into two mutually exclusive categories. Furthermore, in hierarchical dualism, as the term also implies, one side is better or favored over the other side. Simply think about the kinds of people who apply simplistic views of the world around them: my religion is good and true and everyone else's is wrong and evil. People who think about the world in terms of hierarchical dualism are more likely to view women as subordinate to men.

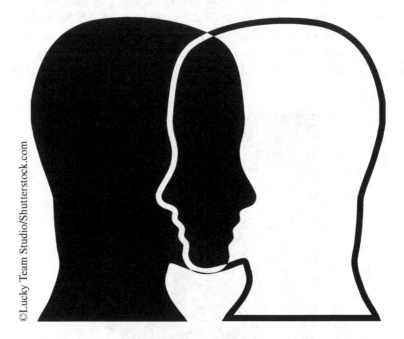

©Lucky Team Studio/Shutterstock.com

Religion, then, clearly plays an important part in maintaining and even strengthening unequal relations between women and men. Conversely, though, it can and has in some areas played a role in creating a more equitable society with regard to gender. Before we turn to a discussion on some of the ways women have been empowered through their religion, let us look at an important historical ideology that was very influential on how women and men were differentially viewed and understood.

SEPARATE SPHERES

The term hegemony first of all refers to the dominant ideology, or collective belief system that appears to be mere "common sense," in a society. Hegemony also refers to the way in which people go along with the dominant ideology even when it does not ultimately align with their own interests. In short, people say that hegemony is the "consent of the dominated." This means that people in power create values that benefit them and, only on the surface appear to benefit everyone else.

A fairly straightforward example of this might be the way advertisers attempt to sway us into buying expensive cars. I might therefore be inclined to spend a great deal of money in order to signal to others that I have a certain social status. On the surface, a fancy car will symbolize that I am wealthy and have "good taste." Ultimately though we know that these symbols are merely social constructions and the real point of having a car is so that I can get to where I would like to go. So when I buy a fancy car I have "bought into" a system that benefits the makers of the vehicle and the marketers who get rich from working with the car manufacturer. What I might have done is rather than buy the fancy car, put the money into savings, invest in some stocks that will accrue interest, or even donate the money in order to benefit a charitable organization.

Hegemony works in a lot of ways and we often do not realize when we are buying into a system of beliefs that will benefit people who have more power or privilege than we do. Sometimes it is only in hindsight that we can begin to see hegemony at work. One such example of this has to do with the hegemonic beliefs that benefit and empower men at the expense of women. In the following example, we can see that what on the surface appears to empower women ultimately reinforces their secondary status in society.

In the 1800s, the most prominent perspective regarding the norms and expectations of women and men is called the "separate spheres" perspective—it was the hegemonic point of view. Accordingly, women and men were believed to contribute to society in different ways. Women and men each had their own set of responsibilities and those sets of responsibilities took place in different areas of daily life. There was a strict separation then in the kinds of activities in which women and men engaged. For men, their "sphere" took place in the public arena of the workaday world, while women's sphere was in the private arena of the home. Men's duties were to engage in social activity that took them beyond the household and into the workaday world as breadwinners. Men were thus expected to be industrious, outgoing, entrepreneurial, hardworking, and exhibit leadership. Women's duties revolved around social reproduction: to bear children and raise those children to be morally in line with their designated roles as girls and boys so that when they were grown, they could fulfill their proper "sphere" in life.

©Everett Historical/Shutterstock.com

The Women's Christian Temperance Union was, as the name suggests, a women-founded and women-led social movement designed to combat alcohol abuse and was a significant factor leading to Prohibition. The organization was formed in the 19th century. And while members fought to win women the right to vote, suffrage was seen as something that would protect the moral sanctity of households, thus perpetuating the notion of "separate spheres." Ultimately, then, men's hegemony over women remained in place since in spite of the power to vote, since the goal was to keep women in the home and thus financially dependent on men.

Why, you might ask, would women participate in activism that reinforces and perpetuates male social dominance? Is it because women are simply being duped? Einwohner, Leamaster, and Pratt note that, "[W]omen find value, fulfillment, and even empowerment in conservative activism that seems to reinforce religious patriarchy" (forthcoming). So even in spite of the ultimate consequences of our actions, our religious priorities and values are such that we can oftentimes feel that what we are doing matters in significant ways to ourselves as well as to other people who are important to us. So to return to my previous example of buying a fancy car . . . I might be fully aware of the fact that the social status achieved in my driving such a car is a fiction propagated by a consumer society that equates owning nice things with being viewed as a successful and important person. Yet, if in fact owning a fancy car impresses others around me, and if their opinion of me matters to me, then I will be inclined to drive the fancy car.

©penton439/Shutterstock.com

However, religion also provides women with the moral justification that allows them to convince others that change is necessary. To provide an example, I will draw on a friend of mine who is a Buddhist scholar. In her work she details the ways in which the Buddha himself was a strong proponent of social equality and justice (Hu, 2011). He even went so far as to encourage his followers to fight against the rigid social caste system that favored people who happened to be born to families in higher classes while denigrating those in lower classes. Buddhist activists then draw on this knowledge of the Buddha in order to justify their beliefs that we should strive for complete social equality regardless of sex, ethnicity, religion, or sexual orientation.

There have been many instances in our society in which women were at the forefront of religious movements and religious leadership. We discuss some examples below.

WOMEN AT THE FOREFRONT

Einwohner, Leamaster, and Pratt point out the following: "At the same time that religious institutions may serve as the target of women's activism, these institutions also . . . provide the necessary resources that women need to plan, stage, and succeed in their activism" (forthcoming). They state that religion does two things that help to empower women. First, religion provides resources through the social networks that can be strengthened in religious communities. When people form connections with another, they are able to draw on those connections in order to strategize, organize, and mobilize one another's resources for change.

There are a number of organizations that are actively working to change the feminization of religion and the lack of women in leadership positions. One notable group is Equal in Faith, an ecumenical (interfaith) organization that "Call[s] for the equitable inclusion of women in religious traditions that persist in excluding them from positions of religious and spiritual authority" (retrieved from URL: equalinfaith.org). As it now stands, though, men still dominate the top ranks within religious leadership. Einwohner, Leamaster, and Pratt (forthcoming) point out that men more frequently hold formal leadership positions. The nature of their title as Pastor or Elder provides them with a certain amount of power and authority because of their designated position within the institution. Women, on the other hand, are more often unofficial leaders who "lead by example" and facilitate informal groups and social networks between groups. This is evidenced by numerous examples in which women have been at the forefront of religious movements that began from the grassroots (or bottom-up) as opposed to those movements that were initiated from institutional leaders occupying the top ranks within religious hierarchies.

©Everett Historical/Shutterstock.com

An important example of this can be found in the case of *The Woman's Bible*. In 1895, Elizabeth Cady Stanton convened a panel of 26 women to examine the Christian Bible and provide commentary through close inspection of its narratives. A strong proponent for suffrage and a contemporary of Susan B. Anthony, Stanton and her colleagues conducted a thorough analysis of the books of the Bible in in order to explore the ways women were at times highlighted as empowered protagonists in the Bible and other times dismissed, disregarded, or otherwise oppresses. Stanton wrote: "The object is to revise only those texts and chapters directly referring to women, and those also in which women are made prominent by exclusion." Stanton and her collaborators provided extensive commentary that relied on historical contexts, authorship of various texts, and multiple interpretations of specific passages. What we begin to see in reading *The Woman's Bible* is the way in which culture shapes how the Bible was crafted and how it is read and applied today. *The Woman's Bible* is a key example illustrating the importance of women to Biblical scholarship and theological studies. Though, by far it is not the only one as we shall see.

Following World War II, the American population increased rapidly (resulting in what we call the generation of "Baby Boomers"). Also, more and more people were moving out to newly created suburbs in the United States. Combined, these factors led to a rise in the number of new churches, synagogues, and temples. Some mainline congregations began allowing the formal ordination of women to become clergy (though women still cannot be ordained in some fundamentalist and evangelical Christian denominations nor in the Roman Catholic Church). All of these new faith communities fueled a demand for more clergy and, as a result, more women began being admitted to divinity schools and seminaries (Allitt, 2003). Many women who attended divinity schools and seminaries did not end up serving in formal leadership roles within churches and synagogues but instead turned to academia to continue their religious pursuits. In other words, many more women were becoming theologians and professors of religion.

In 2010, the field of theology lost one of its most significant scholars. Mary Daly was a feminist theologian who had taught at Boston College (a Jesuit institution) since the 1960s. Raised as Roman Catholic, Daly identified with the Church early on but began drifting away when she became increasingly dissatisfied with what she felt was an intrinsic patriarchal characteristic to institutionalized religion. In fact she would sometimes assert: "[A] woman's asking for equality in the church would be comparable to a black person's demanding equality in the Ku Klux Klan (1986: 6). She believed that religion had privileged men throughout history and continued to rely on outdated ideas that oppressed women.

In 1973, she wrote the seminal *Beyond God the Father: Toward a Philosophy of Women's Liberation*. In it, she raises a number of important theological issues. First, she decries the language we typically use when referring to God in masculine terms: God as the "Father" and our pronoun usage of God as "He" and "Him." Because we generally default to these masculine terms, we naturally tend to associate the divinity with that which is masculine. And because we view God as male, we then tend to view masculine qualities as somehow superior to feminine qualities. Consider, for example, if we always referred to God as "She" and "Her" and "God the Mother." We might then conclude that God has qualities that we associate with femininity: we might see God as being nurturing, caring, sensitive, expressive, and gentle. If that were the case, and if we had been inculcated to always thinking of God as a woman, we might be more likely to revere feminine qualities of human nature and less likely to dismiss such traits. Similarly, what if in the New Testament it was not Jesus who represented the human incarnation of God but instead a woman? Might that also have affected the ways we have historically devalued women, feminine qualities, and the thoughts, feelings, and actions that we so often associate with women? Daly makes a convincing argument that indeed it would and goes so far as to claim that even though Jesus was a man, he would most certainly qualify as what we today call a feminist.

Daly does not argue that we need to view God as a woman. In fact, she attests that any kind of anthropomorphization of the divinity is problematic. She states that any time we view God as being human-like (whether male or female) we put God in a box

©Vibrant Image Studio/Shutterstock.com

that limits our ability to appreciate God as something omnipresent and omnipotent. When we describe God in any terms that are human-like, we are committing a kind of heresy since we are essentially making God out to be far less than God actually is. Even attempting to describe God using our very limited, fallible, inadequate language is to do God a disservice since God is greater than anything our feeble human minds could conceive. Thus, for Daly, theology should avoid trying to make sense of the divinity and instead focus on the actual, concrete forms of oppression and suffering that exist in our world. In other words, God would want us to spend less time trying to "figure out" God, which is an impossible task anyway, and instead devote our lives and our work to figuring out how to make the world a better place.

MASCULINITY

As we have seen, the majority of religious participants, attenders, and members in faith communities are women. This, we learned, is the "feminization" of religion. There have been a number of movements throughout history that have attempted to draw more men into religion. These movements have done so primarily by framing religion as a masculine sort of institution, one that can appeal to men's desire to be "manly" men. For instance, in the latter part of the 19th century when women comprised two-thirds of church membership in the United States, some leaders advocated what they called "muscular Christianity" (Johnson, 2010). Muscular Christianity was a movement started by men in the hopes of getting more men into churches. To accomplish this they spread the message that morality was not a passive or docile quality—that was perceived to be too feminine. Instead Christian morality was something that took strength, guts, and independence. The leaders in muscular Christianity avoided portraying Jesus as weak, gentle, and meek. Jesus was a strong, assertive leader who, after all was a carpenter. Reinforcing the movement was the formation of the YMCA (Young Men's Christian Association) in 1844. The YMCA aligned itself with muscular Christianity by equating physical strength with moral uprightness.

Muscular Christianity enjoyed a brief period of popularity but declined in the early 20th century. However, a more contemporary movement developed that aimed to accomplish similar goals associating masculinity with Christian morality with the evangelical movement called Promise Keepers. "Promise Keepers was the fastest-growing religious movement of the 1990s, a nondenominational organization for Christian men who believed that many of the nation's woes could be blamed on themselves for failing to play their biblically ordained role as strong husbands and fathers" (Allitt, 2003: 242). Started by a college football coach, the group rented out stadiums for day-long revivals in which thousands of racially diverse men participated in worship, prayer, and singing. Religion was masculinized albeit the morality espoused by the movement was a very conservative one that was anti-abortion, anti-feminist, and anti-gay. Promise Keepers began in 1990 and still exists today though it lacks the size, visibility, and robustness that characterized it in the 1990s. Thus, to this day, religion continues to be dominated by men in leadership roles while women make up the majority of religious followers and devote more time than men when it comes to the voluntary work needed to run religious organizations.

SEXUAL EXPRESSION

There is no doubt that our sense of sexual morality bears the imprint of Judeo-Christian views that sex is dirty and wrong except for when it takes place within a narrow frame of expression (only in marriage, only between a woman and a man). In Christianity, Jesus was born to a virgin thus suggesting that sex is somehow not commensurate with that which is divine. Paul in the New Testament was an advocate of sexual purity and abstinence. He even went so far as to imply that if a person could not attain those standards, they should then get married. And of course, Catholic priests are expected to avoid engaging in sexual behavior.

Same-sex sexuality has been a hotly contested issue in the past few years within religious organizations. Some religious denominations continue to equate heterosexuality as the only acceptable form of sexual expression while others have welcomed

©Lightspring/Shutterstock.com

Queer Anything that deviates from what is generally understood as "normal"; odd or strange; any sexuality that is not "straight" or heterosexual.

people who do not identify as heterosexual (i.e., "straight"). Later we will discuss non-heterosexual individuals as existing on an LGBTQ "spectrum"—that is, persons who identify as lesbian, gay, bisexual, transgender/transsexual, and/or **queer**. But before we do, it is useful to understand how sociologists think about sexual expression.

As such, sociologists are informed by some of the pioneering sex research done by Alfred Kinsey in the 1940s. Kinsey conducted in-depth interviews with thousands of people and he found that sexuality actually existed on a continuum and provided us with the Kinsey Scale. The scale goes from 0 to 6 and one end indicates 100% heterosexuality and the other is 100% homosexuality. What Kinsey found was that people indicated they were often on neither end of that scale but somewhere along the continuum (as being more or less heterosexual or more or less homosexual). The reason it is important to acknowledge Kinsey's scale is because it illustrates the complexity and nuance in the variability of human sexuality. Since Kinsey's work, much additional research has revealed that sexual identity/preference can change throughout one's life.

Adding to the wonderful diversity of human gender/sexual expression is an increasing understanding of the 'T' in the LGBTQ acronym. Transgender refers to those persons who do not identify with their biologically ascribed sex. Save for a few exceptions, most religions have not yet begun to address transgender issues in their theology or in their doctrine. And of those that have, many have unfortunately opted for stances that are trans-phobic by either denunciating members of the transgender community or excluding them altogether.

And speaking of diversity . . . many people have additional letters they include in the acronym LGBTQ. Some add an 'I' for intersex (something we discussed earlier in this chapter) and others add an 'A' for asexual. As our scientific appreciation for the variability in sexuality and gender identity expands, religions will inevitably evolve. Many will welcome individuals on the LGBTQ (or LGBTQIA) spectrum and will adapt how sexuality is situated within their moral doctrines. Others will likely continue to derogate people who do not happen to identify as heterosexual—perceiving non-heterosexual people as somehow abnormal, strange, or sinful.

©Lisa-Lisa/Shutterstock.com

But as sociologists we need to be ever vigilant to how we construct categories—particularly categories that have significant consequences on those whom we wish to categorize. Thus, let us take a moment to examine one such important category: normal.

WHAT IS NORMAL?

What is normal? Is normal just another word for "average?" Most of the time when we use the word "normal" it is really just a synonym for "average." So when we say someone looks normal or they are acting normal, then what we are essentially doing is thinking back to all the people we have encountered and then using those experiences as a reference point. When I was in New York City last month visiting a relative I was surprised at how many rats I saw scurrying along the tracks in the subway stations. I pointed this out to my aunt who simply shrugged her shoulders and said, "Oh, that's normal." She was accustomed to seeing rats scurrying in the subway. And when my mother visited me from Florida last winter here in the Detroit area we'd just

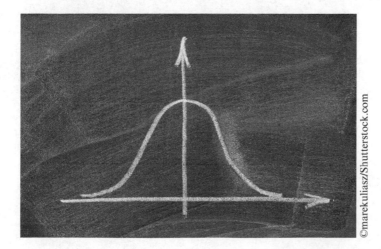

©marekuliasz/Shutterstock.com

had 8 inches of snow. This was remarkable for my mother but for me it was "normal" to have that kind of snowfall in January. So what is normal changes depending on our context and the circumstances. And even then, we can think about normal like we do a statistical bell curve. At the peak of the bell curve, where most people are, we would identify the norm or what we consider to be normal.

For instance, we often hear that the average human body temperature is 98.6 degrees Fahrenheit. In other words, most people, most of the time, have a body temperature of 98.6. But many people stray from that average. In truth, when I go to see my doctor and the nurse takes my temperature I almost always have a temperature of 98.2 which is still considered to be quite healthy. A temperature above 100 degrees Fahrenheit generally indicates someone has a fever. So if we were to put body temperature on a bell curve we might come up with something like this:

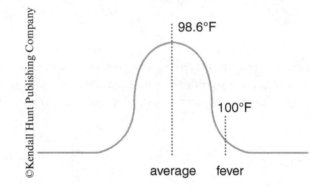

So the average, or what is considered "normal" indicates that someone is considered "healthy" but a temperature that deviates too far from the average indicates that one is not healthy. So one might conclude that average also means "good." That is, it is "good" to have a body temperature of 98.6.

But sometimes, we don't want to be just average. The average IQ is 100 but I would imagine that many people would prefer to be above average when it comes to their intelligence. Or consider a standardized test like the ACT or SAT. Here too, most people would prefer not to be considered "normal" because that would suggest they are "average."

Thus when we think of the word "normal" we get all kinds of associated words like "healthy," "proper," "good," or we can get other words like "average," "plain," or "mediocre."

Now let us look at another word: "queer." What do think of when you read that word? Do you associate "queer" with synonyms like weird, strange, or odd? Or do you think about lesbian and gay individuals?

To some in sociology, including myself, the word "queer" represents a combination of the two: it refers to people along the LGBTQ spectrum and it also means "not normal." But when we say "not normal" in queer sociology we mean it in a positive sense. Just like you likely do not want be of "average" intelligence, some people see being "normal" when it comes to their gender or sexual identity as being "average," "plain," and even a little bit uninteresting. After all, it is nice to live in a world where there are so many different people of so many different complexions, different religious traditions, and different expressions of their gender and their sexuality.

For instance, I teach a course called "Queer Social Theory." In this theory, we address the ways persons who have historically identified along the LGBTQ continuum have been denigrated, debased, and oppressed. However, we also examine the reasons and justifications LGBTQ people have been perceived to be abnormal. Queer studies in sociology examines the ways people who identify along the LGBTQ continuum have been oppressed, victimized, and shamed by people who believe that there is only one normal sexual identity: heterosexual. Queer studies reminds us that normal is just a social constructed category but even more importantly what the field contributes to sociologists more broadly has to do with a linguistic derivation of the word "queer" itself. As a part of speech, "queer" is usually used as an adjective. We might describe something as "queer": a queer woman or a queer man, for instance. Occasionally, "queer" is a noun as when someone might proudly state, "I am a queer." Queer studies add to this usage by suggesting that the word can also be a verb. *To queer* something means to challenge it, subvert it, question it, or rebel against it. I might queer what it means to be a normal man, for instance, by not conforming to societal expectations of what a normal man should be like.

"Queer," then, represents a kind of reclamation, or a way of turning a negative label into something positive. It is as though one is saying—Heck yes I'm queer, and

I'm proud of it. It is a way for people who have been told they are not "normal" to celebrate the fact that they are not normal. Just think about how boring the world would be if everyone had the same religious background, religious traditions, and religious beliefs. We certainly would not be reading this textbook because there would be no complexity of depth to religion. There would be no need to be inquisitive and curious about other people's values because they would simply have the same values as ourselves and everyone else around us.

LGBTQ

Unfortunately, in our society, being heterosexual or "straight" is viewed as natural and normal. Persons who fall within the LGBTQ spectrum are therefore seen as deviant and their sexual orientation is believed to be a choice rather than something as natural and "normal" as heterosexuality. Many people justify their beliefs through their religion. In the Bible, we find such passages as Leviticus 20:13, which says, "If a man lies with a male as with a woman, both of them have committed an abomination; they shall be put to death, their blood is upon them." And in Romans 1:26–28 we find "For this reason God gave them up to dishonorable passions. Their women exchanged natural relations for unnatural, and the men likewise gave up natural relations with women and were consumed with passion for one another, men committing shameless acts with men and receiving in their own persons the due penalty for their error."

At the same time, the Bible contains so many different commandments, prescriptions, prohibitions, precepts, guidelines, and dictates that no individual could possibly be perceived to be faultless. In Leviticus 15, for instance, we learn that women who are having their period are to be considered unclean and no one should be permitted to come in contact with her. And throughout history humans have been selective in the ways they interpret and make use of biblical passages. Oftentimes, this approach has proven to be exploitative and even violent. Take for example slavery. In the ninth chapter of the first book of the Bible, Genesis, Noah curses his son Ham. Because of this curse, Ham and his descendants would all have to live their lives as servants. Slave owners in the United States drew on this story as justification for their actions.

©Morphart Creation/Shutterstock.com

They argued that descendants of Ham were black. As such, white people felt that they basically had God's blessing to take possession of black individuals whose primary purpose in life was to be the servants of whites.

Yet, in the United States so much of our sense of morality centers around issues related to sexuality that sex becomes a focal point for judgment and evaluation. That is a social construction. We might instead choose to focus on eating habits since the Bible also devotes quite a number of passages to the food we ingest. Or we might focus on any number of other areas of human life that are addressed in the Bible. Still we focus on sex and what is considered "normal" and what is considered deviant, sinful, and shameful.

Perhaps you are familiar with the Reverend Fred Phelps and the Westboro Baptist Church in Topeka, Kansas. They are the ones who attend funerals of various people, including American soldiers killed overseas and carry colorful placards that say things such as "God hates fags" and "God hates America." In their view, "proper" sexual morality is so much a priority that tolerance of non-heterosexuality by even a few in the society taints the whole of that society. They believe that God has condemned the entire United States because Americans are increasingly tolerant of a sexually diverse populace. And while the Westboro Baptist Church represents an extreme perspective, there are still a great number of religious communities that feel strongly about condemning people identifying as LGBTQ.

Some religious groups take a strong stand against non-heterosexuality. In 1988, the Southern Baptist Convention passed a resolution stating the homosexuality was "a perversion of divine standards" (URL: http://www.sbc.net/resolutions/610). And there are quite a number of religious-based organizations that are outspokenly anti-gay including the Family Research Council and James Dobson's Focus on the Family.

Some fundamentalist Christian groups considered conversion therapy, for a period of time, as the appropriate means of "correcting" one's homosexuality. Homosexuality in this light was perceived to be a pathology or similar to a mental disorder for which one could seek psychiatric and psychological counseling to become heterosexual. The American Psychiatric Association, the American Psychological Association and even

President Obama have spoken out against such a view and there has been no credible evidence to support that conversion therapy is helpful. If anything, there have been a number of instances in which people who have undergone such "therapies" have suffered significant mental and emotional distress afterward.

©zadirako/Shutterstock.com

Other religious groups have softened their views as evidenced by the number of denominations who have taken an approach that has come to be called the "love the sinner, hate the sin" approach. People with this point of view see homosexuality as one of many "sins" but still wish to provide a more tolerant and welcoming acceptance of people who identify as LGBTQ. Many mainline denominations have only recently begun allowing the ordination of persons who identify on the LGBTQ continuum. Two mainline denominations, the Presbyterian Church USA (PCUSA) and the United Methodist Church were divided in 1990s and much of the first decade of the new millennium as to what their stance on LGBTQ inclusion and ordination should be. While both have become increasingly accepting of LGBTQ members, only the Presbyterians (PCUSA) opted to allow the ordination of gays and lesbians as professional pastors. Eugene Robinson became the first openly gay identifying man to become ordained a bishop in the Episcopal Church in 2003. The move was decried by many Anglican leaders around the world and Bishop Robinson was the target of significant harassment and faced threats to his life.

There are some religious groups that continue to be less welcoming than others—among them are Mormons and Southern Baptists. Also, the sociologist, Richard Pitt (2010), has written on the intersections of race/ethnicity and sexual identity/preference. He notes that "nearly four centuries worth of surveys show that Black Americans are less approving of homosexuality than the White counterparts" and these attitudes are likely a consequence of the African Americans' religious affiliation. That is, many African American churches, in spite of their more progressive stances on politics, class, and even gender, are less so when it comes to non-heterosexuality.

There have been a few denominations that have taken a more progressive approach to welcome members of the LGBTQ community. One such denomination is the United

Church of Christ. They declared that they would ordain gay and lesbian ministers in the early 1980s and have consistently lobbied since then for LGBTQ rights. Additionally, the Unitarian Universalists were among the first advocates of both gender equality as well as sexual equality. The Metropolitan Community Church is an international Christian denomination that formed specifically to address the needs of persons who identify as LGBTQ.

According to the Pew Research Center, there has been a growing acceptance of LGBTQ-identified people in all major religious groups in the United States since 2007 (retrieved from URL. http://www.pewforum.org/2015/11/03/u-s-public-becoming-less-religious/). The study found that as more and more young people come of age within their religious tradition, overall attitudes are beginning to change—even in the most conservative religions and religious denominations. This is a clear sign that when it comes to religiously informed morals around sexuality, religions continue to evolve and adapt to newer understandings of gender identity and sexuality. Furthermore, I would argue that it is a strong indication that younger generations embrace diversity and openness more than ever before.

COMPLEXITY

From the pages above, you have probably gathered that the relationship between gender, sexuality and religion is anything but simple. This is a very complex dynamic that has evolved tremendously over time. There is nothing in the history of religion as a social institution that would suggest that the current arrangements will remain into the future. In fact, if we learn anything about the history of gender and sexuality in the church, it's that the future will contain a constantly shifting and evolving position.

It is true, however, that as these positions have evolved over time, patriarchy continues to be a big part of many religious traditions. The point is that we cannot think of change and evolution in religion as trending inevitably toward some more egalitarian future. If that is to be the ultimate result, it will be because activists, feminists, and others push the institution in that direction.

DISCUSSION QUESTIONS

1. In previous chapters, we have discussed religion as a structure and how structures work to guide the things we do. In this chapter, we consider social scripts as guiding forces for gender performance. Is it possible, then, to also consider social scripts as structures? Why or why not?

2. Explain the concept of "doing gender." Give one example from the chapter and one example from your personal life.

3. What is the "stained glass ceiling?" How does it affect women within the realm of religion?

4. Explain the "feminization" of religion. Why is this peculiar?

5. Who was Mary Daly? What were her ideas about women's roles in the church? Give three examples from the chapter.

6. Compare and contrast ideas of what is "normal" and what is "queer." Account for how these can and do change depending on social environment. How does the church work to dictate people's perceptions of normal and queer?

CHAPTER 7

THE END OF RELIGION AS WE KNOW IT, OR JUST A NEW BEGINNING?

Are baseball and football kinds of religions?

KEY TERMS

- Anomie
- Civil Religion
- Mind-Body-Spirit (MBS)
- Network
- Religion
- Sacred
- Therapeutic Religion

OBJECTIVES:

- Understand that people exist as not just separate entities, but as social creatures that thrive together with others.
- Consider relationships of all types and their importance in the lives of every human.
- Understand how societal or cultural norms work to produce certain behaviors in people that are historically specific, and how they came to be in the first place.
- Grasp the connection between social norms and religion; how something larger than oneself is maintained through human action.
- Understand New Age or **Mind-Body-Spirit (MBS)** types of religions, and how/why many socially conscious millennials adhere to these.

INTRODUCTION

Think for a minute, where does religion come from? If you're religious, how did you "get religion?" This very simple question opens up an extraordinary line of inquiry. Perhaps you answered that you had a conversion experience wherein God communicated with you directly. Maybe you grew up in a household that was religious and can't even remember a time when you weren't religious. But let's move beyond that and think about society as a whole. How does the institution of religion develop? How does it emerge in a society from scratch and develop over the years. And, perhaps most importantly, why?

Mind-Body-Spirit (MBS): Type of therapeutic religion with an emphasis on self-actualization through self-healing facilitated by the mind to create mental and physical well-being; integrates a belief in the spiritual nature or soul of the self.

Religion: The social institution established to incorporate the divinity into everyday life.

One of the founders of the sociology of **religion** also happens to be considered as one of the founders of the field of sociology in a broader sense. Emile Durkheim (1858–1917) lived in France and, before becoming a social scientist, considered going to rabbinical school to train to become a rabbi. However, he had a change of heart, which led him to withdraw from religious participation for the remainder of his life.

Before writing his most famous work on religion *The Elementary Forms of the Religious Life,* he wrote a book simply and starkly titled *Suicide.* Now, when we think about suicide and we ask ourselves why people take their own life, generally people come up with answers having to do with psychological issues. . . they were too depressed or they had a mental illness or they simply could not cope with whatever was taking place in their life.

©Evgeny Atamanenko/Shutterstock.com

What Durkheim pointed out was that if suicide was purely psychological then if we were to compare suicide rates from different countries or different eras of time, then the rates at which people took their own life would be fairly constant. Durkheim points out that this is not the case and that suicide rates vary not only between periods of time and between countries but between all kinds of factors like people's religious identity, whether they are part of a family, or even the state of the economy. He applied rigorous statistical evidence to illustrate that suicide is not merely psychological but social as well.

One of the major concepts that he developed from his study on suicide was that of **anomie**. Anomie refers to a state of normlessness. Norms are the expectations and rules regulating our actions and our thoughts. They are socially established standards for behaviors and beliefs. Durkheim said that humans thrive when there is a healthy set of norms to guide us. Without norms we are left in a state of uncertainty and anxiety and that state he calls anomie. As you might have already speculated, religion is good for protecting us against anomie.

Anomie The state of uncert ainty and anxiety.

Durkheim held a fairly cynical view of human nature, believing that people were inherently selfish and, left to their own devices, would seek constant gratification regardless of the costs to others. So why, then, he asks, does society seem to work as well as it does (in spite of being made up of self-serving, self-involved individual members)? What is the glue that creates social bonding or solidarity? Ironically enough, even though Durkheim himself was not religious, his answer to those questions is rooted in religion, and more particularly with the *sacred*.

Sacred Something/someone that is held in extremely high regard.

Durkheim believed that relationships were special, perhaps even magical. Think about the things that matter most to you in life for a moment. What are they? Likely they fall into one of two categories. The first might be what you consider to be your core values and beliefs regarding what is most important in your life (loyalty, compassion, or generosity, for instance). Was there someone in your life who instilled those values? If so, I will bet that you hold those people in very high regard. Maybe it was someone who was a mentor, a role model, a loved one, or some combination of those things.

©Umkehrer/Shutterstock.com

Or perhaps what is most important to you is some*one*. . . a relative, a best friend, or a romantic partner, very likely. Durkheim would not be surprised with either answer because both have to do with social relationships. For him, our relationships are precious, even *sacred*. Were you to reflect on what were the most painful experiences in your life, you would probably think back to a time when a relationship ended. The ending of a relationship can be devastating. Break-ups, either with friends or lovers, have the potential to leave us feeling lonely, hopeless at times, and insecure. Of course, it is needless to say that when someone we love dies, we can feel more heart-broken and terrifyingly alone than we ever have in life.

©Rawpixel/Shutterstock.com

So our relationships with one another are incredibly special and Durkheim expressed a kind of awe when he thought about the ways in which our relationships interconnected with the relationships of others and even stretched out across the globe. Consider the billions of relationships, all around the world, and consider how for all of those billions of people they consider their relationships to be as magical and special as the ones that contribute to making you the person you are.

So, let us return to the thought exercise and consider our relationships to other people. If you're anything like us, you have a variety of relationships in a variety of different areas of your life. We have co-workers, people we know from our religious communities, neighbors, friends who live far away, our immediate family members, distant relatives, the clerks, cashiers, and servers at the places we frequently shop and dine, and others too.

Each of those different relationships implies a different kind of personal identity in our lives. In other words, we are professors but we are also employees, fathers, aunts, customers, patients, clients, sisters, worshippers, friends, colleagues, and so on. Each of those identities demands we play a kind of role with its own set of behavioral expectations or norms. When the role changes so do some of the norms that help guide our actions.

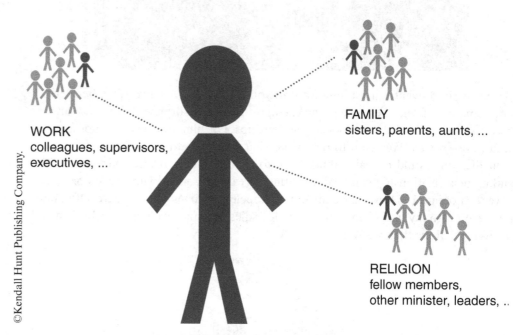

WORK
colleagues, supervisors, executives, ...

FAMILY
sisters, parents, aunts, ...

RELIGION
fellow members, other minister, leaders, ..

©Kendall Hunt Publishing Company.

As you can see from the diagram, the relationships in our lives fan out in a variety of directions and each tends to take on its own unique shape. These patterns of **networks** of people in their various institutional roles are social structures. Durkheim believed that society could be likened to a biological organism that comprised interlocking, interconnected, and interdependent social structures. Or, in the case of a living creature, the structures are comparable to organs.

Three things should be noted about these structures. First, each structure has its own function. Just as the circulatory system in a body conveys oxygen to all the body's parts or the salivary glands create enzymes that help process food, the same can be

Networks Pattern of people in various institutional or personal roles.

said regarding the way society's institutions serve special purposes that contribute to keeping society in proper running order. Police officers ensure people follow the law. Medical professionals develop ways to aid us when we are ill. Universities provide sites for education, and so on and so forth.

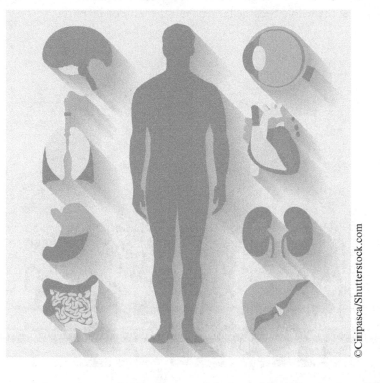

©Ciripasca/Shutterstock.com

The second important point is that any given social structure can affect other structures. Again, one can use the metaphor of a biological organism. If you were to accidentally cut your finger while chopping vegetables and you did not properly attend to the cut, it might very possibly get infected. When that takes place, the change in one organ (your skin is wounded), other organs produce mechanisms like antibodies to eliminate the pathogens. Similarly, in society, when one area of society changes, it affects other areas of society.

For example, Josh lives in northern Colorado that has recently experienced a huge boom due primarily to the oil and gas industry. Almost overnight housing became nearly unaffordable as rents tripled and housing values soared. This was good news for homeowners, but bad news for poor and working class people living paycheck to paycheck as their incomes did not keep pace with the rising cost of living. This changing economy had a profound effect on his city in all sectors from education to politics.

Related to this second point having to do with social structure is the third important point. Durkheim wants us to appreciate that individual social structures cannot be understood in isolation but rather only in terms of how each works within the larger social organism. In other words, it doesn't make sense to try and understand the institution of higher education without understanding what is taking place in the economy at any given time, to use our previous example.

So for Durkheim, our connections with other people create institutions such as education, government, and religion. And those institutions function together with other institutions and from those institutions new social forces are created that impact us personally in ways that are invisible and can be somewhat mysterious. From this, Durkheim asserted that when groups of people came together something extraordinary took place: the whole became larger than the sum of its parts.

©Rawpixel.com/Shutterstock.com

SOCIETY DIVINIZED

Durkheim's book *The Elementary Forms of Religious Life* published in 1912 is one of the most important books in sociology. For me, personally, it is the book I have read the most number of times in my life. In fact, my first encounter with it was what inspired me to become a sociologist in the first place. The book is fairly long and to be perfectly honest, there are a lot of sections that are pretty dry. And then there are some sections that are jam-packed with so much information one could spend a semester merely trying to make sense of all of the heady ideas contained in one page. It might seem contradictory because I just stated that it is one of my favorite books but, in my opinion, it is an incredibly difficult book to make your way through. Yet, the ideas that Durkheim conveys in it are nothing short of radical, profound, and world shifting.

One of the most important concepts Durkheim develops in the book is that of "society divinized" which makes sense only in the context of his overall argument.

What Durkheim does is start from the beginning. And I mean the *very beginning*. That is, he asks us to think about the earliest human groups. Though Durkheim examines early tribal people in Australia, his ethnography of these groups is merely an example. You could use your own example and when I first read the book the images that kept coming to my mind were those of cave people who were just learning to communicate with one another. Cave people had to learn how to work with one another to provide for their basic needs like food and shelter and in doing that they needed to bond together in order to figure out how best to meet those needs. In doing so, they really represent the first stages of society.

©iurii/Shutterstock.com

Remember, how I asked you to take a moment and reflect on what was most important in your life? Again, you probably thought of your loved ones, family, friends, or significant others. To you they are sacred. Well, consider what it must have been like to live life as an early human. The people around you who made it possible to simply survive were also sacred. They made it possible for you to live in a very real, biological sense. Thus, your very existence depended on those people. Durkheim argues that this was where we, as human beings, came up with the notion that there are certain things in life that are sacred.

Now continue to think about this early human existence. . . Each person was part of an extremely close-knit community. In order to ensure that everyone in the group survived, every single person had to play a role. Some people were in charge of hunting, others for providing for shelter, others for maintaining fire for warmth and for cooking, and so on. Thus, each person had a role to fulfill. But what guaranteed that each person would fulfill that role? Durkheim notes that individuals felt compelled by the group to fulfill that role. No one wanted to be guilty of being the lazy individual who sat on his butt and did nothing—and maybe there were even rules that dictated that if you did sit on your butt and do nothing the group would expel you and you would be left to your own devices in order to survive (or at least try and survive since you probably wouldn't last very long on your own out in the wild). So to prevent this, people internalized certain rules and expectations of the group. That ensured that everyone did their part.

These rules, rituals, and regulations that privileged the group and represented the values that were most necessary for life (e.g., community, sacrifice, and selflessness) became "sacred." That is, they were celebrated as essential rules, rituals, and regulations because they were necessary for social stability. Everything else, Durkheim notes, is considered profane. Durkheim uses the term "profane" not to indicate an activity or idea that is damaging or illicit. Rather, he means anything that is simply normal, mundane, and everyday.

©Esteban De Armas/Shutterstock.com

©Nicolas Primola/Shutterstock.com

Durkheim says that the consequence of these sacred rules or norms was the internal feeling that one should act in certain ways. For example, you might be running late for class or for work and you might find yourself driving faster than you ordinarily might. As you are speeding along down the road, you are aware in your gut that you really should not be speeding. Imagine seeing a police car up ahead of you so what do you do? Most likely you will slow down. So not only have you internalized the norm of not speeding but you actually change your behavior.

Durkheim argues that norms actually have a real, tangible force because we act in certain ways, sometimes even when we would prefer not to do so. Now where did the norm come from? You didn't invent it. Rather it came from society. So here is a norm that came from outside of us (society) and now lives inside of us individually (in our consciousness and in our conscience) and has a real force on us since it affects how we behave.

To put this example in technical terms, the norm about speeding is transcendent. It is something abstract and impersonal (since it applies to everyone and not just you or me individually) and it exists above and beyond our own individual existence. At the same time, it is immanent, since we have internalized it and thus the norm, in a sense, lives inside of us. Durkheim concludes that it is the presence of norms, rules, laws, and expectations that first gave human beings the idea of transcendence and immanence and that there are abstract, unseen forces that move about in the concrete world that have a real, felt effect on us.

But where did these norms, rules, codes, and expectations come from? They came from various sources like the government of the United States. Undoubtedly, your campus too has rules and norms. It very likely, for instance, has an honor code that says you should not cheat or plagiarize. The point here is that various institutions in society come up with these norms and rules and they operate like abstract forces that we as individuals internalize and act on. Someone has to tell us that we should not use the ideas and words of other people in our class papers without citing them. Then they have to convince us that that is an important rule. Then we have to accept that as the rule and finally we have to put it into action by properly citing our references and writing our bibliography when we write our papers. So there are all of these steps that move a rule or an idea from the world outside our inner selves to the world that exists inside our mind.

©Diego Cervo/Shutterstock.com

This leads us to Durkheim's next point and that is institutions, like society more broadly, exists prior to the individual. Your university and your country were already in place before you were born. Furthermore, the institutions will continue to exist even after you leave and, most likely, even after you have died. So, for the individual anyway, the institutions have a kind of permanence. You might even say that with respect to our own temporary existence, the institutions (and society more broadly) are eternal. So, you may have guessed what Durkheim concludes from this: we get the notion that there is something abstract, that has a force, that exists outside of us but also within us that is eternal from the very fact that there are social institutions in the first place.

It is important to acknowledge what I mean when I say that societies and institutions are abstract. When I think about my country, the United States, it is impossible for me to humanize it or put a face to it. Though I may disagree with some of my government policies there is no one person who represents the government (though some might wish otherwise and say everything that happens that is wrong with the country is the result of the President—we know that is simply a naïve and simplistic view of how the government works). The United States is much broader than any one person. It is an abstract, faceless entity just like society is an abstract faceless entity. Yet it has a force that again is both transcendent and immanent.

In short, society, Durkheim says, is where we humans came up with the notion that there is a God and religion is the institution that connects humans to that God. It wasn't actually God that gave us the sense of something abstract, transcendent, immanent, impersonal, and all-powerful. It was society.

Characteristics	God	Society
immanent and transcendent	✓	✓
eternal	✓	✓
provides people meaning	✓	✓
people are dependent upon	✓	✓
abstract	✓	✓
provides rules and norms	✓	✓
can be a source of collective effervescence	✓	✓
has sacred totems	✓	✓

©Kendall Hunt Publishing Company

Early humans who were trying to make sense of the powerful and sacred nature of other people in the first stages of society were in fact the first religion. Society, for them, was their God. So for Durkheim, when we are today worshiping God, what we are really doing is worshipping society. God is merely an invention of people who needed to make sense of the ways society had such a powerful force that they felt it and acted according to the norms and rules and expectations of an abstract, faceless, impersonal "thing" like society. So in order to try and make such an abstract "thing" comprehensible, humans created an entity they felt could fulfill that role—a divinity. And religion was the social institution that was established to incorporate the divinity into everyday life.

That is society divinized. God is actually just society. We have taken society and created a kind of proxy for society. God is a human invention designed to stand in for society: an all-powerful, transcendent, immanent, abstract, faceless thing that is eternal, and one that forces us to behave and think in specific ways.

That is, I think you will agree, a pretty radical argument coming from the person who is considered the "father" of the sociology of religion. If you are a religious person, you might even think that it is a little blasphemous. It is nevertheless, an important contribution to the sociology of religion and it gives us a unique perspective on how to view religion as a social institution.

It should be noted that Durkheim's claims here are not intended to reflect on the veracity of any truth claims made by a particular religion. That is, he is not suggesting this line of logic as proof for or against the existence of God. Rather, as the father of what would come to be known as functionalism, he was much more interested in how beliefs are shaped and animated in the world. His perspective about the relationship between society and religion holds regardless of personal belief about the existence or nature of the divine.

One of the outcomes of Durkheim's assertion that God is simply society divinized is that it allowed sociologists to think outside the box. Religion, according to these sociologists should be thought about more broadly. Religion is more than just prayers, songs, clergy members, and temples, churches and mosques. Or, rather, prayers, songs, clergy members, etc. are more than just religion.

In 1967, Thomas Luckman wrote *The Invisible Religion* in which he argued that we needed to widen our definition of what religion is. For him, religion provides one with a sense of morality, a personal identity, and provided us with purpose and meaning. Thus, religion should not be confined to what we ordinarily consider institutionalized conventional religions. This idea took hold and was later termed "implicit religion." An implicit religion could refer to the ways people go to the "church of football" to "worship" their team. Or it could refer to the ways hip hop artists or rock stars are idolized. Or it could refer to the ways Americans experience patriotism, engage in collective rituals like the National Anthem, and consider the flag to be a sacred object. And it is precisely this—the religion of America to which we now turn.

CIVIL RELIGION

The term "**civil religion**" comes from the French philosopher, Jean-Jacques Rousseau, in the 18th century. Rousseau felt that what holds a society together is a unified morality or sense of right and wrong. He thought that individual religions might prove too divisive, so the nation state required something that transcended any one religion in order to get citizens committed to their country.

This might sound so much like a conspiracy theory, but Rousseau and others who champion this idea do not suggest that this was an intentional, strategic, and

> **"Civil religion"** Public religious dimension expressed in a set of beliefs, symbols, and rituals.

manipulative decision by a few elite politicians, but rather as an institution, the nation-state moves in ways to protect its own existence. In this way, a system emerges which privileges stability and devotion.

Emile Durkheim too asserted something similar when he observed that society requires a collective glue that binds people together. The glue, for Durkheim, was religion, though according to him the religion did not require a divinity so much as it required a collective belief system that espoused a commonly understood morality as well as rites and rituals in which everyone could participate. Thus, religion in this sense, could apply to the way Americans are bound together through shared beliefs about what it is to be American and through common ritualistic behaviors in which we participate.

Robert Bellah (1970) is credited with developing the idea with respect to contemporary civil religion. Bellah noted that in the United States, religious beliefs are commonplace. And while there is certainly a wide diversity among individuals' differing religions and religious beliefs, there are some religious ideas and religious language that everyone seems to share or at least with which they are familiar. So while atheists might not believe in God, atheists are sufficiently aware of popular ideas having to do with religion (such as "love thy neighbor") or religious stories or ideas (such as the Ten Commandments). In fact these stories and ideas are so widespread and shared by so many people that they "have played a crucial role in the development of American institutions and still provide a religious dimension for the whole fabric of American life, including the political sphere. This public religious dimension is expressed in a set of beliefs, symbols, and rituals. . . [are] the American civil religion" (Bellah 1970: 171). Thus, civil religion is far more encompassing than any one religious tradition or religious denomination.

Bellah noted something that for him was very illustrative of a civil religion. During the inauguration of John F. Kennedy as President of United States, Kennedy, himself a Catholic, mentioned God three times. Kennedy did not address anything that was specific to the Catholic religion but rather invoked God as broad reference to the importance religion plays in our country. Civil religion does not replace the conventional religion that individuals practice as part of their faith and worship. Instead it works in tandem with those religions.

And it goes further back than Kennedy. Thomas Jefferson talked about how the founding of the United States was like the Israelites coming out of Egypt. But many political leaders have made similar allusions to America being like the Promised Land. Today some politicians quite explicitly say that ours is God's chosen nation. So part of our civil religion refers to the way the history of the country is perceived to be part of a greater, even divinely ordained, plan.

Just like conventional religions, our civil religion has similar components. . . Civil religion has sacred objects. Just think about all the rules concerning the American flag: it should not touch the ground; if it is displayed at night, it should be illuminated; and when it becomes too old and worn out there are specific practices you should do in order to properly dispose of it. Just like Judaism has the Torah and Christians have the Bible, Americans also have sacred texts that are part of our civil religion: The Constitution and the Declaration of Independence.

Similar to the ways Muslims celebrate Ramadan and Christians celebrate Easter, Americans have sacred times such as holidays like the one celebrating Thanksgiving or Independence Day on July 4. Some of these holidays correspond to the "saints" in our civil religion—people like King, John F. Kennedy, Martin Luther King, Jr., or Abraham Lincoln.

Much like Christians, Jews, and Muslims have designated sacred places in the Holy Land, Americans have sacred sites such as the Vietnam Memorial, the Lincoln Memorial, and Arlington National Cemetery.

And think about belief systems and values that we share as Americans. We have sacred common beliefs like the belief in the American Dream of going from "rags to riches," or the American "way of life." These ideas are common to Americans and have the power to unite a diverse nation.

©Joseph Sohm/Shutterstock.com

Finally, we have sacred rituals that require participation. For instance, if you have ever attended a professional sporting event then you have seen this in action. Before the game begins, the national anthem is played. Everyone is expected to stand up (inasmuch as they are able), remove their hats if they are wearing them, and place their hands over their hearts as the anthem is played.

In the above instances, the rituals, sacred objects, belief systems, and values are more metaphorically "religious" and thus those aspects of civil religion would fall under the category of an implicit religion. However, some elements of civil religion though are more literal. Consider the following examples. . . For a number of years, witnesses who were called to give testimony in court had to swear on the bible that they would "tell the truth, the whole truth, and nothing but the truth." Supreme Court sessions include the invocation: "God save the United States and this Honorable Court." If you have cash or coins in your wallet you can read for yourself: "In God we trust." And many schools still require students to stand and recite the Pledge of Allegiance, which of course contains the line "One nation, under God." Following the terror attacks on September 11, 2001, members of Congress gathered together as a body to sing "God Bless America" on the steps of the Capitol Building. And Presidents and other political leaders have often ended important statements by uttering the wish "God bless you and God bless America" or simply "God bless the United States."

©Ahturner/Shutterstock.com

While civil religion is not tied to any one single religion, here in the United States it undoubtedly has a Judeo-Christian flavor. This fact is evident when taking into consideration the way critics of President Barack Obama would derisively refer to him as Muslim and call into question his claims that he is a Christian. What this made clear is that many people can only envision a Christian serving as the leader of our American civil religion.

Also, following the attacks on 9/11, many in the media in addition to some politicians, felt compelled to claim that America was a "Christian nation" and the founding fathers had intended it that way. Though a few of the early leaders and founders were indeed Christian, many were deist (who believed in a divinity but not in a personal God). Yet, in our current version of American civil religion, the dominant theme is one that is Judeo-Christian. That fact then is so powerful that it re-frames the historical narrative of the country.

There are a number of functions of a civil religion. Civil religion provides a unified bond between a very diverse and multicultural nation. Bellah also pointed out that civil religion serves as a kind of moral compass or moral ideal to which our country's leaders should aspire. And of course, civil religion protects against citizens from becoming too self-interested because it reminds us that we are part of something larger than ourselves. It fosters patriotism and loyalty. It is a source of solidarity, a common sense of identity, and the feeling of affinity with others around us. Bellah, like Durkheim, has a pessimistic view of human nature, seeing individuals being basically selfish and inclined to seek what is best for the individual rather than the collective group. But what would happen if both conventional religions and our civil religion lose some of their importance or their strength? That is the topic of our next section.

PRIVATIZATION OF RELIGION

Privatization or religion refers to the process whereby religion becomes more individualized and less pertinent to public institutions. It takes place when individuals make a hard and fast distinction about their own ideas of what is sacred as opposed to more commonly expressed and shared ideas about what is considered sacred. Thus, when people say they are spiritual, not religious they are echoing sentiments of privatization. Religion, in this instance, becomes something intimate and personal and instead of viewing one's religion as something that others should subscribe to, it is only meant for oneself. While preferences may be shared, ultimately, according to the theory of the privatization of religion, one's beliefs are strictly one's own, less subject to institutionalized authorities.

©Lightspring/Shutterstock.com

The problem with privatization is that we all seek to legitimize our beliefs. That is we want to justify why we believe what we do. Legitimation has traditionally come from external sources—people and institutions outside of oneself—rather than from inside oneself. Berger said that one important source of legitimation comes from plausibility structures. These are structural patterns or social arrangements in which people actively practice and talk about their beliefs. Seeing others do these things convinces us that what we ourselves are believing and doing is worthwhile.

Take for example your classroom. Likely your professor says a lot more in her or his lectures than you actually need to know to take a test. It would be virtually impossible to write down everything she or he says and commit all of that information to memory. So how do you know what's important? Sometimes the professor will explicitly say something like, "This is very important," or "This will be on the test." But other times we look around to see what other people are responding to and how much they are writing down. Even the simple fact that others come to class and take notes and ask questions is a signal that something meaningful is going on. Otherwise, the reality of the classroom might disintegrate and we might not take it seriously. It could very well be that some random person has decided to show up in the same room you are sitting in and decided to talk about random pieces of information. The classroom and the people who are in it contribute to creating a plausibility structure. Thus, we recognize it as something meaningful.

Peter Berger argues, "Since the socially significant 'relevance' of religion is primarily in the private sphere, consumer preference reflects the 'needs' of this sphere. This means that religion can more easily be marketed if it can be shown to be 'relevant' to private life than if it is advertised as entailing specific applications to the larger public institutions. . . As a result the religious institutions have accommodated themselves to the moral and therapeutic 'needs' of the individual in his private life" (1967: 147). What Berger is saying is that today, individuals see religion less as something that ought to be related to work or politics or the like. His view is distinctly postmodern since it is implied that religion is something intimate and personal more that social. Thus, if it is highly individualized, then it is congruent with other areas of life that are related to our tastes and preferences.

Think about the rather banal choice of a toothpaste or deodorant. There are a lot of choices on the grocery store shelves and which product we pick is entirely up to one's own preferences. Berger is basically saying that we think about religion the same way we think about toothpaste: since it is for me, why should I concern myself with attributes of it that are not related to my own personal wishes and desires. Thus, we ask—does it do the job that I want it to do?

When we begin thinking about religion on those terms we are essentially redefining religion. In the traditional way of thinking about religion, one of its primary functions is to provide a moral guide (right and wrong; good and bad) to a large group of people. In a privatized religion, one of its primary functions is to serve as a psychological guide that aids the individuals along her or his life journey. Therefore, some say that privatized religion emphasizes the *therapeutic* rather than the moral.

THERAPEUTIC RELIGIONS

While some sociologists predicted that religion in the modern world would become increasingly privatized over time and increasingly therapeutic, there has actually been a long history of such religions. To just name a few examples: Swedenberg in the 1700s gave us "spiritualism" and in that same era Mesmer developed "mesmerism"; Mary Baker Eddy in the 1800s who gave us Christian Science (which later evolved into an additional denomination—unity); and there was the occultism offered by Blavatsky in the 1800s.

©marekuliasz/Shutterstock.com

Or perhaps you have seen Stuart Smalley on Saturday Night Live look in his mirror and give his daily affirmations: ". . .Because I'm good enough, I'm smart enough, and doggone it, people like me." The ritual of giving oneself personal affirmations originated with the one of the founders of New Thought. New Thought began in the early 20th century and its followers believed that God was everywhere including one's self. They also believed in positive thinking and that the mind could heal the body. New Thought has been incredibly influential to **therapeutic religions**, not least of which was the New Age movement that developed in the 1970s and 1980s.

Though quite a few sociologists have studied the New Age movement through the years, few individuals who align themselves with such belief systems would call themselves "New Agers" today. That term has come to take on a more pejorative or negative connotation. What has replaced it both in name and in albeit slightly modified practice is the phrase "Mind-Body-Spirit," or "MBS" in short.

While MBS is a diverse movement, there are some central characteristics. One primary property of MBS is its emphasis on self-actualization and the emphasis on the individual's own practice that enable her or him to realize her full potential. Some say MBS is comparable to "self-help" and other forms of pop psychology and to a degree there are some of those themes present—though MBS also integrates a belief in the spiritual or soulful nature of the self. It demands that individuals be highly introspective and intuitive and some go so far as to include a kind of mystical element. MBS, like the New Thought that preceded it, also seeks to dissolve the conventional boundaries between the body and the mind. The mind, it is believed, can facilitate healing and physical wellbeing.

> **Therapeutic religions** includes self-motivation and positive reinforcement in practice; built around the idea that each of us is "good enough" and that we matter.

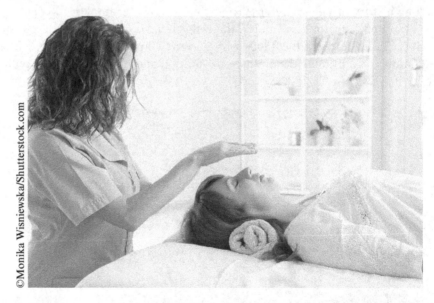

©Monika Wisniewska/Shutterstock.com

Another frequent theme within MBS has to do with its relationship to previous, more established religions, particularly those that originated in Southeast Asia. For example, some people in MBS believe in the power of chakras, which are nodes within one's body, thought to channel the body's life force. The belief in chakras (and the practice of visualizing energy and aligning one's inner balance) comes from early Hinduist philosophies. Others in MBS profess the power of Ayurvedic medicine, which integrates non-Western forms of medical intervention including acupressure, herbal treatments, and other non-conventional (at least to most Westerners) treatments to restore natural internal equilibrium.

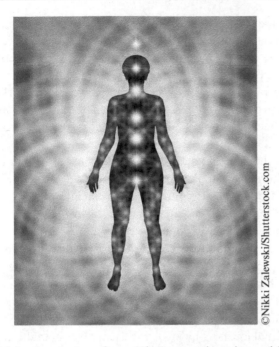

©Nikki Zalewski/Shutterstock.com

Yoga too, which also derives from Hindu practices, is a widely accepted form of exercise that is intended to result in emotional, cognitive, and physical well-being. Practitioners of Reiki believe that a healer can draw on a universal life force and channel it through their hands and can activate the patient's own abilities for self-healing. Some Reiki practitioners work much like massage therapists though touch is light if there is touch at all.

The MBS movement has many critics. Most focus on what appears to be the link between MBS and consumerism. As one such critic writes: "In its original context, feng shui is a serious matter of relating to the spirits of the dead. In Britain, it is a decorating style. Yoga is no longer a spiritual discipline; it is an exercise program. Meditation is not about attaining enlightenment; it is about relaxing. And Ayurvedic medicine is just another cosmetics line from the Body Shop chain" (p. 44).

©Kite_rin/Shutterstock.com

On the other hand, my own research suggests that participants in MBS feel that they are genuinely seeking to connect with something sacred. If reading a book or buying a sacred totem or a package of healing therapies allows them to do that, that does not diminish the power and importance of these products in their lives. After all, we live in a consumer society and even conventional religions market, produce, and sell goods that help people along their spiritual paths. Even traditional religions have products that everyone can go out and purchase (e.g., greeting cards, crosses, menorahs, and jewelry).

Others bemoan the fact that many in the MBS do not belong to a formal community such as a church or temple. Yet this too overlooks the significance of social media to create and sustain social ties around common interests. So while, most people involved in MBS do not belong to any formalized institution, they often belong to loose-knit networks of people who connect via social media.

Furthermore, many in the MBS movement also retain membership in more conventional religions. I have interviewed many individuals who adhere to Native American beliefs such as shamanism or who regularly attend chanting and drum circles or read tarot cards. . . and those same people also continue to attend and invest their time and resources in Christian churches and Jewish synagogues. They are merely compounding their spiritual journeys by involving themselves in multiple traditions.

©everything possible/Shutterstock.com

Technology has always played an important role in religion. The invention of the printing press, for example, made the Bible more widely available and increased individuals' abilities to interpret scriptures and apply them rather than relying on professional clergy to interpret the stories. So too have the technologies of online social media and the rise of a consumer society reshaped the ways individuals make sense of their lives, the world around them, and their responses to what they consider sacred.

Still many sociologists of religion feel that one of the consequences of intense privatization of religion is making too many people too focused on their own individual selves and less concerned about others (a mild version of narcissism). An often cited example comes from the work of Robert Bellah and his co-authors in *Habits of the Heart* (Bellah, et al., 2007). In one anecdote researchers asked a young woman named Sheila to describe her religion since she did not identify with a conventional religion. The woman replied that her religion was "Sheilaism." Sheilaism has become a shorthand way for sociologists to talk about religion that has become so individualized as to be entirely about the person who is practicing it.

But Sheilaism represents more than that. Because when sociologists critique or express concern about Sheilaism they are expressing their worries that Americans are becoming too self-centered. It is generally the same sort of hand-wringing and exaggerated concern that younger generations have somehow lost their way and are not as socially responsible as earlier generations. They worry that these younger people are only worried about themselves and therefore less inclined to act in ways that are not selfish or motivated by their own individual wants and wishes.

What these sociologists miss is the fact that many people who do engage in highly privatized religions or who claim to be spiritual but not religious are also very socially conscious and moral. So while some critics say that MBS and other therapeutic religions are too self-centered, other social scientists provide a different view. This means that the emphasis is less on behaving in such and such a way or conforming to a convention, institutionalized belief system. Rather the emphasis for these individuals is on how religion can ease one's pain and suffering. Thus, it is easy for some people to argue that therapeutic religions because of their perceived psychological benefits and individualistic spiritual concerns are selfish. What this overlooks is the way in which individuals who do in fact adhere to the notion of religion as therapy, also see themselves interwoven with others around them. Hedges and Beckford (2000), for instance, conducted research that found participants were actually trying to accomplish a loss of ego and self-centeredness in order to realize how interconnected they were with others and the world around them.

WHAT ARE WE CELEBRATING NOW?

If religion is simply society worshipping itself, promoting the values, activities, and norms that hold society together and promote stability, then it begs the question, What do our modern religions tell us about contemporary society? When Durkheim began his exploration of religion, he made a distinction between pre-modern societies characterized by mechanical solidarity and modern societies characterized by organic solidarity. The basic difference here is between a society where commonality is established through a shared experience and one where commonality is established through interdependence. These different experiences result in different value systems and different understandings of what is sacred for the functioning of the group.

At the beginning of this chapter, we suggested that a very simple line of questioning could keep sociologists of religion busy for a lifetime, and indeed it has. Even now, there are still myriad questions unanswered that stem from the very basic inquiry about the nature of religious institutions. As you look around the world today, what do you see people worshipping? What norms and values are being reinforced through worship? Do you think these are functional or dysfunctional for a stable, modern society?

DISCUSSION QUESTIONS

1. Think about social structures. How are relationships with people also considered social structures?

2. Explain anomie. Who coined this term? What is their significance to the field of sociology as well as the study of religion?

3. In the chapter, we discussed the idea of the sacred. Durkheim thought that relationships are something in people's lives so important that they held them in a sacred regard. Explain his thinking process about why. Think of the relationships you have in your life. Do you, or could you now, consider any of them sacred?

4. Using a concrete example from your own life, explain how the phenomenon of internalized norms work to produce certain human behaviors in people's actual lives; in other words, explain why people do what they do even in instances where they may not want to—what stops them from doing something else?

5. What does it mean to say society divinized?

6. Explain the sociology of religion's perspective of religion as a social construct.

7. Explain "civil religion". Who coined this term and who is credited with developing its ideas? What are three of its functions? Lastly, give a few examples from the chapter about what makes up American civil religion specifically.

8. What is the privatization of religion? Why does this worry some sociologists? What might they (the critics) be missing?

CHAPTER 8

FROM CHAPELS TO ARENAS

Why do some churches look like shopping malls?

KEY TERMS

- Calculability
- Efficiency
- Irrational
- McDonaldization
- Megachurch
- Predictability
- Seekers
- Technology

OBJECTIVES:

- Understand McDonaldization and what has happened to the institution of religion because of it.
- Understand the role that megachurches play for decentralizing religion as an institution.
- Grasp the connection between consumerism and megachurches.

INTRODUCTION

Quick question, what is the difference between a church and a fast food restaurant? At first, this might seem like an easy question to answer. For starters, there is, typically, a divine component to church that does not exist at Taco Bell. Regardless of how much you revere the CrunchWrap Supreme, most people do not place it in the category of "divinity." But other than that, could you argue that they are the same? That both organizations are simply involved in delivering a predictable product to a lot of people in the most efficient way possible? Or is there something inherently different about the religious experience that makes this analogy fall apart?

On the one hand, Josh thinks of the church his grandmother attends in a small town in Minnesota. She knows everyone there. In fact, she has had dinner at one time or another with virtually every person in the congregation, including the pastor. This small, intimate, very personal church feels far different than a fast food experience. On the other hand, I have personally conducted a lot of field-work in megachurches and, despite the fact that they are from the same Christian tradition as Josh's grandmother's church, I left them feeling the same way I do when I go through a drive through. Sure, I got what I came for, but my presence did not seem to matter to the shape of the organization in any way.

THE THEORY OF MCDONALDIZATION

McDonaldization
The permeation of rationalization into all social institutions.

You will recall that we discussed Max Weber and his concept of rationalization from Chapter 3. George Ritzer updated Weber's theory of rationalization with his own concept of **McDonaldization** (2015). In short, he argues that rationalization has so entrenched its grip on society that we can see its effects in almost all of today's social institutions. McDonaldization refers to the way in which the fast food industry has become a model, or a kind of metaphor for the ways other institutions operate. That is, when you look closely at the processes and the organization and the experiences of a typical fast food restaurant, according to Ritzer, you can begin to see parallels in other places.

Take for instance your experiences on campus. If you have been attending your college or university for at least a year or two, then I would imagine that you have had one of "those" professors . . . and not the good kind. When I was an undergraduate I know had a few of them. They are the ones who put together a bunch of power point slides and basically read their lectures from typewritten notes or from the computer screen that is projecting the power point presentation. It feels dry and stilted; as if they are simply going through the motions. There is nothing unique, personal, or person-able about the professor because she or he could, quite frankly, be a robot.

According to Ritzer's theory of McDonaldization, when we encounter professors who simply show up, read a bunch of material that is presented on a classroom screen, what we are encountering is one of the effects of McDonaldization—specifically in this instance it is the McDonaldization of the higher education. But remember—McDonaldization, according to Ritzer anyway, is everywhere. It is not just in restau-rants and classrooms, but in our stores and our government and politics and, yes, our religion.

©Matej Kastelic/Shutterstock.com

Though Ritzer does not himself directly apply his theory to religion we can easily do so. But in order to see how McDonaldization has crept into the institution of religion, it is valuable to understand the five characteristics of McDonaldization in order to better comprehend how it works and how this impacts people who take part in religion. However, we should also note that just like not all restaurants have been McDonaldized—after all, not all restaurants are like fast food chains—not all religions and religious communities have become McDonaldized. Nonetheless, it is an important concept that is relevant to a portion of religions and religious communities. Furthermore, some people are predicting that the McDonaldization of religion is growing, and while a few people welcome this trend, others fear that it could be detrimental to their sacred communities.

So what are the five characteristics of McDonaldization? The first one is **efficiency**.

> **Efficiency** The successfulness of a way for accomplishing a task; typically understood as how quickly and well something can be done simultaneously.

©Dmitry Lobanov/Shutterstock.com

I don't know about you but at least once every couple of weeks or so, after a long day at work, the last thing I want to do is go home, open the kitchen cabinets, figure out what to make for dinner, and then go through all of the prepping, rinsing, baking, and boiling in order to make supper (not to mention all of the cleaning up afterward). I'm hungry and I just want to eat.

When that happens I have this wonderful little burrito shop that is around the corner from my house. I go in. I place my order and two minutes later I've paid for it and happily and somewhat greedily tearing off the foil wrapper to get at my delicious burrito. It is efficient—it is quick, fairly effortless, and straightforward.

Here is the question: Can churches emphasize efficiency and if so, what kinds of churches emphasize efficiency? Sure they can—particularly those that have a large number of members or employees. They need to make it easy for workers to know what their jobs entail so that they don't have to waste a lot of time (which would, of course, mean wasted money) in order to perform their tasks.

And the members and visitors of the church too have expectations and needs but if you have a sizable number of those people then you would probably want to figure out a system that would take care of as many people as you could in as little time as possible. In other words, you would want a system that is efficient, right?

Of course there are also churches that have two or three or even more services in a single day. So there, too, you might want to make it easy for people to know which service they would like to attend, how to get to that particular service, and then make sure everyone could get there in time and then leave before the next service begins. So would you expect to have services that last two hours or more each week (because certainly there are some churches and worship communities who regularly hold weekly services lasting two hours or more)? No, you would probably want to keep your services relatively short: maybe about an hour long. Again, the emphasis is on efficiency.

We are not saying that efficient churches are bad. Some people like to get in, get what they need, and get out. Others might find that such experiences feel rushed or like they lack substance and depth. It just depends on what the individual feels she or he needs or is looking for in a religious community and worship experience. As I suggested above, most of the time I cook my food, but sometimes, I hit up the burrito shop.

The second characteristic of McDonaldization is **calculability**.

Calculability is related to the first characteristic of efficiency. By calculability, Ritzer means two different things. The first meaning of calculability, he says, has to do with the way that people want to believe they are getting a lot for their money. That is,

Calculability How much something costs compared to the amount or quality of product received; can be figured mathematically.

they want value. And how often is the word "value" used in fast food slogans? A lot. In fact, a great deal of fast food marketing either tends to focus on new products or on the claim that their products are a good value. We want to feel like our money goes a long way.

Now in this first meaning of calculability, we can expand what we mean when we talk about value in terms of money. Instead, let us replace "money" with the word "costs," and then state that people tend to want to *minimize their costs* and simultaneously *maximize their reward*. Sound familiar? Of course it does since that is precisely what the economistic perspective of the sociology of religion says (see our discussion of this in Chapter 2). In that perspective, sociologists assume that we are rational actors and when it comes to religion we think about costs in broad terms like: effort needed to attend a service; amount of commitment people in the community expect; the financial burden of tithing or giving offerings; the time during the week that one is expected to pray, chant, meditate, or study, and so on. And what are the rewards? People report that the rewards they get from participating in their religion include a sense of belonging, feelings of peace or fulfillment, or the assurance that they will see an afterlife.

As we said earlier, people wish to minimize their costs and maximize their rewards, or, in Ritzer's terms: they want to feel like they are getting a good deal and that they are getting a lot of the good stuff for just a little bit of work or effort.

So how does this apply to religion? Well, one of the ways that religions and churches can appeal to people's desire for value is to offer people a lot of goods and services so that just by showing up and maybe occasionally putting some money in the offering plate, one can get a spectacular experience (or, if not an experience that rises to the level of spectacular, then at least one that is entertaining). So when it comes to creating a sense of value, churches might do things like integrate live music into their worship service. Instead of having a boring sermon about a verse in the Bible, or a sermon that implies people are behaving immorally, they might have a dynamic speaker who is energetic and enthusiastic. And she or he doesn't stand behind a pulpit and "preach." Instead they deliver a message that is intended to make the audience members feel good about themselves.

Then there are some little things, like seating. Wouldn't you prefer to sit in a chair that is comfortable, well cushioned, and even has a cup holder for your coffee? Oh yes, and where did that coffee come from? Maybe it came from the little café just outside the sanctuary that you passed on your way in. These are all things that allow people to feel like they get "bang for their back" so to speak. We put in the effort to get up early on Sunday mornings (which is a kind of "cost") but in return we get an enjoyable worship experience (a "reward").

But do these kinds of rewards apply to all churches? Of course not, but if we were to look at churches that do provide these "extras" then what we would find is that they are mostly very large churches. The reason for this is that only these very large churches have the resources to offer the extras. More members equates to more money coming into the organization. It also means that the church can hire more people to offer specialized services. And it also means that they have more money to pay for things like fancy lighting and rock concert-like amplifiers, mixing boards, and PA systems.

©Atosan/Shutterstock.com

©LuckyImages/Shutterstock.com

So that is the first meaning of calculability—one must perceive that one is getting a good *value*. But as we said, calculability has two meanings according to Ritzer and the second one has to do with the kind of calculations needed to run an organization.

In the fast food industry, everything is portioned out in advance: the burgers all must weigh a certain amount so that they come out the same size and even the soda

©wrangler/Shutterstock.com

dispensers automatically start and stop with the press of a button so that a large or a medium always fits in the same size of cup. This allows large businesses to create a down-to-the-penny budget and thus ensures that the company sees a profit.

Now, churches are non-profit organizations so profit is not necessarily their aim. However, all churches must maintain a budget and do their best to avoid going into debt. Lights must be kept on, the minister should have a salary, and the costs of maintaining a building are all necessities for a church. Thus, there is always some degree of calculability in religious organizations. But think about what happens when large churches grow so large that they have dozens of employees and lots of different facilities and operating costs . . . clearly calculability is more of an issue for churches that are very large. The bigger the church, the more important it has to pay attention to the details of the costs and revenues. Thus, the larger the church, the more we can see elements of calculability at work.

The third characteristic that Ritzer identifies as being a critical component of McDonaldization is **predictability**. That is, customers at fast food restaurants want their food to taste the same no matter when they visit or what particular restaurant in the chain they happen to be. I have been to Taco Bells and Pizza Huts in Europe and I can attest to the fact that even in different countries, the menus are fairly similar to the ones back in the United States. In fact, the food pretty much even tastes like what I would have gotten back in the States. That is part of the appeal of fast food chains: we know what we are getting. It is comforting sometimes to know that we can visit a place that is not in our own town or neighborhood and still get the same things we like when we are home.

> **Predictability** The likelihood that something is going to happen; also the likelihood of something to repeat, occur again.

©Matthew Ennis/Shutterstock.com

Here too we can apply this to religions. People want to know what they are getting themselves into. So, in any given week, while the songs during the worship service might change, the style of music remains the same. And even though there is a different message offered by the worship leader, the tone and delivery of the message is fairly predictable. Another way of saying this is that religions try and provide their members with some degree of uniformity. It is comforting and reassuring when we know what to expect. Therefore, predictability is a part of most religious organizations.

Technology
Technique, method, or equipment used to accomplish a task efficiently.

Ritzer says that the fourth characteristic of McDonaldization has to do with the increased reliance on **technology** in order to get things done. I am old enough to remember a time when cashiers at fast food chains had to know the prices of all of the different products and manually punch those prices into the cash register. In some places, they even had to figure out, completely on their own, how much change to give the customer once she or he had handed over some money. This is clearly not the case anymore since this is all accomplished with the push of a couple of buttons. Cashiers are no longer required to have to go through hours of training in order to properly do their job. The same could be said with many jobs in a fast food restaurant. Another word for this process is "de-skilling." Furthermore, it is not only the fast food industry that has seen a de-skilling of its workforce. There are many jobs today that have reduced the need for individuals to have to be extensively trained in order to perform their jobs.

Do we see an increasing reliance on technology in religious organizations? Of course we do. But just like some of the previous characteristics of McDonaldization we tend to see the use of technology more often at very large churches that rely on projection screens, specialized lighting, and web-based operations. In some places, members of the congregation are encouraged to use Twitter to send the minister feedback as she or he is delivering their message, and many people are encouraged to connect via other social media even during the service. Yet, here again, the use of such technologies generally requires a level of monetary resources that only very large churches are able to provide.

The fifth and final characteristic of McDonaldization that Ritzer discusses is a little more complicated and one that some people take issue with: McDonaldization is **irrational**. That is, according to Ritzer, all of these things that the McDonaldization of society do in order to make life simpler, more efficient, and more straightforward are ultimately not good for society. Now, this makes sense if you think about some of the drawbacks to eating fast food all of the time (it might not prove beneficial for your heart or your waistline), or if you consider how difficult it can be for fast food workers to earn sufficient wages to make a decent living. So with respect to the fast food industry Ritzer makes a strong point: the more we try to make things easier, the more we see drawbacks beginning to emerge.

> **Irrational** Not logical or reasonable.

What Ritzer was trying to get at though in a more general way is important: that the McDonaldization of society (beyond just the fast food industry) has the potential to make us feel comfortable without really challenging us to develop fuller lives. It encourages us to seek out uniformity and sameness rather than choosing to take risks and be adventurous with our choices. It also has the potential of separating us from real human contact because technology can now do that work for us. And since the systems and organizations make everything function as well as they do, we no longer have to think for ourselves; it robs us of our individuality and creativity.

©iluistrator/Shutterstock.com

Does this apply to religion or specific religious organizations like churches? It definitely has the potential to do so. But it is not the necessary outcome when you only look at the first four characteristics of McDonaldization: efficiency, calculability, predictability, and the use of technology. Perhaps those four characteristics contribute to irrationality or perhaps they don't.

There are certainly some social scientists who make a convincing case when arguing that religions that take on the traits of McDonaldization can have detrimental consequences. They say that we can easily become too passive and leading religious leaders to merely pander to our desires to feel good about ourselves. Some argue that religion that has become McDonaldized loses what makes it uniquely religious. They claim that in such cases a religion loses its ability to aid our efforts to transform our thoughts and actions. After all one of the goals of religion is to help us become kinder and more compassionate and show us how we might try and make the world a better place. Other social scientists argue the opposite—that because religion is a socially constructed institution that it is a product of our culture. As culture changes, so should religion and there is nothing inherently wrong with a religion that has become McDonaldized.

One thing from our discussion on McDonaldization is certain . . . that if we ask ourselves what parts of religion are most McDonaldized, the one consistent answer is that it has to do with very large churches. Thus, in the next section, we will discuss such churches.

MEGACHURCHES

> **Megachurch** A church that hosts at least 2,000 people over the course of a weekend.

Of the many developments in American religion over the last few decades, the **megachurch** phenomenon has been a significant factor in reshaping the religious landscape. The surging popularity of megachurches is so noteworthy that one sociologist even refers to this movement as the "Third Great Awakening" (Miller, 1997). The megachurch is defined simply as a church which hosts at least 2,000 people over the course of a weekend. These enormous churches continue to expand their membership rolls, while mid-size churches have lost out on membership (Thumma and Bird, 2008). There were previously only about 10 to 20 churches that would fit the definition of a megachurch at any one time in the United States during most of the 20th century (Thumma, 2012). That changed dramatically in the past 30 to 40 years. Now, more than half of all church attendees attend one of the 10% of the largest churches. Thumma says that there are now over 1,350 megachurches in the United States. The largest one is in Houston and occupies the former basketball arena of the NBA team, the Rockets.

The Hartford Institute for Religion Research maintains a searchable database in which you can explore the megachurches in your own area by going to the following website: http://hirr.hartsem.edu/megachurch/database.html

Megachurches often lack denominational ties. As such these non-denominational megachurches are completely separate from other churches with regard to organizational hierarchies and connections. They are therefore free to create their own services and liturgies, hire their own employees, and make other important decisions about the operation of the church. Not all megachurches are independent and non-denominational. There are megachurches that are Baptist, Presbyterian, Lutheran, and so on. But often when they do belong to a particular denomination, a megachurch may downplay its denominational affiliation. So, for example, instead of calling themselves Woodford Methodist Church, they may simply call themselves Woodford Church. One reason has to do with the appeal this has to a broader audience. If someone sees that a church is Pentecostal then they may feel as though that church is only for self-identifying Pentecostals. On the other hand, a church name like Woodford Bible Church has the potential to appeal to a broader segment of the public (a topic that we discuss more fully below).

In spite of the fact that many of these churches are more theologically in line with conservative and evangelical traditions, many of them purposefully avoid including too much conventional Christian iconography (e.g., crosses, pulpits, or stained glass windows) in their buildings. The reason for this is to appeal to people who, again, are more likely to say they are spiritual and not religious and thus such iconography can leave a sour taste in the mouths of those who associate iconography with religion as an institution.

©zstock/Shutterstock.com

While you will find megachurches throughout North America, there are more of them concentrated in the South and the Midwest. They are a specific product of the contemporary American cultural and geographic landscape. And you will frequently see that they are located in suburbs for a variety of reasons. One reason is that megachurches tend to appeal to the same sorts of people who desire to live in suburbs: "[S] uburbs contain growing concentrations of ideal megachurch clientele—middle-class, educated, consumer oriented, uprooted younger families" (Thumma 2012: 580). These are folks who have taken up residence away from their family of origin, oftentimes for job-related purposes.

A second reason they are located in suburbs is due to the nature of their size. Because they take up such an enormous footprint, they need to be located where there is ample land available. Thus, suburbanization, or the ways in which residential patterns have shifted from urban to suburban and exurban developments, have made possible large tracts of land and buildings that figure neatly into a world of strip malls, the so-called big box retailers (think Lowes or Target) and wide lane thoroughfares.

Most megachurches offer multiple different worship services at different times and often you will find that each service is meant to cater to a different demographic. Some are intended for older people who desire a more traditional service while others are geared toward people in their 20s and 30s. When services are tailored toward a particular group of people based on their age, one of the biggest differences between

©Jesse Kunerth/Shutterstock.com

the services is with the style of music that is featured. Oftentimes this is accomplished by simply changing up the musical genre that is used in a service. Is it more rock 'n roll or is it more electronica and indie music friendly?

Indeed, music plays an important role in most megachurch services and is sometimes used from start to finish (even while the minister is delivering her or his sermon). So while the sermon may be slightly tweaked, depending on the age range of the audience, it is often the style of music that is most readily apparent.

The typical megachurch service is engaging and frequently entertaining. The average budget of a megachurch is $6.5 million (Thumma, 2012: 583). So they generally have access not only to greater sources of money than smaller churches, they also have access to more people in the church who may have skills or expertise that lend themselves to creating a polished, well produced, and creative worship experience.

Megachurches typically do not look like churches on the outside. First of all, because megachurches are more often than not a suburban phenomenon, where people more often drive themselves to places, as opposed to taking buses or trains, an adequately sized parking lot must be available. I have attended several megachurches where the parking lot was so large, I had to park my car and then walk to a nearby shuttle stop so that I could be driven to the church's front doors.

©Leena Robinson/Shutterstock.com

If I asked you to tell me what the prototypical church looks like, I'd bet that you would say something like, "It's a rectangular building with a high, steep roof at the top of which is a steeple." Or you might talk about there being a prominent cross perched somewhere, perhaps on top of the steeple, or a bell tower, or some stained glass.

Megachurches rarely have any of these features. The prototypical megachurch does not resemble the prototypical church. And that fact is quite deliberate. Bill Hybels, the pastor of what was one of the original American megachurches (Willow Creek) is quoted as saying: "I was just at the corporate headquarters for IBM in Atlanta Wednesday, and now I come to a church here and it's basically the same" (in Twitchell, 2004: 92).

Why would someone want their megachurch to not look like most other traditional churches? There are a variety of reasons. First of all, think about who the megachurch is trying to get in their doors. They often want people who don't identify with any single particular religion. They also want people who identify as "spiritual but not religious." Both of these groups of people, it is believed, would be turned off by a building that reminds them of "institutionalized" religion or the kind of religion in which they were raised. So architects and designers want to make their buildings as non-threatening as possible in order to avoid the perception that their church is stodgy, old-fashioned, or simply just "too religious." One way of accomplishing that is to design a church that looks like non-religious places but also design the church so that it is a space that feels familiar and comfortable to most Americans.

Megachurches generally have more than just a church sanctuary, some office and additional rooms for small groups or Sunday school classes. Many have bookstores, donut shops, cafes, fitness centers, baby-sitting services, and even hair salons. Some of these retail and service outlets incorporate branded franchises into their churches (e.g., Krispy Kreme or Starbucks).

Megachurches allow for people to attend, consume a worship service, and then leave, all without talking to anyone. Like a big city, it allows one to be completely anonymous while still reaping the benefits of one's setting. On the other hand, Thumma, Travis, and Bird, who have done extensive research in megachurches, find that the majority of people who attend megachurches felt quite connected to others and

©Wayne0216/Shutterstock.com

compared their churches to a "close-knit family" (2005). One of the reasons people can find intimacy in those settings is due to the fact that many megachurches have numerous small groups.

The small groups can be divided up around any variety of variables: a particular interest; lifestyle; demographic; or activity. For example, newcomers might be in one small group, fitness buffs in another, 20–25-year-olds in one, single people in another, people interested in a certain book in one, people interested in learning more about prayer in another. Thumma (2012) describes one megachurch, for example where small groups and activities included: "rock climbing, 4X4ing, motorbiking, sea kayaking, downtown art shows, and clubs such as surfing, island dancing, skateboarding, and martial arts" (p. 575). So in spite of the enormity of the congregation, members can generally find a group that readily suits their interest. But how do megachurches go about recruiting new members in the first place? Many of them rely on what we call "**seekers**"—a topic to which we now turn.

SEEKERS

Many megachurches are what sociologists refer to as "seeker-friendly" churches that aim to appeal particularly to two groups of people. First, they want to attract those persons who likely grew up with a religious affiliation but became dissatisfied with the institutional nature of their religion. They feel like there are too many arbitrary rules in their former religion, or their church was too "preachy" and moralistic, or that everyone in their church was simply "going through the motions." Having been raised at least somewhat in a religious tradition, this first group of people has some familiarity with religion but is *seeking* a faith community that feels comfortable, provides a worship experience that is engaging, and contains messages that are personally relevant to living in the world today.

The second group of seekers includes people who did not grow up religious but are curious or interested in possibly finding a place for religion in their lives. Perhaps they have transitioned into a new period of life (e.g., marriage or the birth of a child)

"Seekers"
Someone who has grown up in a traditional religious church, is dissatisfied with that, and now searching for another form of religion that relies less on what they see as arbitrary rules, and more on community, comfort, and a message that is more relevant to living in the world today; or someone who has grown up with the absence of any religious tradition and is now in search of one that they might identify with.

or they may have dealt a serious setback and are struggling to make sense of it (e.g., the loss of a job or a divorce). In any case, religion is such a pervasive institution in our society that even for those who were not raised in a religious environment or do not identify as religious are aware of religious options.

Thus, because religion is viewed as something that helps people make sense of their lives and the world around them, helps them cope with challenges and struggles, and provides people with a sense of fulfillment and purpose, people who are not religious may begin *seeking* a religious home at some point in their lives. Thus, seeker-friendly churches also want to reach out to people who have little knowledge or background in a religious tradition but who are seeking answers to deep philosophical questions, a purpose in life, or some comfort for their emotional suffering.

Seeker-friendly churches therefore must be a lot of different things to a lot of different people. One means of accomplishing this is to make the service as broadly appealing as possible and to avoid asserting very narrow sets of values and beliefs. In other words, seeker-friendly churches try and steer clear of asserting dogmatic beliefs and of looking too religious. Seeker-friendly churches tend to be accessible, consumer-centric Christian churches that favor a "me-first," therapeutic gospel meant to comfort and reassure rather than shame churchgoers.

As is the case more generally with megachurches, music also plays a vital role in helping to modulate the tone of the service. Sometimes upbeat and other times more somber, the music has the power to set the tone of the different elements of a particular service. The lyrics are usually projected onto a screen rather than relying on traditional hymnals. Called "praise" music, the songs often includes lyrics that are less about God than love songs to God (Roberts, 2004: 354). And when the rhythm so inspires members, swaying, dancing, clapping, and/or jumping up and down are seldom discouraged.

The sermons are less fire and brimstone and more about how to relate the message to one's personal life. So titles of sermons might include things like: "How to Make God's Story My Story"; "Waking up to Your New Life"; "Learning to Love Better"; or "Remodel your Life through Jesus." In many non-seeker church services, passages from the Bible are frequently discussed and sometimes even slowly and carefully pored over and dissected. This is not the case in seeker-friendly services. The famous mega-church pastor Joel Osteen is quoted as saying: "I'm called to plant a seed of hope in people's hearts. I'm not called to explain every minute facet of Scripture or to expound on deep theological doctrines or disputes that don't touch where real people live" (in Sodal, 2010: 41).

©Oscar C. Williams/Shutterstock.com

As you can see, one means by which megachurches appeal to seekers is by presenting themselves less like churches and more like places that don't feel "religious." In fact, some might argue that such churches can seem more like businesses than churches. Kimon Sargeant has studied seekers and seeker churches and writes: "Seeker church experts often proclaim the shopping mall, Disney, and other customer-sensitive companies as models for the twenty-first-century church" (2000: 8). And it is not unique to seeker-friendly churches. As we saw with megachurches more broadly, many such churches are quite calculated about wanting to make their church less "church-like." Megachurches frequently adopt strategies, approaches, and processes from the business world. So that leads us to ask: If a church wants to avoid appearing like a church and begins including stores in the church building, and its leaders want to run the church like a corporation, does this mean that the church is in fact a business? In the next section, we will discuss this very issue.

THE "BUSINESS" OF THE MEGACHURCH

In the 1970s, Bill Hybels recruited a team of people who reportedly went door to door in a suburban Chicago region in order to ask people what they did or did not like about church. He then used this information to create a church that would appeal to the people he had surveyed. He knew they wanted a church that was not boring and that had a message that people found relatable to their own lives. Willow Creek Church was the product of his work and it opened in 1975 outside the city of Chicago.

Willow Creek proved to be hugely popular, so popular in fact that it outgrew its original church facilities. Now there are six churches in the Willow Creek family all throughout that region. Still, the original "campus" has an average weekend attendance of around 23,000. Hybels's church is not only popular among churchgoers it is popular among church leaders who want to mimic the success of Willow Creek. Thus, Hybels established the Willow Creek Association, which includes 13,000 member churches, from 90 denominations, and 45 different countries. Members in the association pay an annual fee that gives them access to discounts on Willow Creek Resources and conferences, as well as a magazine, an audio journal, several web-based ministry tools, and a variety of resources that are intended to assist members of the Association who want to see more growth in their own churches.

©Iakov Filimonov/Shutterstock.com

Rick Warren is a pastor on the West Coast who, shortly after Willow Creek became successful, wished to create his own church. Since he knew that, in general, churches comprised more women than men attenders, Warren wanted to find a way to get more men involved. Not only did Warren go door to door in search of answers, he went so far as to hire marketers to find out what men wanted in a church. Equipped with his own marketing data he founded Saddleback Church in 1980. Saddleback, like Willow Creek before it, proved to be incredibly popular. As a writer for the business magazine *Forbes* states: "If Warren's church was a business, it would be compared with Dell, Google or Starbucks" (p. 201 in DeWaay, 2006). The quote from this business journalist helps to emphasize the connection between megachurches and the business world.

Related to the ways in which megachurches feed of the business world, Warren also benefitted from his friendship with one of the leading management gurus of the time, Peter Drucker. Warren quotes Drucker as having said: "The most significant sociological phenomenon of the first half of the 20th century was the rise of the corporation. The most significant sociological phenomenon of the second half of the 20th century has been the development of the large pastoral church—of the megachurch. It is the only organization that is actually working in our society" (retrieved July 2009 from URL: http://pewforum.org/events/?EventID=80).

Warren was not the only one who was friends with Drucker, the management guru. Bill Hybels also was an acquaintance. As one historian says: "Inside Minister Hybel's office hung a sign: 'What is our business? Who is our customer? What does the customer value?' The questions came from management guru expert Peter Drucker, whom Hybels had befriended, and it bore witness to his business-oriented approach to the job" (Allitt, 2003: 229). What the examples of Bill Hybels's Willow Creek Church and Rick Warren's Saddleback Church illustrate is the way strategies from the business world are increasingly adopted by leaders in religious organizations.

Many megachurch ministers might be considered minor celebrities and some also make money from selling books. Rick Warren of Saddleback Church has published a number of books not least of which was *The Purpose Driven Life*—the best selling hardcover book ever in America (Thumma, 2012). Pastor T. D. Jakes who pastors a Dallas megachurch is also a prominent author of many best-selling books. The same can be said of Joel Osteen in addition to many others.

Reinforcing the notion that megachurches are businesses is the fact there are many related commercial groups. A parachurch is an organization that somehow supports religious participation without actually serving as a conventional church with clergy and congregation members and so on. These include religious marketing or publishing companies, charitable enterprises set up by a religion or a church, religious schools, religious groups on campus, just to name a few.

Particularly relevant to the present discussion is the manner in which some parachurches work to reshape megachurches in order to make them more accessible, entertaining, and welcoming. According to Mara Einstein (2008) for example, there are approximately 5,000 professional church consultants whose job is to figure out what

church "customers" want and how best to create a "product" that will meet those customers' preferences, wants, and needs. For example, the Barna Group was founded in 1984 to conduct marketing research for Christian organizations. It has grown since then to include four different segments within the company, each with its own focus that include books, youth, church strategization, and spiritual leadership. Through books, data sets, DVDs, and professional speaking engagements, they have become leaders in the Christian marketing sector.

ANOTHER PERSPECTIVE

When hearing how megachurches can turn church into a kind of business that "sells" "products" to "consumers," some people disapprove. How is it, they ask, can something sacred like a religious community be so similar to something so profane as commercial advertising? And isn't it wrong to treat sermons and spiritual messages as merchandise that people consume to make them feel better? After all, isn't there that story

about Jesus storming a Jewish temple that had been turned into a marketplace-like, shopping bazaar? That is certainly a reasonable response. However, there is an alternative perspective. There are some sociologists who argue that maybe when we think about money, we automatically think of it as the "root of all evil." Thus, money is perceived to be profane. Therefore religion, which is by definition about the sacred, should be kept at a distance.

Daniel Miller (1998) has done extensive research into the ways people shop for ordinary things like groceries. On the surface, grocery shopping might seem rather banal and not special at all. After all, the act involves the rather ordinary task of going to the store, selecting what you wish to buy, putting those things in your basket, and finally standing in line to check out and purchase the things you want to take home with you. What his research has shown however is that many people do not consciously think of grocery shopping as something very special but when people are asked to examine the process more closely they begin to recognize the potential of shopping to be not just special but *sacred*.

©Kzenon/Shutterstock.com

This is particularly true for people who are buying goods for others as with a family. Think about it . . . there are quite a few rituals one must go through in order to complete the task. And what is so special about that task? Miller's research reveals that grocery shopping is really about acquiring things that will sustain the lives of the ones you care about the most. And if you are a parent you must take into consideration a lot of factors: whether she or he likes some product or another and whether it is good for their health. Sometimes, you might even go out of your way to find something special, a treat of some sort that will bring a small amount of joy to your loved one. These are all matters of care and love. So contrary to the notion that being a consumer is a negative thing and something profane, Miller's work suggests it is the exact opposite; it is sacred.

Another social scientist Geoffrey Clark (1999) examined the ways people bought life insurance—another kind of activity that, on the surface seems rather profane.

Every month a customer sends the life insurance company some money so that if the insured dies, the company will pay the survivors (such as a spouse or children) some allotted amount of money. The whole industry of life insurance was designed to help offset the fact that the person who dies is no longer earning a salary and contributing to the household budget.

Yet, you might ask, how you can place a monetary value on life? Now life insurance is basically a wager. If I take out a $10,000 life insurance policy on a parent, for instance, I am betting that she or he will die before I have paid the life insurance company $10,000. And if I win, then I get $10,000. So am I essentially suggesting that my parent's life is worth $10,000? I could have taken out a larger or smaller policy after all. Betting is in many religions considered sinful so that is certainly one way of looking at it. Money, which is profane, is basically "contaminating" the value of my parent's life, which is sacred.

Another sociologist points out that this is the conventional way of thinking about the relationship between the sacred and the profane (Zelizer, 1994). Yet, why, she asks, does something profane have to always contaminate that which is sacred? Why can't it be the other way around? Why can't something sacred actually make something profane more sacred?

Emile Durkheim in his sociology of religion said that in order for something profane to become sacred, rituals are required. Thus, in communion, the way the bread becomes sacred is through special rituals performed by the priest or minister. Thus, we ourselves are able to make something sacred by enacting particular rituals. When we take into consideration the sacred lives of loved ones around us, something profane like shopping for groceries or taking out a life insurance policy can become sacred. The money we then use to accomplish those tasks has a sacred policy. What these two examples demonstrate is that something profane like money does not necessarily turn something that is sacred into something that is impure or even evil and wrong. Rather, what these researchers' examples illustrate is that something pure and sacred can work in the other direction by turning the profane into something sacred.

©Blend Images/Shutterstock.com

Belk et al. (1989) give another example: consider your home . . . Perhaps you consider your home "sacred" but what makes it so? Belk's work suggests that it has to do with the ritual of moving in, decorating it, arranging the furniture, and so on. The rituals that we take when we move into an apartment or a house turn an ordinary dwelling into something sacred: a home. At the same time, you (or someone) have to pay money for that space you call home—whether it is through a mortgage or the rent that is required per the landlord. So does the money somehow contaminate the sacred quality of your home? Probably not.

In another more anthropological study, a researcher talks about a Catholic practice in Columbia in South America called "baptism of the bill" wherein a godparent hides some money in her/his hand while holding the baby that is supposed to be baptized. In this religious ritual, participants believe that the baptism of the baby also results in the "baptism" of the money. They also believe that as a consequence of this baptism of money, that when the godparents spend the baptized money that they will reap monetary benefits in the future (Taussig, 1977).

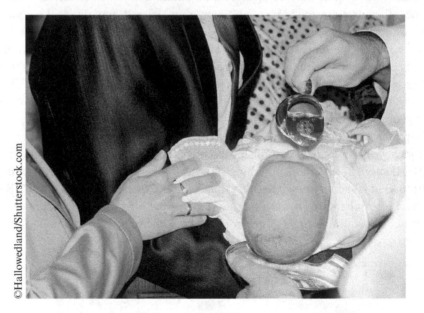

©Hallowedland/Shutterstock.com

The point in bringing up these cases in which social scientists question the assumption that money is something profane, is to point out that, as sociologists, we should not be quick to make value judgments regarding people's beliefs or behaviors. Often, there are alternative views. It is crucial to never take for granted our own assumptions about the meanings people give to their worlds. We should always strive to keep an open mind about the ways people work to create a fulfilling and purposeful existence.

THE KEY DIFFERENCE

As we think with new information, then, about the question posed at the beginning of the chapter, there does seem to be a key difference, other than God, between fast food and religion. Fast food is not intended to be the only, or even the primary, way of eating. Most people, however, choose a church and stick with it. They don't just consume a megachurch version of religion when they are tired or looking for something new. Right?

Well, maybe not so much. As our religious culture shifts to a more spectator-based, McDonaldized approach, our church attendance patterns have shifted as well. A "regular" attendee is now thought by many researchers to be someone who attends as seldom as once a month. So, perhaps our church structures are actually accommodating a consumer pattern that pervades all aspects of modern life, as Ritzer points out. If that's the case, then it raises another interesting question for sociologists. If people are no longer connected to their local congregations in the way that Josh's grandmother is, then how *are* they connected to others in their community?

DISCUSSION QUESTIONS

1. What are the five characteristics of McDonaldization? How can we apply this theory to the sociology of religion? Give a concrete example of each from the chapter and/or from your own experience.
2. What is a megachurch? Give a few characteristics from the chapter. Are these problematic? Why or why not?
3. Compare and contrast "traditional" churches and megachurches. What are some of the defining characteristics of each? Why or why are they not different?
4. What audience are megachurches attempting to reach?
5. What are seekers and why do megachurches rely so heavily on them?
6. What is the role of music in megachurches?
7. Who is Rick Warren and what is his role in the church? What are two examples of his accomplishments?

CHAPTER 9

PAST RELIGION BUT POST-SECULAR

Has religion become a kind of therapy?

KEY TERMS

- **Cult**
- **Edge religion**
- **Modernity**
- **Particularism**
- **Postmodernity**

OBJECTIVES:

- Reconsider the definition of religion, what "counts" as a religion, and what it means to "be religious."
- Understand that although many see religion as belief in God, or gods, a religious belief system does not have to include belief in any deity, and there are in fact many postmodern religions that do not.
- Understand how all the changes occurring in the 1960s fueled such drastic shifts in societal thinking, and what the role of religion was in this period of time.
- Understand that societal ideas about and definitions of religion are always and will always be changing, and in turn, grasp the importance of keeping an open mind when thinking about religion as a social construct.

THE RADICAL LACK

Has there ever been a time in your life when you've felt some kind of nagging feeling like something is just not quite right? Like something is off in your life, despite the fact that you're not exactly sure what it is because everything seems to be going just fine in your life but that there seems to be something…lacking? And that if you were able to put your finger on what it was, you could name it and work toward coming up with a solution and feel more complete or whole? Or maybe it just feels like there is something right around the corner from where you happen to be in life and when you get there, everything will be all right.

It's like your life resembles a jigsaw puzzle, which you have worked really hard and long to complete in order to finish this encompassing, expansive, and beautiful picture. And you sense that you're coming to the end of the puzzle only to discover that one of the pieces is missing. Just one piece! And you don't know where it is. Perhaps a cat swatted it off the table one evening and you are going to need to get on your hands and knees and scour your apartment to find it. Or perhaps it is a defect. Or perhaps the manufacturer forgot to include all of the pieces. But have you ever had that feeling that your life is just like that jigsaw puzzle that is missing just that one, single solitary piece?

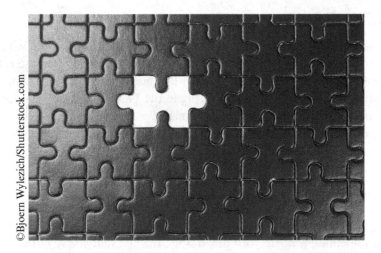

If you've ever felt like what we have been describing, then you've likely engaged in a hunt to identify what that missing piece was and where you might find it in order to feel complete. While the experience may be internal and psychological, some sociologists have tried to address the issue by arguing that one of the functions of society is to offer solutions to what might be thought of as a "hole in your soul."

For instance, some social theorists refer to the missing piece as a "radical lack." It is a "lack" because what it feels like to experience it can be described like we are missing or lacking something that will make us feel whole. And she says it is "radical" because that lack is something that all of us have experienced at one time or another and because it never really goes away.

The radical lack is part of the human condition and this, in turn, leads us to this feeling that there are always "greener pastures" to be found. In other words, we tend to grow dissatisfied with something in our life so then we go about trying to figure out what will bring us renewed satisfaction.

©stickasa/Shutterstock.com

Oftentimes, we feel as though there is a "soul mate" who we are destined to meet and be with. We even use metaphors in our romantic relationships that reflect this attitude. Think about how often you have heard people talk about their "better half," or claim that their partners "complete" them.

Other people feel like if they find that perfect outfit or that hot new car, the radical lack will go away. So for them, retail consumerism is a way of dealing with their radical lack. And for many people as though a spiritual relationship with God or something greater than them will make them complete so that the radical lack will disappear. The point that Peck and others who have talked about the radical lack is that it is something we all share and that one of the most fundamental things that we seek to satisfy that "hole in our souls" is a spiritual life. Increasingly in our world, people are willing to seek spiritual wholeness beyond just the religions we were raised in or the institutional religions that people in earlier generations were a part of. Today, people are more willing than ever to think outside the box in order to construct meaningful lives. Thus, sociologists have had to rethink our core conceptions of what religion is, what can count as a religion, and what resources different forms of religion can provide for people.

POSTMODERN RELIGION

We deliberately titled our textbook *The Air We Breathe* in order to emphasize that religion is all around us. It is vital, and yet often taken for granted. As should be evident by this point, even with the increasing number of people who do not identify as religious, religion still pervades our culture, our political values, and our secular (non-religious) institutions. In this chapter, we will be discussing how culture helps shape new religions and even forces us to ask the question: What exactly counts as a religion? How do we define what is a religion and what is not a religion?

©Lolostock/Shutterstock.com

Some sociologists (and we are among them) think that the definition for what constitutes a religion has changed. Our definitions have become more diffused and less narrow today. Indeed, throughout this textbook, we have reinforced the view that there are oftentimes competing and sometimes contradictory views about religious belief systems even within the one field of sociology. We have discussed religion from multiple perspectives in part because we believe that as social scientists we have a responsibility to understand and appreciate the fact that people who are involved in religion make many different claims about the meaning and purpose of their religion, and the worldviews their religion helps to contribute.

But we also present a diverse perspective because we ourselves, the authors of the textbook, subscribe to our own belief: that we live in a society in which there are more widely differing belief systems than ever. Thus, as sociologists, our job is first to understand those belief systems.

If we go back to the beginning of the sociology of religion and look to what Emile Durkheim said constitutes a religion, we would find that his list of requirements is short and sweet: it had to have rituals, a community of believers, and things those believers considered sacred. You may notice a conspicuous absence from that list that religions had to have a divinity in their list of requirements. Durkheim was correct though. Not all religions have a god in their belief systems and not all religions have a requirement that followers must believe in a god (or gods or goddesses).

©hidesy/Shutterstock.com

Durkheim uses Buddhism as an example. Buddhism is a "non-theistic" religion that is practiced by hundreds of millions of people across the globe. While many non-Buddhists believe that Buddhists worship the Buddha, in reality that is not the case. A lot of Buddhists, especially in the West, are agnostic—they do not know whether or not a divinity exists and that it is not worth even wondering about whether or not there is a divinity. Buddhists believe that the Buddha was nothing more than a wise human being and that individuals can realize their "Buddha nature" through lifelong practice of the Eightfold Path.

So if we return to Durkheim's requirements for what constitutes a religion, we can begin to see that there exists a multitude of possible "religions." Religions do not require belief in a divinity, nor must religions even presuppose the existence of a divinity. Religions must regard some things as sacred, there must be a community of followers, and those followers must participate in ritualistic activities. After all, we discussed how Americanism is a kind of "civil religion" (see Chapter 5). An example in this instance might be: Americans (i.e., a community of people who share the fact that they are American) who are attending a football game, standing in order to sing the national anthem (i.e., engaging in a ritual practice), focused on the American flag which is in the center of the field (i.e., a sacred object).

Now let us use that same example of people attending a football game but focus on just a portion of the people in attendance at the football stadium: fans of the home team. And for the sake of illustration, let us use a concrete example and imagine we are in Denver at the stadium where their professional football team plays—the Denver Broncos. At the beginning of the each game, after the national anthem has been sung, the stadium announcer introduces the teams and when the Broncos are introduced, a man riding a horse (a bronco is a kind of wild horse) charges onto the field with the team players following. When this happens, the fans stand up and cheer and the collective sound is like a boisterous roar.

So now let us ask the following question: Is football, then, a kind of religion? One might reasonably argue that it is. After all it has the three necessary requirements for it to be a religion. First, there is a community of followers (the fans themselves) who gather together a few Sundays each year. At this ritual gathering, fans engage in other rituals: they applaud and yell when their team does something well; they sing and chant; sometimes they participate in the crowd "wave"; many of the fans put on clothing adorned with the team logo, etc. And what is sacred about this "religion"? Certainly the logo is sacred. The horse that runs out at the beginning of the game is sacred (there is even a statue of a bronco at the city's airport), and then there are some of the players who are considered sacred (just think about how invested people get over the health of the quarterback, for example).

So can sports be a religion? Religions provide people with a sense of identity and meaning. Sports can fulfill that function. After all, it means something to Broncos fans who can proudly identify themselves as such. Just think about all of the people you see on a regular basis who wear caps and shirts with their favorite team logo. People who wear these items are essentially identifying themselves with the team represented by the logo. Also, fans find a significant sense of satisfaction and contentment when watching their team play. They invest meaning into the ways their team plays. A team win can be a significant source of pride and joy, and a loss can result in heartache. And while it might be an exaggeration, I have often heard people say things like, "I live for football."

But what about *morality*? One of religion's foremost functions is to provide followers with a sense of right and wrong, or good and bad. Does football do this? Perhaps it does to a small degree. Certainly fans of a given team view their team in more favorable terms than the opposing teams. In fact, like me, you may have even heard someone who denigrates the fans of other teams as being dumb or ill behaved. Or consider the way a referee who makes a questionable call against the fan's team gets portrayed as a villain.

So is football a religion? Undoubtedly there is a portion of people who would say that it is. There are certainly quite a number of Americans who invest more time and money in their "football religion" than in their comparable conventional religion.

Some people have even suggested that making money is a religion. We even have a saying that some people "worship at the altar of the almighty dollar." They might treat money as being so holy that they value it more than they value other people. They offer sacrifices (of considerable time and energy) in order acquire as much as they can and feel as though others in the system of capitalism (especially those who are similar in their devotion to wealth acquisition) are their fellow worshipers. They engage in certain rituals for the primary purpose of connecting with what they believe is sacred: money. Having money gives them a sense of purpose (to get more), a sense of identity (as being someone who is rich), and a sense of right and wrong (capitalism is good, "greed is good," and being wealthy is a sign of good character).

We could go through a litany of other possible religions: baseball, people who are Star Wars fans, people who "religiously" follow musical artists, celebrity worship, and so on. Each time, we might ask the same questions that we addressed in our examples regarding football and money: do these things meet the three requirements of religion that Durkheim identified and do they serve the same functions as conventional religions? Following those guidelines, one can definitely make the case that these are all religions.

We have two points we wish to make by discussing religion as though it is something that is not as clear cut as we generally assume it to be. First, we want to illustrate that what makes a religion a religion is open to interpretation. For people who are part of conventional religions like Christianity, Islam, or Judaism this might not seem like a reasonable conclusion. Yet it is important to recognize because when we open up our definition of religion to refer to non-conventional religions, we begin to appreciate the fact that religion is a social institution. And because it is a social institution it is socially constructed. Because religion is a socially constructed institution it is subject to variability and change. It also forces us to come to terms with the possibility that no one religion has a monopoly on truth and morality. Truth and morality, when it comes to religion, are not things that are universal and absolute but instead can change depending on one's religious tradition.

It is therefore important to be careful about what social scientists call "**particularism**." Particularism refers to the belief that one's own religion is the only one that is true and that others' belief systems are false and will not lead them to salvation. Particularism can be a problem when we start to see "our" way not only as the only way but the only acceptable and good way. Because when we do this, we also tend to view others as being bad, evil, and less valuable or worthy of consideration and care than people who are like ourselves.

This is not to suggest that there are behaviors that cannot or should not be considered universally good (e.g., compassion) or universally wrong (e.g., violence). But what we can conclude from this discussion is that tolerance and respect for religions and religious beliefs that are not one's own is important. In fact, in a world of ongoing religious violence (something that is nearly as old as religion itself) and in a world of increasing human diversity, it is imperative to make every effort to understand how others who are not like us have meaningful and sacred rituals, beliefs, and traditions that are as vital to their lives as our own rituals, beliefs, and traditions are to our lives.

The second point we want to make regarding the way that our definition of what constitutes a religion can be "fuzzy" and open to interpretation, is that this fuzziness is an intrinsic part of today's culture. That is, when we think about how to define our social institutions, not only is there an increasing amount of fuzziness to these definition, there is an increasing acceptance on the part of most people that fuzziness is just a part of life. For example, in Chapter 9, we discussed the ways in which megachurch worship services could be quite entertaining—I have attended some megachurch services that were on par with a concert or a Broadway play. So are those experiences rooted in religion or entertainment? Or is it both? And what about megachurches that have a lot of little shops and cafes as some now have—are we therefore participating in a religious activity or a shopping one? This "fuzziness" about how we think about the distinctions of the social institutions that are part of our life is tied to the present period of time in which we live. We call this period of time "**postmodernity**."

POSTMODERNITY

Social thinkers generally use the year 1968 as the dividing line between **modernity** (before 1968) and postmodernity (after 1968). Now, it should be noted that 1968 is really a kind of arbitrary number and the events that signaled the beginning of postmodernity occurred both before and after. 1968 is used as the year that divides modernity from postmodernity though because so many significant events took place in that year. However, before we discuss postmodernity, let's address modernity.

"Particularism" The belief that one's own religion is the only true religion; all other religions are false.

"Postmodernity" Beginning the year after 1968, acceptance of the "fuzziness" that is life and a rise in skepticism, even of progressive ideas.

Modernity Before 1968, some argue it began with the Enlightenment and others with the rise of industrialization, basic understanding of the natural sciences as revolutionary and the acceptance of "Grand narratives" to guide people.

Depending on whom you ask, modernity either begins with the Enlightenment or with the rise of industrialization. In either case, we can think about modernity as a time period in which people viewed the world in particular ways and those ways differ from the ways in which we view the world today. Primarily modernity affects human thought in two ways. First, people put a great deal of faith in the transformative potential of the natural sciences. In other words, it was believed that science would lead to greater and greater progress in society. As part of that belief, people tended to see progress as something that was always desirable.

Now while we still put a great deal of faith in science, people tend to be a little more skeptical about scientific claims. Consider the following list: eggs, milk, red meat, soy, coffee, alcohol, and salt. At one time or another, science has either told us that those things are very good for us or has told us to avoid those items. So in postmodernity, people are more skeptical about what they read or hear.

New scientific technologies have benefited us in more ways than we could possibly know. However, these same developments have also made it easier for thieves to steal our identity or for big corporations to spy on us as we surf the web. So technological progress is not always a positive thing for us. The increased skepticism and wariness regarding progress is more postmodern than it is modern.

The second primary characteristic of modernity has to do with what we call "grand narratives." Grand narratives are like stories that bind large segments of a society together, such as a society's set of worldviews. One example of a grand narrative for the United States in the middle of the 20th Century was that American Democracy was always good and Soviet forms of Communism were always bad.

©vagant/Shutterstock.com

Grand narratives also encompassed other widespread beliefs: that men were supposed to be breadwinners and women homemakers; that the views of persons of color were less important than those of whites; that homosexuality should be suppressed; that an ideal life consisted of owning a home with white picket fencers and having multiple children; and, among many other things, that the United States was a Christian nation.

©jessicakirsh/Shutterstock.com

Nowadays, for the most part, we see these views as quaint and old-fashioned. We are increasingly a multicultural society made up of people with diverse ethnic and religious backgrounds. We also tend to be more tolerant of gender and sexual fluidity. This is in part due to the weakening of the grand narratives of modernity. Technology and mass media have exposed us to a wide array of perspectives and views.

Additionally, it could be said that modernity was marked by a strong belief that there were certain universal and absolute truths. In other words, people believed that there was "Truth with a capital T." What do we mean by the phrase: Truth with a capital T? If you or someone you know believes that faith in Jesus Christ, for example is the one and only vehicle to getting to Heaven, that is, a Truth with a capital T. Or someone who believes that science has all the answers; or that there is absolutely, positively no God. Each of these are considered Truths with capital Ts.

In postmodernity, however, more and more people adhere to less stringent views about truth and knowledge. They are more open to the possibility that truth is relative, that there are a variety of perspectives that contradict our own assumptions about what is real or what is false. Thus, we say that where modernity is exemplified by "capital T Truths," postmodernity is characterized by a belief in "small 't' truth-claims." That is, we are more skeptical of things we read or hear about and less inclined to accept certain things as completely factual. Less inclined to accept that there is some absolute, universal truth, we are more readily inclined to presume people make claims about something.

So now why then was 1968 such a watershed year or, better still, why were the late 1960s a turning point in which the United States and other Western industrialized nations shifted from modernity to postmodernity? Think about all the events we discussed in Chapter 4 that took place during this period… Among other things, Vietnam launched the Tet Offensive (marking what some consider the beginning of the Vietnam War). Martin Luther King, Jr. was assassinated, as was Robert Kennedy. Student riots took place in the United States and Europe. There were also demonstrations in Chicago around the Democratic National Convention in which police were video-taped violently attempting to silence protesters. There was a symbolic "bra-burning" protest by feminists during a Miss America beauty competition. African American athletes raised their fists in solidarity for Black Power during the Summer Olympics. And the My Lai massacre took place in which American soldiers slaughtered hundreds of unarmed civilians.

©ColorMaker/Shutterstock.com

©Keith Tarrier/Shutterstock.com

All of these events functioned to do a couple of things. First, the media coverage exposed many white, middle class Americans (i.e., "Middle America") to the reality that there was still a great deal of injustice and inequality in their country. America still had a long way to go when it came to recognizing the humanity of an ever-broader diversity of citizens. Second, it forced Americans to reconsider the faith they placed in progress, science, their government, and their civic leaders as never before. So, as you can imagine this period marked a significant turning point in the ways Americans viewed their government, their elected officials, and law enforcement officials. Ongoing struggles for Civil Rights for African Americans as well as equal rights for women and gays and lesbians were salient in popular media, illustrating the fallibility of white, patriarchal dominance.

So what does all of this have to do with religion? Two things: first, during the tumultuous period in the late 1960s and early 1970s America saw the birth of quite a few new religious movements. Even though some have disappeared, this rise in new religions made quite an impact on society that lasts to this day. Second, the shift to postmodernity has changed how we think about religions and religious movements. The definition of what constitutes a religion is a bit more "fuzzy." As people have changed how they view religion and have begun finding that they could get the same things that they used to get in religion from secular institutions, sociologists have had needed to adapt as well. We address both of these developments below but let us begin first by examining how we define "religion."

HEAVEN'S GATE

Marshall Applewhite and wife Bonnie Nettles thought that the Apocalypse was near and that they were divinely ordained to help fulfill biblical prophecy. Specifically, they believed themselves to be incarnations of two characters described in the Book of Revelation and as such they had special insights regarding the end of the world. In the 1970s, the two traveled around the country and preached their message while amassing a small group of followers. Their belief system was a complicated amalgam of Christianity and New Age as well as beliefs in the existence of UFOs and extraterrestrial visits from other planets. Eventually the group, called Heaven's Gate, settled in Southern California.

In 1997, Comet Hale-Bopp was about to make a once-in-a-lifetime appearance since it passes near the earth only about once every 4,000 years. For the members of Heaven's Gate, this was a message from God. Applewhite and Nettles informed their followers that hidden in the tail of the comet was a spaceship. When the comet passed the earth, the planet would be destroyed. The only people who would survive would be the true believers. They would be physically resurrected on the spaceship trailing the comet.

As Comet Hale-Bopp neared, members of Heaven's Gate readied themselves. On the night that the comet was closest to the earth they dressed in matching black outfits and Nike sneakers and wore patches that said "Away Crew." The group of 39 people gathered together and consumed a batch of cocktails infused with poison. All 39 died shortly thereafter.

What do you think of when you read the word "**cult**?" If you are like many people, you think of a small group of people that give all of their money to a powerful leader and who have bizarre beliefs and participate in weird rituals. As you were reading the story about Heaven's Gate, did that word come to mind?

"Cult?" A religion far outside societal norms, generally consisting of a small groups of followers who devote their lives to their cult leader/their cult ideas; generally understood as something negative although many new mainstream religions started out as what we now understand as cults.

A sociological definition of a cult is quite variable. Generally speaking, a cult refers to a new religious movement that exists far outside the social norm. As such, there are a handful of traits that are common to cults: a highly charismatic leader to which people are readily drawn; a sudden and dramatic withdrawal of a member from her or his previous community of friends and family; a heavy focus on proselytizing in order to gain new members; an expectation that members invest a significant amount of labor and time to the group; an intensely strong bond between members or members and their leader; a belief system that is in stark contrast to mainstream societal beliefs; and leaving the group is made particularly challenging and members who do leave the group are ostracized. They also tend to lack formal organizational structure as one would find in more bureaucratic groups.

The term "cult" though clearly carries a negative connotative baggage. Also, it is difficult to define since, for the most part, when we say "cult" the word refers to "deviant" religious social movements. But what does it mean to be deviant? How we characterize what is deviant and what is not is open to interpretation depending upon a number of factors—primarily place and time.

©Solomnikov/Shutterstock.com

Take this case for example: in Greek, the first letter in each of the following words "Jesus Christ, Son of God, Savior" translates into the Greek word for "fish." Early Christians, to avoid persecution by Roman soldiers, met secretly but the way other Christians would know that a place was friendly to them was to use a drawing of a fish. The fish was a secret code. Yet these groups believed things that were in stark contrast to what most people believed at the time. An itinerant carpenter/teacher raised someone from the dead? He walked on top of water? It sounds pretty fishy (pardon the pun). When we think about what a cult is today, we would probably attach that label to this early group of Christians.

In fact, many groups that we might label as cults began life with rituals and beliefs that were considered deviant and non-normative by mainstream society but later either evolved internally into a more normatively acceptable religion or maintained such longevity that it was accepted as a normative religion in spite of its controversial origins and non-normative beliefs.

Some sociologists of religion, therefore, avoid using the term "cult" altogether. The word has such a negative meaning that when we use it, it almost automatically puts a group in a bad light. This makes it more difficult for social scientists to study and publish their research on groups who are labeled as cults because people might be predisposed to assumptions and negative attitudes. The other reason some sociologists give for avoiding the label is due to the way the label changes depending on the social context. What is a "cult" in one era, as we have seen, can be accepted as a mainstream religion in another.

Rather than "cult" many sociologists use "new religious movements" (or NRMs for short). Because it can be difficult to know how long a group can be in existence before it is no longer new (is a group that has been around for one year now? What about 10 years? 20 years?) and because there is some fuzziness between what makes a group a movement versus what makes it a full-blown religion, we prefer to use the term edge religions. The broad term "**edge religion**" allows one to acknowledge the religious nature of the group but recognize that the group is not considered mainstream (thus, exists on the edges of the mainstream rather than in its center). In the section below, we discuss some examples of edge religions.

> **"Edge religion"**
> A religion not fully understood as such by mainstream society; generally existing on the outskirts, or "edges" of society and its norms; the politically correct term for "cult".

EDGE RELIGIONS

Some edge religions have been considered highly controversial and no matter how much we appreciate the value of different perspectives there is no doubt that some of these groups proved to be extremely harmful. However, we should note at the outset that only a very small percentage of groups that one would consider an edge religion are actually dangerous. In fact, oftentimes a benign and mostly harmless group will be castigated and demonized in the media; their strangeness gets exaggerated. Any misdeeds become blown out of proportion for the purpose of scapegoating what are typically easy targets (people who are often young or part of minority groups are frequently scapegoats). When this takes place it is called a "moral panic." An example of a moral panic that took place when I was a kid had to do with what was thought to be an explosion of people who worshipped Satan.

©Heartland Arts/Shutterstock.com

©TDS Photography/Shutterstock.com

The media ran stories about human sacrifices that were part of supposedly satanic rituals. Teachers, parents, and even politicians began decrying the influence of heavy metal music that preyed on the young and brainwashed them into worshiping the devil. The whole thing turned out to be very little at all. It was, in point of fact, a moral panic. Although the purported "boom" in Satan-worshipping metal-heads did not amount to much, this is not the case with "The People's Temple."

In the 1970s, Jim Jones was a charismatic preacher who recruited people from all walks of life to be a part of his new religion that advocated social justice, economic equality, and a strong ethic of love for one's neighbor. Originally identifying with the mainstream denomination the Disciples of Christ, Jones left the group feeling it was not sufficiently radical in its beliefs and values. Jones asserted that Christians had a responsibility to actively work to revolutionize society and to eradicate racism, poverty, and injustice. His messages of equality resonated strongly among women and people of color who comprised the majority of his followers. At the time, his goals seemed, by most measures to be admirable, if a little overly ambitious. Nevertheless though, he quickly developed a sizable following in San Francisco and he and his followers created the "People's Temple."

As time went on and Jones became increasingly more and more popular, his message began to devolve and his behavior became increasingly suspicious. He began claiming that he was divinely ordained and a prophet who could conduct miracles like healing and even raising the dead. His followers deified him and many left their family and friends altogether in order to devote their time exclusively to the People's Temple.

This alarmed quite a few of the loved ones left behind and they were worried that Jones's followers were being victimized through exploitation and abuse.

As the People's Temple began receiving more unwanted attention from media and civic officials, Jones decided to move his followers out of San Francisco, indeed out of the country. Jones next established his own community in Guyana where he and his followers could sequester themselves away from the public. The name of the community that was founded there was "Jonestown." While some members of the People's Temple did not move, hundreds relocated to Jonestown in Guyana in 1977 where they constructed dormitories and set up farms for the residents there.

©Gail Johnson/Shutterstock.com

Some members of the People's Temple left the group before Jones departed for Guyana. These ex-members became outspoken with allegations of sexual and physical violence inflicted by Jones and his top leaders. They and other members' loved ones were able to mobilize and as a result they formed the Committee of Concerned Relatives. The Committee was able to convince federal officials to look into what was taking place in the People's Temple. They were even able to persuade a California Congressman and some reporters to actually travel to Guyana to investigate Jones's community.

When the investigating group arrived in Jonestown in 1978, reporters with the congressman and his entourage attempted to help some of the more wary members of the People's Temple leave to return home to California. Jones's leaders intervened and shot and killed most of the delegation that had come from California. This was followed by what Jones had intended to be a mass suicide. However, not all of the members were willing to take their own lives. In the end, Jones and his leaders laced drinks with cyanide. Some members drank the poison seemingly of their own accord but many were coerced. Over 900 people died on that tragic day.

Jones and the People's Temple were a product of the 60s and 70s and just one of many religious and quasi-religious groups to emerge during the period. Almost all of these new groups were benign. The "Jesus People" or "Jesus Freaks" were born out of the hippie movement and believed Jesus to be the original hippie. And while many practiced open relationships (i.e., "free love") and a renunciation of materialist culture, they were for the most part harmless when it came to their relationship with the general public.

©Jessmine/Shutterstock.com

The same might also be said of ISKCON (International Society for Krishna Consciousness), whose members are generally referred to as Hare Krishnas. "Hare Krishna," for short, has its roots in Hinduism. Imported into the United States in 1965, Hare Krishna had its most popular period in the late 1960s and 1970s. They were visibly distinctive with their shaved heads (save for one strand or knot of hair in the back), colorful robes, and their practices of dancing and chanting ("Hare Krishna, Hare Rama"). Hare Krishnas were often seen in public venues and airports handing out religious tracts and distributing flowers as they attempted to convert additional followers. In Hare Krishna, the Hindu god Lord Krishna is considered the highest divinity and practitioners hope that through their emulation of Lord Krishna's traits, they can attain "Krishna consciousness." Some of their core values include vegetarianism and the abstaining from intoxicants.

One of the members of The Beatles, George Harrison, drew on their core chant to produce the popular song "My Sweet Lord." Thus, Hare Krishnas were for a number of years deemed tolerable if a little fanatic by many, and at worst a pesky nuisance by some people in the mainstream who felt they had to put up with interference while traveling through airports.

After some time though, particularly during the 1980s, when more people in the public became worried about cults' potential to brainwash people, the visibility of Hare Krishnas in public venues diminished. In the 1990s, though Hare Krishna became a little more popular again. The slight resurgence was at least partly fueled by straightedge punks and the popularity of hardcore punk bands such as The Cromags, Youth of Today, and Shelter. Those in that strand of the punk movement found a sense of identity among others who shared values of vegetarian and veganism, abstinence from alcohol and drugs, and avoidance of sexual misconduct.

Developing around the same period as the Hare Krishnas, the Reverend Sun Myung Moon moved from Korea to the United States to establish the Unification Church. Loosely based on Christian principles, as the name of the church suggests, Moon's primary message emphasized the need for people to come together in love. One of the things he became known for was the way he conducted large-scale group marriages. In addition to their size, what also made these weddings unique was the fact that many people who were married to one another were not even previously acquainted.

Moon was deified by many of the church members who believed he was an incarnation of Jesus Christ. He and his wife were (and continue to be) referred to as "Our True Parents."

Like the Hare Krishnas, church members could be found in airports and other venues selling flowers and candy. Members were expected to devote their entire lives to the church, to the chagrin of family members and friends who were basically expelled from members' lives. This earned members a nickname by the mainstream: followers of Moon were derogatorily referred to as "Moonies". Members spent a great deal of time going out into the public to raise money for a variety of church charities. Their efforts contributed to the church's ability to amass a veritable fortune. Unfortunately, at least some of those funds were misused and Moon was convicted of tax fraud in 1982. Nevertheless, at the height of its popularity the Unification Church had around 10,000 members in the United States. (Williams, [1990] 2002).

As we earlier stated, the 1960s and 1970s were a fertile period for the emergence of new religious groups. Another group that rose during this time was The Family. For many years, they were viewed with suspicion and a degree of fear. They, like so many other religious groups, slowly have settled into the mainstream. Today they are a fairly unremarkable organization when compared to their more provocative and eyebrow-raising earlier period.

The story of The Family begins in the 1960s with David Berg. Raised as a Protestant Christian, Berg believed he received divine visions from God who had ordained him to spread God's message. Specifically, Berg felt that God wanted him to convey to people that their society was irrevocably and irredeemably corrupt and that the end of the world was nigh. Berg traveled around the country preaching and trying to convince as many people as he could to become part of his Christian-derived religious community. At some point during this period he took on the name of "Moses David." Later he became simply known as "Mo."

In 1969, Mo crafted a series of documents that discussed God's vision for his religion and shared those documents with his followers. These writings later became known as "Mo's Letters" and were considered by members of The Family to be a sacred text; though Mo's Letters did not replace the Bible, they only supplemented it.

Members of The Family lived in communal homes where household responsibilities were equitably allotted. Each home played a unique role in supporting The Family—for instance, one might be designated for the purpose of child care, another for proselytizing to potential new members, another might play an economic role in supporting other homes, and so on. And within individual homes, a great deal of emphasis was placed on apportioning household responsibilities in an equitable manner. During its high point, membership in The Family numbered in the thousands and there were hundreds of communal homes in numerous countries outside the United States.

As we have attempted to make clear throughout this textbook, religion shapes non-religious institutions just like non-religious institutions shape religion. Or, to put it differently, religion and society are so bound up together, Mo's Letters and the beliefs and values of the members comprising The Family reflect just this sociological truism, which is evidenced by the group's interpretation of Jesus's teachings filtered through the hippies' progressive stance on sexuality in what Mo called The Law of Love.

For instance, members of The Family were permitted to get married (and many did). However, the spouses were not romantically or sexually exclusive to one single partner. Instead, even married people were free to have sex with others residing in their communal homes. This was due to Mo's belief in the "Law of Love." One can find in Mo's Letters the following edict: ""Jesus' Law of Love can also be applied to our sexual interaction with others... that loving heterosexual relations between consenting adults, even outside of marriage, are permissible as long as others immediately affected by these actions are not hurt" (in Chryssides and Wilkins, 2006: 179). The Law of Love meant that sex, in short, was considered to be a sacred act and therefore was something to be shared openly and freely.

Beyond the practice of free love and open relationships, Mo also developed the practice of "flirty fishing" as a way of attracting new members. As the name implies, the practice involved members of The Family flirting with non-members in order to establish a connection and ultimately convince people to join the group. Sometimes flirty fishing led to sex but, again, because sex was considered sacred, this was perfectly acceptable.

Furthermore, members of The Family believed that the love of Christ was inside of each of them and could be so strong that others could sense it and be drawn to the members. Thus, if people out in the public were attracted to members engaged in flirty fishing, then that was a sign that the love of Jesus was so strong that it was emanating through the members. The other person who was the target of the flirty fishing was not actually attracted to the member of The Family but to Jesus. The member of the Family was simply a proxy or stand-in for the love of Christ.

The Law of Love supported members' belief that sex was a highly spiritual activity and one that should be shared. Unfortunately, some members took this to mean that sex between adults and minors was acceptable and even sex within one's biological family. Eventually Mo intervened and attempted to put an end to illicit sex. He wrote new letters informing members of The Family that sex should only take place between consenting adults. Nonetheless, by the 1990s stories of sexual misconduct began making their way into the public forum. Amid allegations of sexual abuse involving minors, communal houses in Spain, France, Argentina, and Australia became the targets for criminal investigations. Members' children were removed from the communal homes in which they lived. Ultimately though all charges were dropped. Since then, the organization has instituted strict regulations regarding sex and the group, now called The Family International, subscribes to a more mainstream and normative set of beliefs and values.

What should be clear at this point in our discussion of edge religions is that religious communities can evolve and become more acceptable by the mainstream. And it also works the other way as well. Society too changes and what may have been deemed unusual in one era can be considered quite normal in another. There are though, some religious groups who have proven over time to be both sustainable and enduring. Despite this, the mainstream view of those groups may continue to be tenuous, unsettled, or just uneasy. Scientology is one such group. Is it a religion? Is it a lifestyle? Is it dangerous? Attitudes related to Scientology vary enormously and recent publicity in the United States has likely done little to aid in the credibility and legitimacy of the group and its members.

Scientology was founded on the work of L. Ron Hubbard who published a bestselling book called *Dianetics: The Modern Science of Mental Health*. Scientology is undoubtedly as complex as it is controversial. Scientologists assert that people are essentially souls (called "thetans") trapped in physical bodies. "Engrams" are events, memories, perceptions, thoughts, and the like that cause us continued suffering. Through "auditing," which is a kind of training and education that is done with someone who is specialized in the practice, one can free oneself from engrams in order to attain a state of "clear." Its self-identified goals are the following: "A civilization without insanity, without criminals, and without war, where the able can prosper and honest beings can have rights, and where man is free to rise to greater heights, are the aims of Scientology."

E-Meters are hand held devices that ostensibly measure electric pulses felt in the body as a consequence of engrams. E-Meters are a central instrument used in auditing. In 1963, the U.S. FDA confiscated more than 100 E-Meters from the Church citing that the E-Meters made unsubstantiated claims that their use could promote better health. In court, the Church won their case and the judge ordered the E-Meters be returned in spite of referring to their use as "quackery" (Cowan and Bromley, 2008: 42).

The Church of Scientology is highly compartmentalized and bureaucratic, like most other conventional religions. The Church provides people with a sense of meaning, identity, purpose, and morality. It includes other characteristics too of mainstream religions such as rites and rituals, and sacred objects. Scientologists themselves are unequivocal in their assertion that theirs is a religion and continue to seek acknowledgment of that through recognition by governments around the world.

One means is through attaining the legal rights that governments grant other religious organizations. In the United States they have accomplished that right. In a 1993, court battle with the Internal Revenue Service, Scientology won 501(c)3 status. Such status is largely used by faith-based organizations in order to receive some tax exemptions. The court decision, therefore, was a tacit acknowledgment on the part of the U.S. government that Scientology meets many of the qualifications of a religion. In fact, Scientology also received similar recognition by Australia, New Zealand, and Italy. Still, other countries including Greece, France, and England have refused to grant Scientology similar status as a religion (Cowan and Bromley, 2008).

CONCLUSION

In a postmodern world, identifying what counts and what does not count as a religion is an ongoing challenge for sociologists. More and more people in the field are choosing to withhold their judgment when it comes to defining emerging religious groups. After all, when sociologists impose their own classification schemes on others they are implying that their judgment is somehow better than the judgment of the people they are studying. Thus, it is important as social scientists to allow people to speak for themselves and to assert their own agency, rather than privileging the scientist as the "expert" of someone else's view of reality.

©SK Design/Shutterstock.com

What Scientology (and other religious groups that exist on the edges of the mainstream) illustrates is that the sociology of religion is not complete. It never will be. Society's ideas about what religion is and what it does for people are always changing. It is more important than ever to keep an open mind about what provides people with direction and meaning in life. In the science of sociology, we have a responsibility to be inquisitive and curious about what people do, what they believe, and what they say. By honoring these things we are able to better set aside our own personal values in order to conduct ethical, scientific research.

©supergenijalac/Shutterstock.com

DISCUSSION QUESTIONS

1. What are the three things that make up a religion, according to Emile Durkheim?
2. How can sports be considered religion? Give a concrete example from your own life. Be sure to use Durkheim's three elements of religion in your answer.
3. What is particularism and how is it problematic?
4. Explain postmodernity. What is the difference between postmodernity and modernity? What are the primary characteristics of each? Also, provide some specific beliefs from each ideology for the chapter for each.
5. What does it mean to say "truth with a capital 'T'"? Which period of time does this idea belong to?
6. What was "Heaven's Gate"? Who were prominent people in this religion? Would you consider it a cult? Explain why or why not using your knowledge about cults from the chapter.
7. What was the "People's Temple" and who was its leader? Give three specific facts about it from the chapter. Lastly, how did it come to an end?
8. What are two more examples of edge religions from the chapter? Give some defining characteristics of each.
9. What is Scientology and who was its founder? Explain its main teachings.

CHAPTER 10

TRENDS IN RELIGIOUS AFFILIATION

Why are millenials leaving the church in record numbers?

KEY TERMS

- **Dones**
- **Moralistic therapeutic deism**
- **Religious marketplace**

OBJECTIVES:

- Appreciate the complexity of individuals' relationship to institutionalized religion.
- Understand how people can still be religious while not identifying with a particular religion.
- Comprehend the changing patterns in people's religious commitments.

INTRODUCTION

Think about your own friends and family. Are any of them religious? Do any of them attend a mosque, church, or synagogue? Do you? Taking it a step further, which answer would you give if you were presented the following question on a survey: What is your present religion, if any? Are you Protestant, Roman Catholic, Mormon, Orthodox such as Greek or Russian Orthodox, Jewish, Muslim, Buddhist, Hindu, atheist, agnostic, something else, or nothing in particular?

If you answered "nothing in particular" you would be among the largest documented trend of "**nones**" in American history. Increasingly, people are choosing NOT to affiliate with a particular religious tradition. While the rates of religiosity, adherence, and affiliation remain high in the United States relative to our European counterparts, there has been a distinct downward trend in recent years that mirrors a more general turn away from institutions to organize social life.

The American religious landscape is undergoing unprecedented shifts as people increasingly forego traditional religious communities. In fact, the number of people claiming no religious affiliation is at an all-time high in the United States as people leave organized religion in record numbers.

Led by a generation of millennials who are rejecting social institutions in a variety of forms, this movement of people away from the church promises to have dramatic consequences for a nation with traditionally high rates of religious participation and a significant reliance on church and faith-based organizations for delivering social services, organizing civic engagement, and facilitating social connections. Thus, it is paramount that we understand what is driving people away from religious institutions in order to assess what impact this movement will have not only on the field of religion, but also on American social institutions more generally.

Recent research has attempted to empirically document the breadth of this phenomenon by accounting for exactly how many people mark their religious affiliation as "none" (Vargas 2012; White 2014).At the same time, research by Lim, MacGregor, and Putnam (2010) tries to understand this phenomenon theoretically by articulating a concept of "religious liminars," those people who are neither secular nor religious. More recently, work by Packard and Hope (2015) addressed the central question of how a person actually makes the decision to move away from organized religion, and Ammerman (2013a; 2013b) documents the shift into a more spiritual "everyday" life where religion is no longer constrained by its own institution.

Each of these investigations addresses a different aspect of the same, inescapable phenomenon. Namely, institutional religion is going through a period of massive upheaval in the United States as people opt for more individualized, customized and personal expressions of faith. For a country with strong historical ties to institutional religion, this trend is bound to have significant ramifications.

This chapter is primarily concerned, then, with addressing the following questions: Why are people increasingly moving away from organized religion? What factors influence these decisions and how and why do some people come back to organized religion after claiming no religious affiliation? Furthermore, what does it mean for a society when traditional religious expressions fall away or transform?

WHERE ARE WE NOW?

Religious disaffiliation, or the active choice to select "none" as a religious preference, is a growing phenomenon in the United States. A 2012 report from *The Pew Forum on Religion and Public Life* reports that "[o]ne-fifth of the U.S. public—and a third of adults under 30—are religiously unaffiliated today, the highest percentages ever in Pew Research Center polling" with recent years seeing massive increases (Funk and Smith 2011:9). Furthermore, the percentage of U.S. adults who identify as Protestant has declined from a recent peak of nearly 80% in the late 1970s to around 55% by 2014 (Funk and Smith 2011). Others, non-Christian faiths, have picked up a larger share of members, but they still account for less than 6% of the overall religious landscape in America (Funk and Smith 2011).

And yet, by many other measures, people are every bit as religious as they once were. Polling by Gallup shows that the percentage of Americans claiming that religion is "very important" in their lives has remained more or less steady at around 60% since the early 1990s. Furthermore, the percentage of people who believe in God has

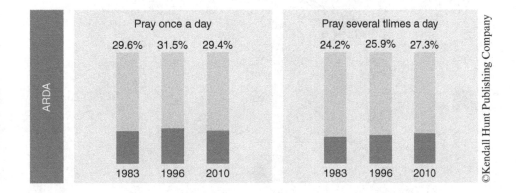

declined only modestly from 95% in 1944 to 86% in 2014 (See http://www.gallup.com/poll/1690/religion.aspx)while spiritual practices like daily prayer have actually seen an uptick in recent decades (Association of Religion Data Archives. See http://www.thearda.com/quickstats/qs_104_t.asp).

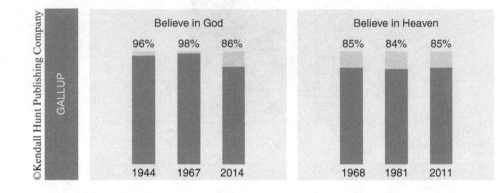

Mark Chaves, a prominent sociologist of religion, picks up on these same trends. While affiliation and participation with traditional religious organizations is declining, he points out that "the percentages of Americans who know that God exists (64%) say they've had a born-again experience (36%), and who pray several times a week (69%) have remained steady since the 1980s" (Chaves 2011b:1–2). Rather than calling current trends a decline in overall religious behavior, he prefers to designate the current era as a "softening" of involvement with traditional religious structures.

So what are we to make of this mish-mash of data? How are we supposed to understand a world where affiliation is down while belief and practice hold relatively steady or even increase?

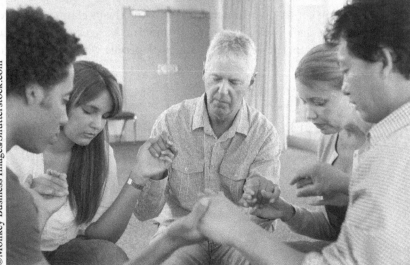

Further complicating this issue is that we know comparatively little about how people come to identify as religiously unaffiliated in the first place. Existing research has suffered from a lack of sustained interest and full-scale studies devoted to the issue. As long ago as 1968, Vernon (1968) lamented that religious "none" was a "neglected category," but his article failed to inspire much serious investigation. Similarly, Condran and Tamney (1985) wrote a 25-year history of the category in their article in *Sociology of Religion* hoping to spur on some research, but their article has been only cursorily noted as well. More recently, Baker and Smith (2009a, 2009b) revived work in this category by identifying the predictive factors of someone claiming "none" as a status and then articulating categories of religious nones as either atheist, agnostic, or unchurched. This is, as you may have surmised by this point, not an exhaustive list of possibilities.

Is it not possible to claim no religious affiliation while also retaining a belief in God? Of course it is. This is but one illustration of many throughout this text that underscores the importance of having a firm connection between empirical reality and theoretical categorization. The theories matter, because they tell us what to look for (and what to ignore) in the data. Without better theoretical constructs than "affiliation" to account for people's organized religious behavior, we have been left with a sub-par understanding of how people actually experience religion in the 21st century.

©Castleski/Shutterstock.com

I first gained insight into this issue when I was researching for my book *The Emerging Church: Religion at the Margins* (Packard 2012). Consistent with the Pew report, I found many people forgoing corporate worship experiences because they were dissatisfied with organized religion in general rather than with any particular doctrine, teaching, or pastor. Following Hammond, (2001) I referred to these people as the dechurched. Later, working with Ashleigh Hope (Packard and Hope 2015) I came to call this group the "**dones**" in explicit opposition to the "nones" described above. The "dones" still claim a religious affiliation, but they do not attend institutional church (i.e., they are "done" with church). Instead, they choose to organize their faith lives

> **"Dones"** People who consider themselves to be religious but who do not belong to a faith community nor regularly attend one.

outside of the institution in more informal gatherings with friends, neighbors, and colleagues. Eschewing the traditional, pastor-led model, these people gather in homes, volunteer at non-profits and generally spend more time engaged with their local communities rather than being active in their local congregations.

Nancy Ammerman (2013a) refers to this shift in the organization of religious belief and practice as a move toward a more spiritual "everyday life." While many have taken the numbers about rising number of "nones" as a confirmation of the long-awaited decline of religion in the United States, Ammerman argues that religion has not disappeared, rather it has shifted. She writes that "in a time of significant change, we cannot assume we will find religion in the predictable places or in the predictable forms. And if we do not find as much of it in those predictable places as we did before, we cannot assume that it is disappearing" (Ammerman 2013a:6). These findings stand in stark contrast to the earlier understanding of secularization (discussed in Chapter 2) which sees a less conventionally religious world as one where religion is necessarily less important.

Ammerman goes further in her conceptualization of religion in everyday life when she advances the idea that ALL institutional boundaries have become more porous, not just religious institutional boundaries. Work no longer stays at work. Indeed, the things we consider "work" are no longer confined to just those things that pay wages and conversely our wages increasingly are not paid by a single employer. Further, politics, civic engagement, and a whole host of other social institutions have similarly undefined or blurred boundaries.

©Brian A. Jackson/Shutterstock.com

So also with religion. Our individual beliefs might remain strong as we carry religion with us throughout our daily lives into all of the various spheres that we move through in the course of a day, while actual institutional participation could be on the decline. Moving into a world where institutions are no longer the dominant organizing force of religious expression is uncharted territory. What effect do you think this will have on our society? What other social structures will we need to build up or create if religious institutions decline?

HOW DID WE GET HERE?

Instead, what is emerging is a picture of modern religion and spirituality that transcends institutions and traditional expressions. We can turn to Christian Smith's research to understand some of the roots of this modern behavior. His work, most notably with Melissa Lundquist Denton in *Soul Searching* looks at the religious and spiritual lives of teenagers and other young people in America. Drawing heavily on the National Study of Youth and Religion, they find that the characteristics that make up as religion for many of Americas youth can be summed up as **Moralistic Therapeutic Deism**. Young people believe that God (1) exists, (2) wants people to be nice, (3) wants people to be happy, (4) is available when you have a problem, and (5) brings people to heaven when they die (Smith and Denton 2005).

Summing up this position, they write that God is "something like a combination of Divine Butler and Cosmic Therapist" (Smith and Denton 2005:165). That is, God is always on call, ready to serve you when you need something, and God is there to help you solve problems either with advice or, occasionally, intervention. Gone are the days when young people believed in a retributive and jealous God who stood ready to punish people for their sins.

> **Moralistic Therapeutic** The idea that a divinity exists and one that is invested in individuals' happiness and psychological wellbeing.

©KieferPix/Shutterstock.com

This is quite the turnaround. In just a generation the faith of an entire portion of our population has shifted dramatically. I think here about my own parents, one raised Lutheran and the other Catholic. While their understanding of God included aspects of grace and love, there were also very real components of moral accountability, judgment, and punishment. There were, in short, consequences in this world and beyond for daily behaviors.

When I present this position to my students in a Sociology of Religion course, their responses vacillate between disbelief and disgust. Many of them cannot even comprehend that there was a time not long ago where those characteristics were the dominant components of mainstream Christian faith in the United States, and others can certainly believe it. . . and it angers them. Regardless of which position they take, exceedingly few of them express that their own understanding of God, Christian or otherwise, fits into that same paradigm. In fact, my students tend to express views very much like ones uncovered by Smith and Denton. Even my agnostic and atheist students explained how they believed others experienced God in that same way.

Essentially, they express that God is a friend you can call on in times of need. God is wise and can offer insight in to making your relationships and life better. God loves you like a good parent loves you. But God doesn't get too involved in telling you what to do every minute of every day.

While this may sound like a watered-down version of faith that is not actually practiced by serious believers, ask yourself this question: How often have you implored God to help you on an exam or in a sporting event? How often have you turned to God with your problems? Or, if you do not believe in God, think about the times and places where you have heard and seen others do these things. The way we interact with God signifies a great deal about the assumptions that underlie our beliefs. Petitioning God with our problems is based on an assumption that God cares and that prayer will be an effective way to solve these issues.

©Lolostock/Shutterstock.com

While it may seem that the idea of a caring and interested God should be assumed, this has not always been the case. In fact, in many religious traditions, especially the Christian ones that make up the vast majority of belief in the United States, this is a relatively recent turn—one which reflects the push toward individualism on all levels.

Over 30 years ago, Robert Bellah and his coauthors wrote *Habits of the Heart* wherein he famously documented the beliefs of Sheila. Sheila explained her faith to him by saying, "I believe in God. I'm not a religious fanatic. I can't remember the last time I went to church. My faith has carried me a long way. It's Sheilaism. Just my own little voice...It's just try to love yourself and be gentle with yourself. You know, I guess, take care of each other. I think He would want us to take care of each other" (Bellah et al., 1986: 221). Sociologists and others took this startling admission as a sign of the decline of traditional religious authority.

Instead of people adhering strictly to a set of beliefs offered by Christianity or Buddhism or some other religious tradition, the latter part of the 20th century saw a shift toward an explicitly and intentionally constructed religion. Individuals increasingly claimed to be **"spiritual but not religious" (SBNR)** where they refused to identify with any particular religious tradition or system. Sheila summed up these sentiments perfectly in her description of her own spirituality.

Putting in this context, then, the idea that religious expression is shifting outside of the institution in modern times is not so far-fetched an idea. People are increasingly growing up in an individualized and atomized society where even connections are mediated by technology in the form of social media. It is no wonder, then, that we have cultivated religious expressions that are similarly tailored.

©iurii/Shutterstock.com

SO, WHERE ARE WE GOING?

While it is somewhat easy to trace back the more recent historical antecedents to the decline of institutional religion in the United States, it is a bit more difficult to project into the future. In order to begin projecting the future of religion and religious participation, it is important to understand the particular dynamics that make up the **religious marketplace** in the United States.

In his exhaustive work on the social history of the church in America, Rodney Stark, working with various colleagues, helped to pioneer a market-based approach to understanding the ebbs and flows of religious adherence and affiliation. This position takes as its basic premise that the field of religion is a marketplace where various belief systems and groups compete for members on the basis of promised rewards. These rewards might be present in this world (e.g., self-fulfillment, peace, financial gain) or saved for the afterlife (e.g., heaven). We discussed this in Chapter 2. The result of this competitive marketplace is that various religious organizations are constantly innovating in order to attract members and sustain their operations. Without members coming in and supporting the organization with time, talent, and money, the organization will simply die away.

This stands in stark contrast to the state-supported religious systems found in much of Europe and other places in the world where an official church is supported through taxation from a centralized government.

Religious marketplace The sociological view that understands the various religions within a society as competing to attract and retain members.

The long history of religious innovation in this country can be traced through multiple spiritual revivals, Great Awakenings, the development of new sects, the most recent major world religion (see Mormonism) and countless denominations and types of religious expression. Through these events and movements, religious entrepreneurs have managed to consistently attract a large swathe of the American population with innovative religious "products."

As one example of this, let's look at the modern megachurch movement. Borne out of the first attempt to apply market-research principles to religion, the megachurch movement developed first in Chicago with Willow Creek in the late 1970s. Surveying the suburbs of Chicago revealed that the thing people disliked most about church was that it was boring. Armed with this insight, Bill Hybels, the founder of Willow Creek, set out to create, first and foremost, a church that wasn't boring.

This simple innovation brought about a massive transformation in the way that evangelical Christianity was produced and delivered over the last 30 years in this country. In the process of attracting massive amounts of people to these congregations, traditional, denominationally affiliated, liturgically based churches have seen a steady decline.

The shift toward these large, corporatized religious expressions in turn spawned their own innovation, the Emerging Church Movement (ECM). The ECM is a movement within Protestant Christianity in the early decades of the 21st century that distinctly resists institutionalized religious organization. Rather than cultivating the religious spectacle and performance oriented worship that characterizes the megachurch, the ECM turned toward smaller and less well organized gatherings, often in people's homes. Occupying this niche in the religious field allowed them to attract a segment of the religious marketplace that would not otherwise have gone to church.

This dynamic is but one example of how change in the religious marketplace is not simply a natural evolution, but rather the outcome of a distinct process of innovation by entrepreneurs who articulate new messages and offer new products. Spinning this process forward, it would seem that the current decline in religious affiliation, coupled with relatively strong levels of belief in general would lend itself to a period of substantial innovation.

Assuming this religious marketplace thesis is correct, what would you think is the next great innovation in religion in this country? What kind of religious expressions will resonate with millenials and the generations that follow?

©alexreynolds/Shutterstock.com

STEPPING BOLDLY INTO THE FUTURE

So what are we to make of the future of religion? Is it declining as a social force or is it simply waiting for the next great innovation to drive it forward? Should we, as social scientists, continue to care and think deeply about this venerable social institution? So many scholars over the years have predicted the decline and eventual disappearance of religion as a global social force, and so many have been wrong, that it seems foolish to think that religion will completely disappear or even diminish to the point of irrelevance.

As we have documented elsewhere throughout this text, religion continues to play an important role in everything from local politics to global terrorism to the way people construct meaning in their individual lives. As an institution, it still manages to compel massive amounts of dollars, volunteer hours, and adherents. While it may be simmering down in some places, if we look beyond our own borders we find that religion remains a potent and universal force.

The sociological study of religion undergirded the very first questions that sociologists asked about the world. Durkheim was interested in the way that religion as a social institution held people together, Marx understood the ideology of religious systems as an important mechanism for achieving social control and for the powerful to retain their power, and Weber recognized the central role that religious systems played in justifying and creating cultural systems. Despite this, there have been repeated and regular calls for sociologists to give up the study of religion, academic jobs for sociologists of religion are few and far in between (indeed, your co-authors for this book were hired to teach and other things and are grateful they are "allowed" to advance a research agenda that takes religion as a central focus), and religious research has regularly been downplayed even among sociologists. Indeed, in the 110-year history of the American Sociological Association there has not been a single President who took the study of religion as her/his central focus.

And yet, looking at recent global events, it is impossible to understand our current social world without at least a passing understanding of how religion works to organize people. Without a sociological understanding of religion, one cannot understand modern global terrorism, American politics, climate change, the importance of shift in policy, and tone introduced by Pope Francis, the politics of marriage in America and around the world, and countless other examples.

We cannot assert the importance of religion for understanding the world around us while continuing to ignore it in the academy. As you read this, you probably sit in Sociology of Religion course. Maybe you have even chosen to take this class as an elective. Hopefully, you chose it because you were interested in the topic and not just because it was the last class left that fit in your schedule and filled a requirement!

In any event, as you have come to the end of the course, what thoughts do you have? Is this a worthy topic of study? Should your tax dollars, spent to support public universities, be spent to support the academic study and teaching of religion? On a more practical level, as you take this bit of sociology with you out into the world, how will your life be impacted? What types of things do you think about differently now?

A sociological perspective on a topic as personal and intimate as religion is difficult to obtain. Whether you are religious or not, you almost certainly had ideas about religion when you began this course. Were those rooted in a sociological perspective or personal experience? Our sincere hope is that at this point we have not eradicated your ideas about religion rooted in personal experience, but that we have managed to enhance them by offering a sociological component. We want you to carry both of these things, the personal and the sociological, with you as you forward and think, feel and experience religion.

DISCUSSION QUESTIONS

1. Are people as religious as they were 40 or 50 years ago? What empirical evidence supports your answer?
2. What is meant by the concept "dechurched" and what are the factors that contribute to people who are dechurched?
3. What is meant by "religious disaffiliation" and what generation is most likely to disaffiliate from institutionalized religion and why?
4. Who is most likely to subscribe to moralistic therapeutic deism and why?
5. What is the Emerging Church Movement? How does it reflect the contemporary patterns in religious affiliation?
6. What is "Sheila-ism"? Do you think Sheila-ism is common amongst your peers? How do you think people in your grandparents' generation would think about Sheila-ism?

GLOSSARY

Achieved: something one can be born into but is either solely or also chosen/selected by the individual.

Agency: individual's ability to act on her or his own accord.

Alienation: the separation caused by modern capitalism that takes place between people and within individuals that keeps people at odds with one another and even with their own inherent nature.

American exceptionalism: the belief that the United States is unique, special, and blessed by God.

Anomie: the state of uncertainty and anxiety.

Ascribed: a social category one is born into.

Biblical inerrancy: the idea that the Bible is the literal word of God, is completely factual, and contains no errors.

Bureaucracy: the kind of organization in which groups are compartmentalized according to specific purposes, activities, and functions.

Calculability: how much something costs compared to the amount or quality of product received; can be figured mathematically.

Civil Religion: public religious dimension expressed in a set of beliefs, symbols, and rituals.

Color-blind racism: the belief that racism no longer exists, which ignores how race continues to play a role in ongoing inequalities.

Commodity fetishization: when, as a result of the global capitalist economic system, people begin to value goods over human beings and begin to treat human beings as though they were things.

Complementarianism: the view that women and men are essentially different and thus have separate but equal and necessary roles to play.

Conspicuous consumption: the purchasing of ostentatious items that are meant to show off one's wealth to others.

Consumerism: the belief in modern society that the purchasing of goods and services is a valuable activity in support of a capitalist economy.

Cult: a religion far outside societal norms, generally consisting of a small groups of followers who devote their lives to their cult leader/their cult ideas; generally understood as something negative although many new mainstream religions started out as what we now understand as cults.

Cultural-ethnic Jew: someone who is Jewish by birth and/or marriage, identifies as Jewish, but does not belong to a synagogue.

Dispensationalism: the idea that God has divided history into well-defined eras of time.

Dones: people who consider themselves to be religious but who do not belong to a faith community nor regularly attend one.

Double Consciousness: term, coined by W.E. B. Du Bois, referring to how certain groups of individuals are forced to maintain two different perspectives simultaneously; for example, African Americans historically were forced to view themselves not only as their own community of African Americans does, but also how White society views them.

Economist perspective: view that all religious organizations can be interpreted as religious "producers" and they compete for a limited number of consumers.

Edge religion: a religion not fully understood as such by mainstream society; generally existing on the outskirts, or "edges" of society and its norms; the politically correct term for "cult".

Efficiency: the successfulness of a way for accomplishing a task; typically understood as how quickly and well something can be done simultaneously.

Essentialism: the belief that men and women are essentially, or "naturally," different based solely on biological characteristics.

False consciousness: the state of mind in which people do not see their own oppression and exploitation.

Functional differentiation: process whereby individual institutions have an increasingly narrow specialization with regard to what each provides for people in everyday life.

Gender: socially constructed understanding of one's masculinity or femininity, generally understood as one of two categories, woman or man; more recently many terms describing people who do identify somewhere else or nowhere on a "gender spectrum" have emerged.

Institutionalized racism: policies, laws, or regulations that either intentionally or unintentionally help members of one racial group while preventing members of another racial group from accessing valuable resources.

Institutions: communities, organizations, or collectivities that are made up of bundles of roles.

Irrational: not logical or reasonable.

Islamophobia: the irrational fear of Muslims.

Liminal period: the stage between an old identity and the new identity.

McDonaldization: the permeation of rationalization into all social institutions.

Megachurch: a church that hosts at least 2,000 people over the course of a weekend.

Mind-Body-Spirit (MBS): type of therapeutic religion with an emphasis on self-actualization through self-healing facilitated by the mind to create mental and physical well-being; integrates a belief in the spiritual nature or soul of the self.

Modernity: before 1968, some argue it began with the Enlightenment and others with the rise of industrialization, basic understanding of the natural sciences as revolutionary and the acceptance of "Grand narratives" to guide people.

Moralistic therapeutic deism: the idea that a divinity exists and one that is invested in individuals' happiness and psychological wellbeing.

Neoliberalism: the ideology that values laissez-faire-style government and emphasizes individual agency.

Network: pattern of people in various institutional or personal roles.

Norm: a behavior or thought that is socially acceptable and generally socially expected.

Normal: something/someone that is generally perceived as good and/or healthy; can also be understood as average or plain.

Particularism: the belief that one's own religion is the only true religion; all other religions are false.

Plausibility structure: the set of interactions and behaviors of a group of people that help to make a situation real.

Polity: the way in which religious organizations are structured.

Postmodernity: beginning the year after 1968, acceptance of the "fuzziness" that is life and a rise in skepticism, even of progressive ideas.

Predictability: the likelihood that something is going to happen; also the likelihood of something to repeat, occur again.

Privatized: when something becomes relevant to individuals on a personal level rather than to groups on an institutional level.

Proselytizing: when a religious group actively seeks out new members, attempting to convince people to convert to their religion via persuasion.

Queer: anything that deviates from what is generally understood as "normal"; odd or strange; any sexuality that is not "straight" or heterosexual.

Rationalization: the process wherein society becomes increasingly ordered and structured according to rules and regulations.

Reaffirmation: the means by which a person chooses to adopt the religion in which they were raised.

Reify: to confirm something to be true or exist.

Relativistic: point of view that there is no single version of the truth or single path to salvation; each group is true "in its own way".

Religion: the social institution established to incorporate the divinity into everyday life.

Religiosity: socially constructed idea to describe the level at which someone is or is not religious; measures vary.

Religious "nones": a growing group of people who identify as spiritual but not religious.

Religious marketplace: the sociological view that understands the various religions within a society as competing to attract and retain members.

Religious pluralism: there are a wide variety of religions that are available to people.

Rite of passage: a ritual, often formal and required, that one undergoes marking the transition from an old personal identity to a new one.

Roles: personal identities that are characterized by a set of norms.

Sacred canopy: an institution that functions to protect us from feeling like existence is meaningless; a metaphor for religion.

Sacred: something/someone that is held in extremely high regard.

Secularization: the "dereligioning" of society; stems from the word "secular," which generally means anything that is not religious; the process by which sectors in society and culture are removed from the denomination of religious institutions (Berger).

Seekers: someone who has grown up in a traditional religious church, is dissatisfied with that, and now searching for another form of religion that relies less on what they see as arbitrary rules, and more on community, comfort, and a message that is more relevant to living in the world today; or someone who has grown up with the absence of any religious tradition and is now in search of one that they might identify with.

Sex: biological understanding of oneself as either male or female; with the exception of intersex (ambiguous genitalia).

Social Construction: something that does not exist except in the fact that collective "we" think it does.

Social drift theory: a gradual process of changing religious ideas; suggests there are both "push" and "pull" factors that drive us away from a current religion or lack thereof and guide us to a new religion or lack thereof, in order to find meaning.

Socialization: process wherein an individual learns and internalizes the appropriate norms that allow them to fulfill their roles within an institution.

Solipsism: the belief that we live in a completely isolated reality, in which we can never know for certain whether or not we or anything/anyone else around us is real.

Symbol: something that stands for something else.

Technology: technique, method, or equipment used to accomplish a task efficiently.

Therapeutic Religion: includes self-motivation and positive reinforcement in practice; built around the idea that each of us is "good enough" and that we matter.

BIBLIOGRAPHY

Albanese, Catherine L. "Metaphysical Movements," in *The Cambridge History of Religions in America, Volume II, 1790–1945*, ed. Stephen Stein (Cambridge, UK: Cambridge University Press, 2012), 435–56.

Aldridge, Alan. *Religion in the Contemporary World: A Sociological Introduction, 3rd Edition*. (Cambridge: Polity Press, 2013).

Allitt, Patrick. *Religion in America since 1945: A History* (New York: Columbia University Press, 2003).

Ammerman, Nancy. *Bible Believers: Fundamentalists in the Modern World* (New Brunswick, NJ: Rutgers University Press, 1987).

Ammerman, Nancy. *Sacred Stories, Spiritual Tribes: Finding Religion in Everyday Life* (New York: Oxford University Press, 2013a).

Ammerman, Nancy. "Spiritual but not Religious? Beyond Binary Choices in the Study of Religion." *Journal for the Scientific Study of Religion* 52 (2013b): 258–78.

Baer, Hans A. *The Black Spiritual Movement: A Religious Response to Racism* (Knoxville, TN: University of Tennessee Press, 1984).

Baker, Joseph O'Brian, and Buster Smith. "None Too Simple: Examining Issues of Religious Nonbelief and Nonbelonging in the United States." *Journal for the Scientific Study of Religion* 48 (2009a): 719–33.

Baker, Joseph O'Brian, and Buster Smith. "The Nones: Social Characteristics of the Religiously Unaffiliated." *Social Forces* 87(2009b): 1251–63.

Belk, Russell W., Melanie Wallendorf, and John F. Sherry. "The Sacred and the Profane in Consumer Behavior: Theodicy on the Odyssey." *Journal of Consumer Research* 16(1989), 1–38.

Bellah, Robert N. *Beyond Belief: Essays on Religion in a Post-Traditional World (New York: Harper and Row, 1970)*.

Bellah, Robert, Richard Madsen, William Sullivan, Ann Swidler, and Steven Tipton. *Habits of the Heart: Individualism and Commitment in American Life* (Berkeley, CA: University of California Press, 1985).

Bendroth, Margaret. "Fundamentalism," in *The Cambridge History of Religions in America, Volume II, 1790–1945*, ed. Stephen Stein (Cambridge, UK: Cambridge University Press, 2012), 569–594.

Berger, Peter and Thomas Luckmann. *The Social Construction of Reality* (Garden City, NY: Doubleday, 1966).

Bonilla-Silva, Eduardo. *Racism without Racists: Color-blind Racism and the Persistence of Racial Inequality in America* (New York: Rowman and Littlefield, 2013).

Bruce, S. "Secularization and the Impotence of Individualized Religion." *Hedgehog Review* Spring/Summer (2006): 35–45.

Capps, Kriston. 2015. "How Real-Estate Brokers Can Profit from Retrieved from Racial Tipping Points." *Atlantic*. Retrieved March 21, 2016, from URL: http://www.citylab.com/housing/2015/03/how-real-estate-brokers-can-profit-from-racial-tipping-points/386674/?utm_source=SFFB.

Chaves, Mark. *Congregations in America.* (Cambridge, MA: Harvard University Press, 2004).

Chaves, Mark. *American Religion: Contemporary Trends* (Princeton, NJ: Princeton University Press, 2011a).

Chaves, Mark. 2011b. "The Decline of American Religion?" (ARDA Guiding Paper Series). State College, PA: The Association of Religion Data Archives at The Pennsylvania State University, from http://www.thearda.com/rrh/papers/guidingpapers.asp.

Chryssides, George D. and Margaret Z. Wilkins, ed. *A Reader in New Religious Movements* (London, UK: Continuum, 2006).

Clark, Geoffrey. *Betting on Lives: The Culture of* Life Insurance *in England, 1695–1775* (Manchester, UK: Manchester University Press, 1999).

Condran, John G. and Joseph B. Tamney. "Religious 'Nones': 1957 to 1982." *Sociology of Religion* 46 (1985): 415–23.

Cowan, Douglas E. and David G. Bromley. *Cults and New Religions: A Brief History* (Malden, MA: Blackwell, 2008).

Daly, Mary. [1968]. *The Church and the Second Sex* (Boston, MA: Beacon Press, 1985).

Daly, Mary. *Beyond God the Father: Toward a Philosophy of Women's Liberation* (Boston, MA: Beacon Press, 1973).

Davidman, Lynn. *Becoming Un-Orthodox: Stories of Ex-Hasidic Jews.* (Oxford: Oxford University Press, 2014).

Dewaay, Bob. *Redefining Christianity: Understanding the Purpose Driven Life Movement* (Springfield, MO: 21st Century Press, 2006).

Du Bois, W.E.B. *The Souls of Black Folk.* (Mineola, NY: Dover, 1994).

Einstein, M. *Brands of Faith: Marketing Religion in a Commercial Age* (London: Routledge, 2008).

Einwohner, Rachel L., Leamaster, Reid J., and Benjamin Pratt. "Push, Pull, and Fusion: Women's Activism and Religious Institutions" (Forthcoming).

Ellison, Christopher G., Boardman, Jason D., Williams, David R., and James S. Jackson. "Religious Involvement, Stress, and Mental Health: Findings from the 1995 Detroit Area Study." *Social Forces* 80 (2001): 215–249.

Emerson, Michael O., Mirola, William A., and Susanne C. Monahan. *Religion Matters: What Sociology Teaches Us About Religion in Our World* (Boston, MA: Pearson, 2011).

Farnsley, Arthur E. "Faith-Based Initiatives," in *The Sage Handbook of the Sociology of Religion*, eds. James A. Beckford and N. J. Demerath, III (Los Angeles, CA: Sage, 2007), 345–56.

Fausto-Sterling, Anne. *Sexing the Body: Gender Politics and the Construction of Sexuality* (New York: Basic Books, 2000).

Finke, Roger and Rodney Stark. *The Churching of America, 1776–1990: Winners and Losers in Our Religious Economy* (New Brunswick, NJ: Rutgers University Press, 1992).

Funk, Cary and Greg Smith. "'Nones' on the rise: One-in-five adults have no religious affiliation." *Washington, DC, Pew Research Center* (2012).

Glock, Charles and Rodney Stark. *Religion and Society in Tension*. (San Francisco, CA: Rand McNalley, 1965).

Hammond, Mary Tuomi. *The Church and the Dechurched: Mending a Damaged Faith* (St. Louis: Chalice Press, 2001).

Hedges, Ellie and James Beckford. "Holism, Healing and the New Age," in *Beyond New Age: Exploring Alternative Spirituality*, eds. Bowman, Steven Sutcliffe and Marion (Edinburgh: Edinburgh University Press, 2000), 169–87.

Iannoccone, Laurence R. "Why Strict Churches Are Strong." *American Journal of Sociology* 99 (1994).

Iannoccone, Laurence R. *Rational Choice: Framework for the Scientific Study of Religion*. (New York: Routledge, 1997).

Johnson, Benton. "On Church and Sect." *American Sociological Review* 28 (1963): 539–49.

Johnson, Sarah E. "Gender," in *The Blackwell Companion to Religion in America*, ed. Philip Goff (Malden, MA: Wiley-Blackwell, 2011), 147–62.

Johnson, Sylvester. "The Black Church," in *The Blackwell Companion to Religion in America*, ed. Philip Goff (Malden, MA: Wiley-Blackwell, 2011), 446–67.

Johnston, Erin F. "'I Was Always This Way…': Rhetorics of Continuity in Narratives of Conversion." *Sociological Forum* 28 (2013): 549–73.

Katzenstein, Mary F. *Faithful and Fearless: Moving Feminist Protest Inside the Church and Military* (Princeton, NJ: Princeton University Press, 1998).

Kelley, Dean. *Why Conservative Churches are Growing*. (Macon, GA: Mercer University Press, 1996).

Kozol, Jonathan. *Savage Inequalities: Children in America's Schools* (New York: Broadway Books, 2012).

Lim, Chaeyoon, Carol Ann MacGregor, and Robert D. Putnam. "Secular and Liminal: Discovering Heterogeneity among Religious Nones." *Journal for the Scientific Study of Religion* 49 (2010): 596–18.

Lippy, Charles. *Pluralism Comes of Age: American Religious Culture in the Twentieth Century*. (New York: Routledge, 2000).

Lofland, John. *Doomsday Cult* (New York: Irvington, 1977).

Luckmann, Thomas. *The Invisible Religion* (New York: Macmillan, 1967).

Marx, Karl. *Critique of Hegel's "Philosophy of Right."* (Cambridge: Cambridge University Press, 1977).

McGuire, Meredith B. *Religion: The Social Context* (Belmont, CA: Wadsworth, 1992).

Miller, Daniel. *A Theory of Shopping* (Ithaca, NY: Cornell University Press, 1998).

Miller, Donald A. *Reinventing American Protestantism: Christianity in the New Millennium* (Berkeley, CA: University of California Press, 1997).

Moosa, Ebrahim. "Post 9/11: America Agonizes over Islam," in *The Cambridge History of Religions in America, Volume III, 1945 to the Present*, ed. Stephen Stein (Cambridge, UK: Cambridge University Press, 2012), 553–74.

Morrill, Susanna. "Women," in *The Blackwell Companion to Religion in America*, ed. Philip Goff (Malden, MA: Wiley-Blackwell, 2010), 376–94.

Morris, Aldon. "The Black Church in the Civil Rights Movement: The SCLC as the Decentralized, Radical Arm of the Black Church," in *Disruptive Religion: The Force of Faith in Social Movement Activism*, ed. Christian Smith (New York: Routledge, 1996), 29–46.

Olson, Laura R. "Religious Affiliations, Political Preferences, and Ideological Alignments," in *The Sage Handbook of the Sociology of Religion*, eds. James A. Beckford and N. J. Demerath, III (Los Angeles, CA: Sage, 2007), 438–57.

Packard, Josh. *The Emerging Church: Religion at the Margins* (Boulder, CO: Lynne-Rienner/First Forum, 2012).

Packard, Josh and Ashleigh Hope. *Church Refugees: Sociologists Reveal Why People Are DONE with the Church, but not Their Faith* (Loveland, CO: Group Publishing, 2015).

Pitt, Richard N. "'Still Looking for My Jonathan': Gay Black Men's Management of Religious and Sexual Identity Conflicts." *Journal of Homosexuality* 57 (2010): 39–53.

Procter-Smith, Marjorie. "Women and Religion in Modern America," in *The Cambridge History of Religions in America, Volume III, 1945 to the Present*, ed. Stephen Stein (Cambridge, UK: Cambridge University Press, 2012), 488–510.

Ritzer, George. *The McDonaldization of Society* (London: Sage, 2015).

Roberts, Keith A. *Religion in Sociological Perspective, 4th Edition* (Belmont, CA: Wadsworth, 2004).

Roberts, Keith A. and David Yamane. *Religion in Sociological Perspective, 6th Edition* (Los Angeles, CA: Sage, 2016).

Roof, Wade Clark and William McKinney. *American Mainline Religion: Its Changing Shape and Future* (New Brunswick, NJ: Rutgers University Press, 1987).

Sargeant, K. H. *Seeker Churches: Promoting Traditional Religion in a Nontraditional Way* (New Brunswick, NJ: Rutgers University Press, 2000).

Smith, Christian and Melinda Lundquist Denton. *Soul Searching: The Religious and Spiritual Lives of American Teenagers* (New York: Oxford University Press, 2005).

Sodal, Helje Kringlebotn. "'Victor, not Victim': Joel Osteen's Rhetoric of Hope." *Journal of Contemporary Religion* 25 (2010): 37–50.

Sointu, Eeva and Linda Woodhead. "Spirituality, Gender, and Expressive Selfhood." *Journal for the Scientific Study of Religion* 47 (2008): 259–76.

Stark, Rodney and William S. Bainbridge. *The Future of Religion: Secularization, Revival and Cult Formation.* (Berkeley, CA: University of California Press, 1985).

Taussig, M. "The Genesis of Capitalism Amongst a South American Peasantry: Devil's Labor and the Baptism of Money." *Comparative Studies in Society and History*, 19 (1977), 130–55.

Thomas, William I. and Dorothy Thomas. *The Child in America.* (New York: Alfred Knopf, 1928).

Thumma, Scott, Travis, Dave, and Warren Bird. 2005. "Megachurches Today." Retrieved March 1, 2016 from URL: http://hirr.hartsem.edu/megachurch/megastoday2005_summaryreport.html.

Thumma, Scott and Warren Bird. *Changes in American Megachurches: Tracing Eight Years of Growth and Innovation in the Nation's Largest-Attendance Congregations* (Hartford Institute for Religion Research, 2008).

Turner, Victor. *The Ritual Process: Structure and Anti-Structure* (Chicago, IL: Aldine, 1969).

Twitchell, James B.. *Branded Nation: The Marketing of Megachurch, College Inc., and Museumworld.* 2004 (92).

Vargas, Nicholas. "Retrospective Accounts of Religious Disaffiliation in the United States: Stressors, Skepticism, and Political Factors." *Sociology of Religion* 73 (2012): 200–23.

Weber, Max. *The Protestant* Ethic *and the "Spirit" of Capitalism and Other Writings.* (New York: Penguin, 2002).

West, Cornel. *Race Matters* (New York: Vintage, 1994).

White, James Emery. *The Rise of the Nones: Understanding and Reaching the Religiously Unaffiliated* (Grand Rapids, MI: Baker Books, 2014).

Williams, Peter W. *America's Religions: From Their Origins to the Twenty-First Century* (Urbana, IL: University of Illinois Press, [1990] 2002).

Wuthnow, Robert. *After Heaven: Spirituality in America Since the 1950's.* (Berkeley, CA: University of California Press, 1998).

Zelizer, Viviana. *The Social Meaning of Money* (New York: Basic Books, 1994).

INDEX

A

Abortion, 135
Abrahamic religion, 16–18
Active churchgoers, 10
African Americans
    after slavery, 103–107
    agency and structure, 97–100
    black power, 113–115
    institutionalized racism, 107–111
    1950s and beyond, 111–113
    racial equality, 101–103
    Social Gospel, 115–118
Agency and social structures, 97–100
Alienation, 74
Allitt, Patrick, 136
American exceptionalism, 137
American religious landscape, 241
American Sociological Association, 253
Ammerman, Nancy, 130, 246
Anomie, 170
Applewhite, Marshall, 227, 228
Asuza Street Revival, 104
Atheists, 180
Auditing, 236
Ayurvedic medicine, 186

B

Bakker, Jim, 134
Bakker, Tammy Faye, 134
Baptism of the bill practice, 212
Barna Group, 209
Bauman, Zygmunt, 88, 89, 91, 92
Becker, Howard, 11

Belief, 34
Bellah, Robert, 180, 183, 189, 248
Berger, Peter, 11, 14, 42–44, 46, 184–185
Beruf, 82, 83, 84
*Beyond God the Father: Toward a Philosophy of
    Women's Liberation* (Mary Daly), 157
Bible Believer: Fundamentalists in the Modern World
    (1987), 130
Biblical inerrancy, 121, 122
Black Christian churches, 112
Black cultural armor, 117
Black liberation theology, 115
The Black Manifesto (James Forman), 115
Black power, 113–115
Black Theology and Black Power
    (James Cone), 114
Blockbusting practice, 110
Book of Genesis, 151
Book of Revelation, 125–127
Born-again experience, 121
Brown v. Board of Education, 111
Buddhism, 22–24, 219
Bureaucracy, 79
Bush, George W., Sr., 135, 138, 139

C

Calvin, John, 82
Capitalism, 69, 70, 74
Catholicism, 81
Catholic Worker, 115
Catholic Worker Movement, 115
Chaves, Mark, 10, 244
Christian Broadcasting Network, 133
Christian Coalition, 134

Christian evangelicalism, 121–123
Christian fundamentalism, 121–123
  Bible Believer: Fundamentalists in the Modern World
    (1987), 130
  Book of Revelation, 125–127
  end of world and Christ's reign, 126
  "The Fundamentals: A Testimony of the Truth,"
  historical background, 123–124
  Israel and international politics, 132
  Left Behind, 131
  in modern world, 130–132
  televangelism, 133–138
  in 20th century, 127–130
Christian Identity Movement, 101
Christian Right, 120–121
Christian Science, 185
Church of Scientology, 237
Civil religion, 179–183
Civil Rights Era, 111
Civil Rights movement, 112
Clark, Geoffrey, 210–211
Color-blind racism, 116–117
Comet Hale-Bopp, 228
Commencement ceremonies, 55–56
Commitment, 93
Commodity fetishism, 72–74
Communist USSR, "Evil Empire," 134
Complementarianism, 122
Conflict theory, 68–70
Congregational polity, 25
Congregations, 9, 96
Consequential dimension, of religiosity, 34–35
Conservative politics, 120
Conspicuous consumption, 87–88
Consumerism, 88, 89
Content analysis, 6
Conversion therapy, 165, 166
Cult, 228, 229
Cultural-ethnic Jews, 17
The Culture Wars: The Struggle to Define America
    (1991), 136

D

Daly, Mary, 157–158
Davidman, Lynn, 36
Day, Dorothy, 115

Descartes, Rene, 11–14
Dianetics: The Modern Science of Mental Health
    (L. Ron Hubbard), 236
Disenchantment (Max Weber), 77–78
Dispensationalism, 126
Double consciousness, 105, 106
Drucker, Peter, 208
Du Bois, W. E. B., 105, 106
Durkheim, Emile, 170–178, 211, 218, 219, 252

E

Economic determinism, 75
Economic system, 75
Economistic perspective, 58
Eddy, Mary Baker, 185
Edge religions
  The Family, 234–236
  ISKCON, 231–232
  moral panic, 230
  People's Temple, 231–232
Einstein, Mara, 208
The Elementary Forms of the Religious Life (Emile
    Durkheim), 170
Embodied knowledge, 35
Emerging Church Movement (ECM), 251
The Emerging Church: Religion at the Margins
    (Packard), 245
E-Meters, 236
Enchantment, 77
Engrams, 236
Episcopal polity, 25
Equal in Faith, 156
Equal Rights Amendment (ERA), 130
Era of Fordism, 89
Essentialism, 145
Evangelical Christians, 120–122
Evangelical *vs.* mainline churches, 60–61
Experiential consumption, 35, 36
Experiential dimension, of religiosity, 35

F

Faith, 83, 247, 248
False consciousness, 71
Falwell, Jerry, 134
The Family, 234–236
The Family Research Council, 136

Federal Communications Commission (FCC), 133
Feminism, 142–143
Feminization, of religion, 150
First stages of society, 175
Five Pillars of Islam, 19
Flirty fishing practice, 235, 236
Focus on the Family, 136
Football religion, 219–221
Ford, Henry, 89
Functional differentiation, 43, 46
Functionalism, 179
Functions, of civil religion, 183
"The Fundamentals: A Testimony of the Truth,"historical background, 123–124

G

Gay rights movement, 129
Gender
  in religion, 143, 148–152
  and sex, 144–148
General Social Survey, 5
G.I. Bill, 108
GINI coefficient, 69
Glass ceiling concept, 148
Glock, Charles, 32
God, 157–158, 243, 244, 247–248
Graham, Billy, 133
Grand narratives, 224
The Great Migration, 107

H

Habits of the Heart (Robert Bellah), 189, 248
Hare Krishnas, 233–234
Hartford Institute for Religion Research, 200
Heaven's Gate, 227, 228
Hegemony, 152–154
Hierarchical dualism, 152
Hinduism, 21–22
Hole in your soul, 216, 217
Homosexuality, 160, 165, 166
Hope, 117
Hubbard, L. Ron, 236
Hunter, James Davidson, 136
Hybels, Bill, 203, 207, 208, 250

I

Implicit religion, 179
Institutionalized racism, 107–111
Institutional religion, 242
Institutions, 47
Intellectual dimension, of religiosity, 33
The Invisible Religion (Thomas Luckman), 179
Islam, 18–21
Islamaphobia, 21
Israel and international politics, 132

J

Jakes, Pastor T. D., 208
Jefferson, Thomas, 180
Jehovah's Witnesses, 58
Jones, Jim, 231–232
Judaism, 17
Judeo-Christian flavor, 183

K

Kennedy, John F., 128, 180
Kennedy, Robert, 129
King, Martin Luther, Jr., 80, 95, 101, 112, 115, 117, 129, 181, 226
Kinsey, Alfred, 160
Kinsey Scale, 160
Ku Klux Klan, 101

L

Law of Love, 235, 236
Left Behind, 131
Legitimation, 184
LGBTQ spectrum, 160, 166
  and Bible, 164–165
  Pew Research Center, 167
Life, 215, 216
Liminal period, 57
Liquid modernity, 88
Liquid religion
  and commitment, 91–93
  description, 90
Lofland, John, 50, 51
Love-bombing concept, 49
Love the sinner, hate the sin approach, 166
Luckman, Thomas, 179

Luther Bible, 82
Luther, Martin, 81, 82

M

Malcolm X, 113, 114
Manson murders, 130
Marx, Karl, 69–72, 74, 75, 103
Masculinity, 158–159
McDonaldization
  calculability, 194–197
  description, 192
  efficiency, 193–194
  irrationality, 199
  predictability, 197
  reliance on technology, 198–199
The Meditations (Rene Descartes), 12
Megachurches
  average budget of, 202
  business of, 207–209
  definition, 200
  music, 202
  non-denominational, 200
  resemblance of, 203
  small groups, 204
  suburbanization, 201
Mesmerism, 185
Meta-institution, 106, 107
The Metropolitan Community Church, 167
Millenarianism, 125–127
Miller, Daniel, 210
Mills, C. Wright, 4
Mind-Body-Spirit (MBS), 189
  Ayurvedic medicine, 186
  and consumerism, 187
  power of chakras, 186
  property of, 186
  Reiki practitioners, 187
  Yoga, 187
Modernity, 226
  characteristics of, 224
  effects on human, 223–224
  universal and absolute truths, 225
Modern megachurch movement, 250
Montgomery bus boycott, 112
Moralistic therapeutic deism, 247
Moral Majority, 134

Moral panic, 230
Moral science. *See* Sociology
Muhammad (Prophet), 18
Muscular Christianity, 158–159

N

National Association for the Advancement of Colored
  People (NAACP), 111
Nation of Islam, 113, 114
Neoliberalism, 138–140
Nettles, Bonnie, 227, 228
Networks, of people, 172
New Age movement, 186
New religious movements (NRMs), 230
New Thought, 186
9/11 attack, 137
Nixon, 130
Noble Eightfold Path, 23
Non-denominational megachurches, 200
Nones. *See* Religious nones
Normal, 161–163
  way of being man and woman, 148
Norms (sociology), 47
  consequences of, 176–177

O

Occultism, 185
Operation Rescue, 135
Optimism, 117
Organizational homophily, 149
Osteen, Joel, 206, 208

P

Parachurch, 208
Participant-observation strategy, 5
Particularism, 222
Patriarchy, 142
Pentecostalism, 105
People's Temple, 231–232
The Pew Forum on Religion and Public Life, 243
Pew Research Forum, 9–10
Phelps, Fred, 165
The Philadelphia Negro (Du Bois), 106
Pitt, Richard, 166
Plausibility structure, 53, 54

Political conservatives, 120
Polity, 24
Postmodernity, 222–227
Postmodern religion, 217–222
Power of chakras, 186
Praise music, 206
Predestination, 82–83
Presbyterian Church USA (PCUSA), 166
Presbyterian polity, 25
Privatization, of religion, 45, 183–185
Profane, 176
Promise Keepers, 159
Prosperity gospel, 87
Protestant Christian churches, 96
The Protestant Ethic and the Spirit of Capitalism
    (Max Weber), 81
The Purpose Driven Life (Rick Warren), 208

Q

Qualitative methods, sociology, 5–7
Quantitative methods, sociology, 4–6
Queer, 163–164
Queer Social Theory, 163

R

Race and religion, 95, 96
Race Matters (Cornel West), 117
Race relations, 80
Racial equality, 101–103
Racially diverse American churches, 11
Radical lack, 217
Rationalization, 78–80
Reaffirmation, 48
Reagan, Ronald, 134, 137
Redlining, 109
Reiki practitioners, 187
Relationships, 171, 172
Relativism, 62
Relativistic point of view, 59
Religion, 15, 41, 103–104, 169, 190
    Abrahamic, 16–18
    Buddhism, 22–24
    civil religion, 179–183
    and consumerism, 88–90
    Durkheim's requirements for, 218, 219
    edge religions, 230–238

functional differentiation, 43, 46
function of, 11–15
future of, 251–253
fuzziness, 222
gender in, 143, 148–152
Hinduism, 21–22
institutional religion, 242
Islam, 18–21
particularism, 222
privatization, 45, 183–185
sacred, 170, 171
secularization, 42–44, 46
socially constructed institution, 222
technology in, 188
therapeutic, 185–189
and women, 143–144
Religiosity, 32
    belief, 34
    consequential, 34–35
    experiential, 35
    intellectual, 33
    ritual, 33
Religious affiliation
    "dones," 245
    market-based approach, 249
    in United States, 241, 243–244
Religious denominations, 11, 24–25
Religious disaffiliation, 243
Religious economy
    description, 57
    economistic perspective, 58
Religious liminars, 242
Religious marketplace, 249–251
Religious nones, 8, 25–29, 245
Religious pluralism, 58–59
Religious socialization
    definition, 47
    emotional intimacy, 52
    newcomer/visitor, attention to, 52
    proselytizing, 50
Reuther, Rosemary, 152
Rite of passage, 55, 57
Ritual dimension, of religiosity, 33
Ritzer, George, 192–199
Ritzer's theory of McDonaldization. *See*
    McDonaldization
Robertson, Pat, 133–135

Roberts, Oral, 134
Robinson, Eugene, 166
Roles, 47
Romans 1:26–28, 164
Rorty, Richard, 14
Rousseau, Jean-Jacques, 179–180

S

Sacred canopy (Peter Berger), 11, 14
Sacred common beliefs, 182
Sacred places and sites, 181
Sacred rituals, 182
Sacred rules, consequences of, 176–177
Sacred texts, 180
    for Jews, 17
Sacred times, 181
Saddleback Church, 207
Salem witch trials, 145–146
Sargeant, Kimon, 206
Satanic rituals, 231
Schlafly, Phyllis, 135
Scientology, 236, 238–239
Scopes Monkey Trial, 128
Sect-church model (Ernst Troelsch), 63–65
Secularization, 42–44, 46
Seeker-friendly churches, 204–206. *See also*
    Megachurches
Separate spheres perspective, 154
Serial and episodic concepts, 91, 92
The 700 Club, 135
Sex and gender, 144–148
Sexual expression, 159–160
Sexuality, 151–152
Seymour, William, 104
Sheilaism, 189
Shias, 18
Social construction
    college classroom, 39–41
    people's attitudes, 41
    reification, 38, 39
    symbols, 37–38
The Social Construction of Reality (Berger and
    Luckmann), 37
Social drift theory, 49
Social Gospel, 115–118

Social stratification
    capitalism, 69, 70, 74
    commodity fetishism, 72–74
    conflict theory, 68–70
    economic determinism, 75
    economic system, 75
    false consciousness, 71
Social structure and agency, 97–100
Social structures, 172, 173
Society and God, 178–179
Society divinized, 174–179
Sociological analysis
    levels of, 7–11
    types of, 4–6
Sociologist, defined, 2
Sociology
    definition, 1–4
    founding figures of, 67
    micro-level *vs.* macro-level analysis, 7–11
    race, class, and gender, 67
    of religion, 7 (*see also* Religion)
    theoretical paradigms, 67
Sociology of Religion (Condran and Tamney), 245
Solipsism, 14
Soul Searching, 247
The Souls of Black Folk (Du Bois), 105
Southern Baptist Convention, 165
Southern Christian Leadership Conference (SCLC),
    112
Spiritual but not religious (SBNR), 45, 249
Spiritualism, 185
Spiritual life, 217
Stained glass ceiling concept, 149
Stanton, Elizabeth Cady, 156–157
Stark, Rodney, 249
Stonewall Riots, 129
Strictness, 60
Suicide, 170
Sunnis, 18
Supernatural compensators, 61, 62
Surveys, 6

T

Talmud, 17
Technology, 188

Televangelism
    Billy Graham, 133
    Christian Broadcasting Network, 133
    Federal Communications Commission, 133
    Jim Bakker, 134
    Oral Roberts, 134
    Pat Robertson, 133
    and politics, 134–138
    Tammy Faye Bakker, 134
    Trinity Broadcasting Network, 133
Therapeutic religion, 185–189
Theravada School of Buddhism, 23
Thomas Theorem, 102
Thomas, W. I., 102
Torah, 17
Transgender, 160
Transubstantiation, 41
Tricks of the Trade (Howard Becker), 11
Trinity Broadcasting Network, 133
Troelsch, Ernst, 63–65
Turner, Victor, 57

U

Unitarian Universalists, 167
United Church of Christ, 167
United Methodist Church, 166

V

Veblen, Thorstein, 87

W

Warren, Rick, 207, 208
Washington, T., 105

Weber, Max, 77–84, 86, 87
Weber's thesis
    Catholicism, 81
    faith, 83
    modern capitalism, 81
    predestination, 82–83
    prosperity gospel, 87
    Protestantism, 81, 82
    race relations, 80
    work, 85, 86
Westboro Baptist Church, 165
West, Cornel, 116, 117
Willow Creek Church, 207
The Woman's Bible (Elizabeth Cady Stanton), 156–157
Women
    activism, 154–156
    vs. men, 141–143
    and religion, 143–144
    in the world, 141–143
The Women's Christian Temperance Union, 154
Woodford Bible Church, 201
Woodford Methodist Church, 200
Work, 85, 86

Y

Yoga, 187
Young Men's Christian Association (YMCA), 158

Z

Zen school, 23
Zero-sum resource, 68

CPSIA information can be obtained
at www.ICGtesting.com
Printed in the USA
LVHW010239131120
671420LV00001B/6

9 781465 287519